The Sense of the Avant-Garde

The Sixth Sense of the Avant-Garde

Dance, Kinaesthesia and the Arts in Revolutionary Russia

IRINA SIROTKINA and **ROGER SMITH**

methuen | drama

LONDON • NEW YORK • OXFORD • NEW DELHI • SYDNEY

METHUEN DRAMA
Bloomsbury Publishing Plc
50 Bedford Square, London, WC1B 3DP, UK
1385 Broadway, New York, NY 10018, USA

BLOOMSBURY, METHUEN DRAMA and the Methuen Drama logo are
trademarks of Bloomsbury Publishing Plc

First published in Great Britain 2017
This paperback edition published 2019

Cover design: Louise Dugdale
Cover image: Aleksandra Ekster, *Salome. Dance of the Seven Veils*.
Moscow, Russia (© Bakhrushin State Theatre Museum)

ISBN: HB: 978-1-350-01431-2
        PB: 978-1-350-08740-8
        ePDF: 978-1-350-01433-6
        eBook: 978-1-350-01432-9

Typeset by RefineCatch Limited, Bungay, Suffolk
Printed and bound in Great Britain

To find out more about our authors and books visit www.bloomsbury.com
and sign up for our newsletters.

CONTENTS

LIST OF
ILLUSTRATIONS

ACKNOWLEDGEMENTS

This book is a fully rewritten and expanded version of Irina Sirotkina, *Shestoe chuvstvo avangarda: tanets, dvizhenie, kinesteziia v zhizni poetov i khudozhnikov* (The Sixth Sense of the Avant-garde: Dance, Movement, Kinaesthesia in the Lives of Poets and Artists), published in the series 'Avant-garde', copyright the European University Press in Saint-Petersburg (EUSP), Russian Federation, in 2014, republished in a third edition in 2018. This English-language version is published by arrangement with EUSP, whose involvement is gratefully acknowledged. We sincerely thank the editor of the Russian text, Andrei Rossomakhin, for his deep interest and support.

The book owes much to a wide range of scholars and Russian institutions. It crosses borders between Slavic studies, dance and performance studies, history of art and literature, cultural history and history of science in order to draw on the riches of research in the humanities. The notes indicate our debts. Amidst all the scholarship on the Russian avant-garde, it is hard to overemphasize the contribution by a scholarly couple, John E. Bowlt and Nicoletta Misler. In addition to their own prolific writings and curatorship of exhibitions, they edit *Experiment: A Journal of Russian Culture*, twenty-one volumes (1995 to present) including academic inquiries into ballet, ballroom dance, theatre, gymnastics and body culture in early twentieth-century Russia. They have generously contributed their enthusiasm and knowledge to our project.

We also would like to thank Caryl Emerson, Lynn Garofola and Dee Reynolds for their encouraging interest in and support for the book.

The English text, based on a translation from Irina Sirotkina, *Shestoe chuvstvo*, is our own. We thank Sergei Zhozhikashvili for many explanations of the Russian language and much patience with his student, Roger Smith.

We are happily indebted to our experience of the Russian tradition of 'musical movement', to our teachers Aida Ailamazian and Tatiana Trifonova, and to all those with whom we have shared movement.

We acknowledge the following permissions:

Extract in chapter 2, from Rainer Maria Rilke, *Sonnets to Orpheus*, trans. J. B. Leishman (1936), reprinted by permission of the Random House Group Ltd.

The epigram to chapter 6, © Vladimir Mayakovsky, author, and George Hyde, translator, from 'How Are Verses Made?', Bristol Classical Press, an imprint of Bloomsbury Publishing Plc.

The epigram to chapter 7, from Friedrich Nietzsche, *Thus Spoke Zarathustra*, trans. R. J. Hollingdale, copyright © R. J. Hollingdale, 1961, 1969, reprinted by permission of Penguin Random House UK.

NOTE ON THE TEXT

All translations are our own, unless otherwise acknowledged. We transliterate Russian names and words according to a modified US Library of Congress standard; where more familiar versions of names are in common use (e.g. Dostoevsky), we adopt that form. Where we cite sources, we copy names as they appear in that source.

Where ellipses (. . .) appear in quotations, they are our insertions, unless noted as being in the original text.

Where emphases are added to quotations, this is noted.

LIST OF
ABBREVIATIONS

GAKhN	Academy of Art Sciences (All-Russian, and after 1926, State)
GARF	State Archive of the Russian Federation
GINKhUK	State Institute of Art Culture (Petrograd)
INKhUK	Institute of Art Culture (Moscow)
Mastfor	'Masterskaia Foreggera' (Foregger's theatre-workshop)
MGU	Moscow State University
Narkompros	People's Commissariat of Enlightenment
NEP	New Economic Policy
NOT	scientific organization of labour
Okna ROSTA	'Windows of the Russian Telegraph Agency', propaganda posters created by artists and poets within the ROSTA system
OPOIaZ	Petrograd Society for the Study of Poetic Language
Proletkul't	*Proletarskaia kultura* (proletarian culture), Soviet institution to promote culture and art of working people
RATI	Russian Academy of Theatre Art
RGALI	Russian State Archive of Literature and Art
RGGU	Russian State Humanities University
RSFSR	Russian Soviet Federative Socialist Republic
tefizkul't	*Teatralizatsiia fizkul'tury* (theatrialization of physical culture), a project of Ippolit Sokolov and Vsevolod Meyerhold supported by Vsevobuch
TEO	Theatrical Section of Narkompros
TsIT	Central Institute of Labour
UNOVIS	*Utverditeli Novogo Iskusstva* (The Champions of the New Art), a group of Russian artists founded by Kazimir Malevich in Vitebsk
Vsevobuch	Main Directorate of General Military Education
VSFK	All-Russian Council of Physical Culture

FIGURE 1 *Vera Maya's Studio. Photo: S. Rybin, 1927. Courtesy A. A. Bakhrushin State Central Theatre Museum, Moscow.*

Introduction: Movement and Exuberant Modernism

To be is to sense, to feel; in that sensing and feeling, to know, to be aware. All sensing is movement.

A young woman jumps, leaps, takes to the air. We do not know her name, only that she flies in the free dance studio of Vera Maya in Moscow, perhaps in 1927. She indeed flies free, even if the photographer carefully sets up the shot from a low angle to give an impression of height. It may well be that dancer and photographer rehearse over and over again to get the effect they want. The exact place is not important; but it is essential that the flight is in the open air – in nature, as people say. This is not a lady at a ball, but a woman setting out to be her 'natural self'. She shows the surprising capacity of the human body to lift off. We see this in the back-flip of the high-jumper and the somersaulting spring of the acrobat, and we see it in the arts of dance. We also see it in animals. The eminent physiologist C. S. Sherrington, fascinated by the magic of a falling cat turning to land upright on its four paws, examined the nervous system in order to understand just such feats of bodily organization. In leaping, flight or free fall, a person (or cat) attains for a brief moment the unattainable, life in the air, elevated, higher, 'trailing clouds of glory', inspired, closer to perfection, if not indeed to heaven.[1] The woman aspires to be yet higher. Her stretched and extended limbs show the force which she puts into the effort. The wind of movement catches her hair and tunic. The force creates the illusion that she flies, and because she creates the force, it is no illusion that her spirit flies. Mind and body transcend what language and philosophy so often keep separate. To achieve this, a person, if not the falling cat, has to train the body, to attain bodily skill, not mental reason. But the leap questions these categories: the woman *feels* with the body and there is *knowledge*. The woman holds the artificial and the natural in forceful tension: posed picture and free leap. If mind is to culture as body is to nature, this leap is close to nature. Yet it is cultivated, as it is the art of a studio, and, moreover, the studio is in a large city: Moscow after the Revolution, transforming with chaotic haste. The leap is a modern one, confirmed by the woman's dress, or relative undress for Russia at this time: her gymnast's costume and flowing tunic.

Eighty or ninety years later, the photograph has become well known, having appeared in exhibitions on modernism and physical culture and the covers of books. The woman has a public. Yet the image still has the power to undermine and to transcend description. We might be tempted to think that there is no need to say anything: this is a moment of beauty and liberation, performed not stated. The dancer's jump, however, leads us to a number of large claims, the themes of our book, themes at one and the same time historical and philosophical. Our conclusions must be tentative, especially in a short book of large scope. Nevertheless, we aim to focus attention on and advance discussion of a number of related issues.

First and foremost, we make a large claim for *kinaesthesia, the sense of movement*, as both a source of personal knowledge and a resource for innovation in the arts and wider culture. We show this was the case in the personal lives and in the public achievements of the artists, poets and performers of the Russian avant-garde at the beginning of the twentieth century. Further, we set the historical culture we describe in the context of a larger discussion, very much current in the performance arts, dance most obviously, and in philosophy and physiology, about the primacy of movement and the movement sense in knowing and expressing being human, being alive. As some others have done, we name the sense of movement 'the sixth sense', intentionally alluding to the associations of this name to intuition, to a 'sense' that goes beyond the senses. We explain the historical and conceptual background to this in the first chapter.

The argument starts from what no one doubts: sensing, feeling, knowing and awareness have a breath-taking qualitative variety. There is no definitive separation between what one senses or knows, and what one feels or is aware of. The English language permits using 'sense' and 'feeling' interchangeably, or saying, 'I'm aware of that', meaning 'I know that'. We feel, and know, our bodies, other people and the world. The flexibility and nuance of language matches the variability and delicacy of awareness. As a result, there has long been, and still is, large debate about proper description of mental states. The everyday being of a person is, so to speak, immersed and then uncovered in the tide of this variety, advancing and receding.

Yet a belief is prominent in contemporary culture: amidst all this variety in sensuous life there is one sense, one form of awareness and one type of knowledge underlying the rest. This, it is said, is the sense of movement, or kinaesthesia. Maxine Sheets-Johnstone wrote: 'At their most fundamental level, subjective experiences are tactile-kinaesthetic experiences. They are experiences of one's own body and body movement; they are experiences of animate form.'[2] People very often refer to this sense as a dimension of what they broadly call touch or, using the now fashionable term, the haptic sense. Clearly, the sense of movement is of paramount interest in the performance arts of dance, acrobatics or acting, and the arts of film or multi-media conceptual art that go with them. It is also central in sport, climbing, gymnastics and all the varieties of physical culture that have become so large a part of so many people's commitment to health and well-being. Nor should we ignore 'simple' walking.[3] All these activities presuppose some sense and knowledge of movement. Once there is recognition of this, it is not a large step to believe that the sense of movement is actually intrinsic to being a living animal. Animals move, and while we can conceive of movement sustaining life without sight or hearing or smell, we cannot conceive of this without the presence of touch in some form. To move is to be alive; to be alive is to move.

Partly as a result of such understandings, contemporary Western culture has taken a large turn towards valuing the body as the foundation on which to build secure knowledge for life, and also secure knowledge for science and for the arts. Language referring to the body and embodiment is everywhere, from cognitive neuroscience to film theory. What is perhaps not so widely appreciated is that this cultural life takes for granted the existence of movement sense. Indeed – and here we state the conceptual, as opposed to historical, theme of our book – belief that the sense of movement of the body underlies other experience, or is the foundational element of experience, has achieved a prime position. We start to ask how and why this has happened, how and why the sense of movement of the body, in many commentaries, has been posited as the most elementary, and secure, element of awareness and knowledge. The formal, philosophical defence of this claim depends on a phenomenological argument, going back in its modern form to Edmund Husserl, elaborated psychologically in the work of Maurice Merleau-Ponty and finding modern expression in such writers on touch and movement as Maxine Sheets-Johnstone, Jean-Luc Petit and Matthew Ratcliffe.[4] Sheets-Johnstone and Petit have also striven to link their philosophical argument with biology, with the empirical, scientific evidence that we can take the body and the body's sensitivity to (if not knowledge of) its own movement as constitutive of 'life'. Merleau-Ponty's work is a reference point, at the basis of contemporary appreciation of the embodied nature of perception, even when writers, like Sheets-Johnstone, criticize his arguments for ignoring the centrality of kinaesthetic sense for the phenomenology of the body.[5]

It would seem that the contemporary turn 'to the body' addresses a longing for some firm base. This may be understandable, as it follows hot on the heels of what many people feel are the relativistic excesses of postmodern culture, not to mention the depredations of capitalist production rendering everything, even 'life', in the form of commodities. It is not our view that the body, or the natural science of the body, in a direct way, provides such a firm base, but the belief is powerful and prevalent. Moreover, modern performance surely creates the means with which both performers and audience, via bodily life, feel in re-possession of agency and autonomy. What interests us in this book is the place that kinaesthesia has had historically in the search for the foundation of experience, agency and performance. Put in its simplest form, the claims for kinaesthesis hinge on the argument that this sense gives unmediated contact with the world, while the other senses offer a mediated relationship. The very word 'contact' communicates the point: in movement and touch there is contact, a direct relationship *with*; in the other senses there is not. With touch and movement, a person is at one with the world; with the other senses, so it may be felt, there is subject and object, self and other. In this way of thought, dance becomes the most powerful metaphor, and it also becomes the reality, of unmediated being alive as part of a world. It follows that the implicit knowledge of the body in movement, in action and performance, 'knowledge how', may be a person's most secure knowledge. Many artists have conceived of movement as the unmediated presence of being human in the world; they have sought to transcend the subject-object opposition and to know the self 'in contact with' what they have understood to be 'the real'. We are going to explore this conclusion through its historical expression. Our interest is the claim, at times implicit and at others explicit, that kinaesthesia is the 'highest' sense: not so much the sixth sense, but the first and the most important sense.

We would like to suggest that there was substantial precedent in intellectual culture, and also in the everyday discourse of practical engagement with people and things, for a notion of 'the real' given by touch and movement senses. There was a long tradition, developing as the analysis of touch and muscular sensation, distinguishing knowledge or experience of the primary, foundational qualities of what exists from secondary or acquired experience and knowledge. It is not that the modernist artists all built on the literature of this tradition; they characteristically did not. But they did live in a cultural world deeply informed by the metaphors of touch, movement and life, that is, by metaphors of bodily sensing thought to transcend social and artistic conventions.[6]

This takes us to the second theme, reflected in the subtitle to this chapter, 'exuberant modernism'. We start with 'modernism' since this is the heading under which a vast literature has tried to understand and explain innovative changes in the arts in the decades on either side of 1900 and continuing into the mid-twentieth century. The search for an essential definition has surely been misguided. It was led, in part, by the effort, in abstract terms, to determine the politically progressive or regressive content of the arts in relation to modern conditions of life ('modernity'). For our purposes, however, modernism is a family name (to use Wittgenstein's phrase) for a host of innovative work. For us, then, for instance, it is not important to argue when modernism began (and, indeed, reference to 'the new' in the arts and intellectual culture was a cliché from the 1860s onwards), or to claim that, in essence, the achievement of modernism was abstraction and the complete break with naturalism and realism. Modernism involved controversies and tensions; it required keeping the opposites in the air, in play, making them dance. Thus, for example, modernism was as much about policing the line between mind and body as about bringing them together, as much about disciplining the body as about letting it loose.

Beginning in the mid-twentieth century, there has been an explosion of research on modernism and the body. As a result, it has become widely accepted that 'early modernism was by, for, through, and about the body'.[7] Recently, researchers have reconsidered the thesis, attributed to Theodor Adorno, treating the 'early modernist concern for the cultivation of the body as a symptom of false consciousness, a quasi-Taylorist discipline masquerading as social liberation'.[8] They have also reassessed the position attributed to Clement Greenberg, which held that the essence of modernism was abstraction, understood as a move away from embodied forms of representation. Collectively, this rethinking has established bodily experience and kinaesthesia as highly significant to the arts of the modern era. A number of scholars have drawn out different parts of the picture. Guillemette Bolens, for instance, wrote on kinaesthesia in gesture and literary narrative, Dee Reynolds analysed uses of rhythm and energy in modern dance, and Robin Veder examined 'the conjoining of physical practices and aesthetic theories' which she termed 'kin-aesthetic modernism', and she linked her study to 'the economy of energy', arguing that 'kinesthesia organized its expressions'.[9] Veder's project was not dissimilar to ours, though her focus was on modern art and body culture practices in the United States in the 1910s through to the mid-1930s. She recognized that 'while the turn-of-century kinesthetic body cultures [especially where they concerned the cult of the will] most obviously appear to be disciplinary projects of false consciousness ... kinesthetic awareness was a cultivated *skill* with particular meanings and techniques'. Happily, we might say, there was also a brighter side, not disciplined: these bodily cultures involved 'inquiry into energy, manifested in the human body's subtle, enforced, and exuberant movements'.[10] Our project concentrates precisely on the 'exuberance' rather than the 'discipline' intrinsic to kinaesthesia. Living art was expressed in exuberant individual lives as well as in the creations of artists, and it is this exuberance in the body that we place in modernist culture.

Recent work on the arts has sought to show that there is a much more direct relationship between physiological science in the second half of the nineteenth century and the arts than has been acknowledged. Indeed, both Robert Michael Brain and Robin Veder, the former discussing mainly Parisian culture in the 1880s and 1890s, the latter modernism in the United States in the first half of the twentieth century, have distinguished what they called 'physiological aesthetics'.[11] There are perhaps two pertinent dimensions to this concept. The first is a general shift to naturalism, looking to the physiological or evolutionary nature of human beings in addressing questions such as 'what is art?' or 'what is beauty?'. This certainly had a significant input from experimental science, of which Etienne-Jules Marey's use of photography to record and analyse the components of movement and Theodor Lipps's psychological studies of *Einfühlung* (translated into 'empathy' in 1909, introducing this word into English) are famous examples. Marey's contribution to the new art of the cinema has been extensively documented, while empathy theory has become an important part of dance research.[12] A second issue concerns the actual inspiration derived from science in artistic innovation. There are clear examples: Brain turned to the distinctive case of the painter, Georges Seurat, and Veder provided a persuasive account of Georgia O'Keefe's interest in the psycho-physiology of motor imagery. Such examples, however, do not necessarily diminish the appropriateness of the more established attribution of innovation to the artists' imaginative reconstruction of existing aesthetic practices.

'Exuberance' is synonymous with 'dance', and the centrality of dance to the avant-garde is our book's third theme. The changes in the arts, we write, hinged on a large and special appreciation of the sense of movement. Some scholarship has certainly recognized this in specific instances: for instance, there has been appreciation of the link, through rhythm, of the influence of dancers on poetry, at least since Frank Kermode's essays in the late 1950s.[13] There also is new literature on the sense of touch. In spite of this, it remains the case that writers about modernism have neither done full justice to the place of dance in the changes across the arts nor sufficiently appreciated how kinaesthesia, as a sense, played a central part.[14]

Innovative artists, searching for new certainties, but painfully aware of the uncertainties of the socio-political world, in the period from the 1880s to the First World War drew heavily on a range of linked polarities: real–false, natural–artificial, insight–convention, deep–superficial, objective form–decoration, true feeling–sentiment and so on. To these we may add life–death, movement–stasis, contact–distance. These were polarities that made a turn to bodily movement significant and highly symbolic. In particular, there was noteworthy artistic activity for which striving 'to be in contact with' nature, or with the flux of life, or with cosmic movements and forces, was central. This was very clear in the dance of Isadora Duncan or Rudolf Laban, or in the spectacular new forms of the Ballets russes.[15]

In the 1880s and 1890s and in subsequent decades, it hardly needs to be said, the arts were transforming, sometimes with great speed, and sometimes radically. What we would argue for is the place of bodily movement, and of sensibility to movement, certainly linked to the other senses, in this.[16] The historical content of the later chapters on avant-garde culture in Russia in 'the Silver Age', beginning in the 1890s and ending, transformed by the Revolution, in the 1920s, will show just what a rich contribution this was.[17] The Russian case is certainly pertinent to larger and more general claims. A central reason why it is hard to characterize the modernist arts in any straightforward way is that these arts took such a range of expressive forms. Indeed, this *range* of creativity in new forms (tonal music, abstraction, the stream of consciousness in writing and so forth) must be part of any portrait of modernism. Only later was all this range to receive a collective name. Yet all modernist voices rejected a contemporary culture said to have reduced art to academic or bourgeois conventions and to have failed to uphold an art of higher values. Individual artists took it upon themselves to establish what higher values are. Each artist was her or his own authority, though, of course, artists shared lives as well as techniques and inspiration. The cutting-edge of this social world, preoccupied with innovation, became the avant-garde, constantly and self-consciously renewed, dismissing predecessors. In Russia, this self-consciousness had a special quality. The tsarist state claimed divine legitimacy and imposed autocracy. As a consequence, a broad swathe of educated opinion formed itself in opposition and took up liberal, if not radical, causes. It was a context which fostered idealist dreams, often associated with a turn to 'life'; as a result, many artists were to welcome the Revolution, if many also did not, or quickly turned away in disillusionment.

In the Russian context, we find innovation in technique and expression often very strongly linked to a turn 'to nature', the very direction which some later commentators held to be anti-modernist. The turn 'to nature' – this is the main point – depended on experiencing and expressing movement, most specifically performing dance, as the vital link between being human, 'life' and 'the real', thereby breaking with academic artistic conventions, like the classical ballet.[18] At the centre of avant-garde groups was a cult of innovation, the declaration of cultural autonomy, free agency for the artist, expressed through new techniques and through new forms of representation, followed by new scepticism about the possibilities of representation, belief in the formal properties of media as the proper basis of art, and so on. In our usage, the avant-garde refers to those Russians who self-identified as innovators in their respective media and grouped together in mutual support, sometimes with political intent, and for social pleasure – not least, to dance together.

Most Russian artists were very well educated and widely read in several languages, and they would have had some knowledge of scientific authors like Wilhelm Wundt (writing on physiological psychology), Ernst Haeckel (evolution and the nature of life), Henry Maudsley (the brain and mental illness) and Pierre Janet (automatism).[19] In the case of the Russian avant-garde, we find little reference to experimental science. Where there most obviously is a connection, if indirect, is in relation to the appreciation of breathing and rhythm, an appreciation that linked patterns of aesthetic expression with belief in the underlying wave-like energies of living, if not cosmic, forces. Historians writing about the connection between psycho-physiology and the arts in order to locate both as expressions of modernity have therefore explored 'the pulse', economy, speed, technology and urban transformations of modern times.[20] Such transformations, we need to note, were also underway in Russia, before the Revolution, and it was a reaction against them, as much as celebrations of them, that motivated the artists we discuss.

Modernist art movements were international; indeed, the way in which innovations broke through the borders of national cultures was intrinsic to modernism. Many Russian artists lived and worked in, or at least travelled to, Paris, Munich and London. Fewer artists made the journey in the opposite direction, though some did, and Isadora Duncan did with great effect. The Russian impact in Europe and North America was well recognized, most spectacularly with the debut in Paris, in 1909, of the Ballets Russes. After 1918, there was a strong Moscow–Berlin connection, fostering Constructivism in art, design and architecture. Vladimir Nabokov wrote his first reflexively literary novels, and Viktor Shklovsky his Formalist compositions, de-familiarizing the everyday world, in Berlin.[21] Our Russian story is thus part of a larger epic.

The Russian experience also gives us the sources to develop a large claim about why the movement sense has been regarded, as we argue it has, especially around 1900 and now, as the highest, most significant and most authoritative, sense. From ancient times, and in many cultures around the world, there is evidence of a human longing to gain knowledge transcending the everyday senses, senses so apt to deceive. In mystical religious practices, in dreaming, in the life of the imagination, in philosophical reason, there is a long history of search for intuition, sometimes called a sixth sense, to ground knowledge in a higher realm than the one revealed by the mundane, material senses. In Russia, utopian longings, linked to worldviews rich in imagination for the place of humans in the cosmos, were of special importance. We argue that this search for a higher sensibility, at least in part, transformed in the modern age into a range of beliefs about kinaesthesia as a higher sense. It is in this context that we find significance in the belief that the movement sense gives both unmediated expression to being-in-the-world and unmediated knowledge of the world. The sense has been held to transcend the separation of subject and object and to realize the ancient hope 'to know' by rendering the knower *part of* the larger whole, not an *outside* observer of it. This, we suggest, is a modern recreation of intuition, insight and belief in higher, or most profound, knowledge. The modern dancer is its personification, its celebrant. The belief holds that knowledge is *in* the body, and the body the vessel of truth. This argument connects our historical story with present debate about the nature and understanding of dance and embodied performance. This reference to performance requires brief comment.

There is a growing body of scholarship on embodiment, materiality and praxis, in which authors argue that texts, architecture and other art forms are not objects or things but behaviours, practices or, in short, *performances*. This is part of a reassessment of the entire area of inquiries into culture, promoting the view that 'performance studies start where other disciplines end'.[22] The success of the term 'performance' is partly due to its multiple meanings. In business, sport and sex, to perform means both to do something up to a standard and to succeed, to excel. In the arts, to perform is to put on a show, a play, a dance, a concert. In everyday life, to perform is to show off, to go to extremes, to underline an action for those who are watching. As one of the most energetic speakers on behalf of performance studies, Richard Schechner, argued, all these usages grow from the same root: in ancient Athens, theatre festivals were simultaneously ritual, art, sport-like competitions and popular entertainment.[23] In the twenty-first century, many people have come to feel that they live, as never before, by means of performance. Yet the functions of performance, it would seem, have separated. Dance emphasized movement, theatre emphasized narration and impersonation, sport emphasized competition and ritual emphasized communication with transcendent forces or beings.

As a result of this, at least in part, the contemporary tendency is to seek unification rather than separation of different kinds of performance. Thus aesthetic performances have developed, including performance art, mixed-media, happenings or inter-media, that cannot be located precisely as theatre or dance or music or visual arts. These activities, Schechner claimed, 'blur or breached boundaries separating art from life and genres from each other. As performance art grew in range and popularity, theorists began to examine "performative behaviour" – how people play gender, heightening their constructed identity, performing slightly or radically different selves in different situations.'[24] Linking performance and identity brought studies of the arts close to the social sciences. The ethnographer Victor Turner was influential in this connection, as he wanted the professional discourse of cultural studies to capture the struggle, passion and practical engagement of village life that he had so relished in his studies in the field. 'The language of drama and performance gave him a way of thinking and talking about people and actors who creatively play, improvise, interpret, and re-present roles and scripts.'[25] For such reasons, *Homo performans* has made his entrance into academia. Recently, the introduction of the category of everyday-life performance (ELP) has made the argument even stronger. Nathan Stucky, for instance, stressed that 'in ELP, I "become" the other character, but I don't make it up'. This happens, he claimed, due to 'deep embodiment' (a term evoking Clifford Geertz's 'thick description' and 'deep play'), 'total immersion, using all of the evidence available, getting inside':

> As I try to organise my movements, move my mouth, extend my limbs, the body tells me something about what it feels like to move in new ways. My habitual movements become shifted into other habitual movements, to the other's habitual movements. I in/habit an/other's space.[26]

All this has considerably raised consciousness about the place of kinaesthesia and movement in the arts. Some authors, indeed, taking the embodiment argument further, have criticized the founding fathers of performance studies, Turner and Schechner, for stressing vision at the expense of the other senses. Peggy Phelan expressed suspicion of their 'faith' in the potentially omniscient standing of vision, and she nursed an alternative, looking to ' "points of contact" – to take up Schechner's inviting phrase . . . [to] sustain the field in the next century'.[27] Referencing and understanding embodiment appeared to her, as to many others, to be the way forward. 'Clearly,' Catherine M. Soussloff and Mark Franko argued, with the moving body in mind, 'something is lost when performances and images become texts.'[28] The dance scholar Jane Desmond even called for a specific movement-studies methodology, not then available within cultural studies. 'Much is to be gained,' she wrote, 'by opening up cultural studies to questions of kinesthetic semiotics and by placing dance research (and, by extension, human movement studies) on the agenda of cultural studies.'[29] Likewise, Dwight Conquergood welcomed a passage 'from nouns to verbs, from mimesis to kinesis, from the textualized space to co-experienced time'.[30] This shift from analysing movement in geometrical space to locating movement in experiential space-time seems to be particularly important (and in this context there has been a revival of interest in the philosophy of Henri Bergson). In an article on 'the dwelling body', Suze Adams therefore called for a

> new understanding of the relationship between body and place. . . . It is a matter of paying full attention and shifting that attention away from the known, of refocusing embodied engagement and bodily posture, of (repeatedly) expanding awareness from body to place and from place back to body

again . . . of dwelling simultaneously in the body *and* dwelling in place.[31]

Performance studies have the great ambition to capture what tends to get lost on other paths of scholarship: subjectivity, experience and the irreducibly personal aspect of emotion.[32] In consequence, there is currently a tendency to speak about 'the affective turn' instead of 'the performative turn'. In the words of Susan L. Foster, 'when properly cultivated by the choreographies, dance movement can unite both dancer and viewer in the experience of fundamental human emotion'.[33] A further large ambition, significant for these arguments reconfiguring cultural studies, is to theorize anew, through kinaesthesia, the relation of aesthetics and politics. This, it is envisaged, is a way to 'break down conceptual divisions of choreography/improvisation, innovation/tradition, sound/movement, and collective/individual'.[34] Soussloff and Franko recalled Jacques Derrida's saying: 'No one can any longer separate knowledge from power, reason from performativity, metaphysics from technical mastery.'[35] To performance studies is assigned the capacity to transform existing disciplinary formations. This is because embodied knowledge, which integrates cognition, praxis and ordinary life, is assigned to performance. Thus, James Loxely argued that 'because performance studies attends to our lives as practice, as embodied, in the way that it does, it is well placed to insist on the importance of these other, marginalised, "nonserious" modes of experience, modes whose marginality is a function not of their insignificance but of their repression'.[36] The study of performance appears to restore the political to the everyday. The dancer and scholar, Naomi Bragin, for instance, used 'the idea of (kin)aesthetic politics to ask how street dance might imagine alternative modes of relating that define performances of being connected and dislocated, belonging and dispossession, escape and capture'.[37]

This returns us to the great hope, to which we allude in referring to the distinction between knowing how and knowing that: by capturing the experiential component of living processes, performance studies may open up a novel epistemology, new ways of sensing and knowing both the world and ourselves. Terms widely used recently, such as 'embodied cognition', 'experiential knowledge', 'the cognitive body' and 'the learnt body', also point in this direction. What is at issue is not just knowledge that artistic performers have, but what they gain in performance. Moreover, this is at issue for both audiences and scholars. For Turner and Schechner, action and awareness are one: the action of reflection, or reflexivity, is central to performance – 'the relationship between studying performance and doing performance is integral'.[38] Conquergood argued that 'the communicative praxis of speaking and listening . . . demands co-presence even as it decenters the categories of knower and known'. Communication, he claimed, introduces 'vulnerability and self-disclosure', the opposite to closure and authority as constituted by the gaze, and it is exemplified by the performance of movement.[39] Elsewhere, he brought discussion of varieties of knowledge into the argument, distinguishing propositional knowledge, 'knowing that' and 'knowing about', and 'active, intimate, hands-on participation and personal connection', that is, 'knowing how' and 'knowing who'. 'Knowing who,' he explained, 'is a view from ground level, in the thick of things. This is knowledge that is anchored in practice and circulated within a performance community, but is ephemeral.'[40] It is the sort of knowledge the dancer has improvising in a group.

All in all, as Tracy C. Davis playfully wrote:

> the performative turn is . . . a turn that is alternately a technique of dance (pirouette), leads to unconventional routing (detour), championing social change (revolution, social or otherwise), bends for new use (deflection), proudly questions the culturally normative (deviation), like a sail propels us forward yet is obliquely positioned to the wind (tack), and though unsteady is wide open (yaw), depending upon what is apt.[41]

This brings us back to the realm of the senses and sensuousness, of which kinaesthesia is part, that is, to the feeling of muscular joy, or kinaesthetic pleasure, the exuberance, even ecstasy, brought by free movements. We suggest, talking of avant-garde art, that it is not enough to point to technical matters. It is necessary to think of the engine, or spirit – the choice of metaphor may matter – that moves artists to make radically new art. This is to bring in a teleological cause of innovation. We locate this engine, or spirit, in the affectivity linked to movement, in what the title of this book calls 'the sixth sense', the feeling of one's body moving in a free and creative way. We would like to demonstrate that the deeper, intuitive knowledge the avant-garde artists sought, and sought to perform, was coupled with sensuousness and affectivity, and kinaesthesia was the foundation.

A conception of kinaesthesia has thus not only taken root but has gradually grown in the appreciation and disciplined study of the arts, as it grew in the research of the psycho-physical sciences in the nineteenth century and subsequently. In addition to 'kinaesthetic intellect' and 'kinaesthetic empathy', there is talk about 'kinaesthetic perception', with the help of which a person, freeing herself from normative, habitual means of moving, creates new moving images and 'happenings'. There is a distinction between the self-perception of movement (kinaesthesia) and the perception of movement of another person (kinesia).[42] There is research dedicated to how precisely, with the help of which psycho-physiological mechanisms, the viewer perceives the movements of the dancer.[43] And, as we discuss (chapter 5) in connection with the place of movement in esoteric practices, there is considerable interest in the notion of 'presence', a special state in which the human person as observing subject (whether performer or spectator) comes to feel, and perhaps to be, one with the world.[44] We return to these arguments, which place kinaesthesia in the centre of performance, at the end of our book. This will be after our discussion of the Russian revolutionary arts has shown how kinaesthesia was indeed 'in the thick of things'.

The Greek root *kine* is present in both 'kinaesthesia', the sense of bodily movement, and 'cinematography', the art of moving images. In the early 1920s in Russia, there was in fact an attempt to create a science of *kinemalogiia* (kinematology) to study movements in activities as various as dance, sport, physical labour, photography and cinema.[45] The idea originated with Kandinsky and his colleagues in the State Academy of Art Sciences (GAKhN), who saw the possibility of studying movement abstractly and as abstraction. It was a sign of recognition that, in the words of Jacques Rancière, 'cinema is not the art of the movie camera – it is the art of forms in movement, the art of movement written in black-and-white forms on a surface'.[46] However, the early 1920s attempt to institutionalize 'kinematology', movement studies, as a single discipline in Russia was not successful, partly because the disciplinary boundaries between photography studies and dance studies had already been established. Although, later, there were multiple lines of rapprochement between the two, the scope of our research does not include cinematography.[47] Owing to the way film represents movement, the gestures and pantomimic performance of actors, the close connections between filmic and other art forms, and the empathetic response of audiences, there is surely a story involving kinaesthesia to be told. It can be said, all too briefly, that public cinema developed in Russia before 1914 as elsewhere in Europe and North America, but there were no significant specifically Russian innovations. The avant-garde artists took an interest, to be sure, but we are not aware that it was a medium of particular importance for them. Later, after the Revolution, this of course changed, once the Bolsheviks understood the propaganda value of film. The 1920s and early 1930s, as is well known, then saw a wave of artistic inventiveness and technical innovation, associated with directors like Sergei Eisenstein and Dziga Vertov.[48] Eisenstein, before he became famous as a film director, moved in the Russian avant-garde circles that we discuss.

Many of the contributions of the artists of the Russian avant-garde are well known, greatly admired and much studied. This attention, however, has extended less to the way movement, and the sense of movement, entered into the content and technique of their creations, *and* entered into the way they lived. Consider literature. The avant-garde Moscow Linguistic Circle formed in 1915, and a year later the Petrograd Society for the Study of Poetic Language (OPOIaZ); together they gave rise to what is known to history as literary Formalism. A founder of this movement, Shklovsky, wrote about the early years in Petrograd and described how he and his colleagues had the thought that, in general, poetic language is different from prosodic, that it is a special sphere in which the movement of the lips is important. That is, they implied, the world of poetry is a world of dance, a world where the muscles of movement give delight. In the world of art, delight is held back, indulged, re-formed: 'in fashioning an Art of Love out of love, Ovid counsels us not to rush into the arms of pleasure'.[49] The consequence, it would seem, is that only a person who has her or himself experienced this muscular delight can write. The artists were not armchair scholars; young and warm, they fell in love, were active in sport, danced and fought. A happy imprint of energy, vitality and embodiment lies in their works and in their reflections on the avant-garde.

The sheer amount of studies of the Russian avant-garde confirms that it was and remains an influential cultural movement, however diffused and merged with other streams in the arts. Authors have looked for explanations, for the motor behind the burst of creative energy of the phenomenon and for the influence that it had. Nina Gurianova argued that the avant-garde artists were driven by anarchist ideas of freedom, elimination of boundaries and deconstruction of logic.[50] By contrast, Sara Pankenier Weld diagnosed the 'child within' and 'the nonspeaking subject "infans"' that determined some of the distinct features and theories of the avant-garde. She referred to 'the naïve perspective of the child' and 'childish alogism', while she wrote that 'infantile primitivism' accounts for 'an infantilist aesthetics', a version of minimalism in art. She therefore suggested that it was 'the naïve perspective that perceives everything with a defamiliarized eye' that allowed Shklovsky to establish the fundaments of Formalism.[51] Other scholars have concentrated on technicality and materiality as possible sources of innovation. Isabel Wünsche, for example, examined the concept of *faktura* – literally, texture – a quality to be achieved in a work of art through the successful use of appropriate combinations of materials. In her view, artistic creation is a result of the human desire to work with *material*.[52] Julia Vaingurt argued that 'technology provided a new cultural framework wherein an artist could redefine knowledge, art, and self, and find new ways of seeing the world and his and her art in it'. She showed that Shklovsky's uses of the word *'priem'* (technique) in relation to art is highly relevant: the Greek *techne* is synonymous with *poiesis* – 'bringing forth' – revealing or delivering something to the world; *techne* is 'poetic' by definition. The triad *techne/technique/technology*, Vaingurt argued, is responsible for reconfiguring human affectivity in the time of industrial revolutions. Thus, in his epistolary anti-novel of 1922, *Zoo, ili pisma ne o liubvi* (Zoo, or Letters Not About Love), Shklovsky confessed: 'It is bad for me to talk about love', and he suggested, 'Let's talk a bit about automobiles.' Vaingurt commented that 'Shklovsky's *Zoo* does not substitute technology for love as a new aesthetic subject, but rather offers a new technique for thematizing love, underscoring the extent to which thinking and even feeling are conditioned by the technological revolution'.[53]

Much of the work of Russian avant-garde artists, like Malevich's *Black Square* or Eisenstein's *Battleship Potemkin*, was to become internationally famous and influential. But such works were only a small part of an extraordinarily brilliant and productive regional culture. Often enough, but not always, the men and women who participated adopted unconventional, or oppositional, lifestyles, reflecting the fact that modernist movements were concerned with remaking humanity and were not just aesthetic in intent.[54] In Russia, the class known as the 'intelligentsia' denoted (unlike some later English language usages of the term) a large group of people, well educated and highly cultured, but with no particular social status. Though they often belonged to the professions like acting, medicine or journalism, they certainly had no political power in tsarist society. The artists we discuss nearly all came from the intelligentsia, and because of the existence of this class there was no sharp line dividing a radical avant-garde and more bourgeois participants in new art movements.

This is a book about Russian artists, about how bodily kinaesthetic practices invigorated their art, and about the way this made the art innovative, with a lasting influence. We look at the artists and poets of the Russian avant-garde to discover how their involvement with various bodily practices on the everyday level affected their art. Personal movement influenced art. Our subject is the life of this avant-garde world rather than modernism, as if the latter were something that could be studied in itself, or studied as the false consciousness of the modern economy of work.

We conclude this introduction by briefly indicating the arrangement of the book. In the opening chapter, we point out that, by the early nineteenth century, there was a literature differentiating touch and movement senses. It then became a standard feature of discussions to claim that the sensory couple, movement and resistance to movement, gives an unmediated sensory awareness of 'the real'. This claim was associated with an appreciation of the role of bodily feelings in general in creating knowledge of self and other. The possible epistemological, even existential, significance of hand touching hand, for recognition of which people now cite Husserl, had been the subject of comment since at least the mid-eighteenth century. Throughout nineteenth-century thought, we can find assertions of the fundamental place of touch and movement in knowledge (not least knowledge of the spatial qualities of visual perception). This history leads us to suggest that when modernist artists, including dancers, turned to movement as a source of truth, in their terms turning from convention and society to creation and nature, they enacted in art what had long been asserted in the theory of how people come to knowledge of themselves in the world.

Twentieth-century phenomenology recreated the argument in philosophical terms. Subsequently, in recent neuroscience theories of motor cognition, philosophy and science have offered each other mutual support in claiming for movement the prime place in an organism's knowledge (know-how, if not conscious cognition).

Our story follows general issues as they came to expression in the lives of particular people. So to speak, we read these lives as gestures, all the more lively for their innovative and passionate form, of the human world of movement. In chapter 2, we introduce the ideal of 'higher sensitivity' and its exemplification in Kandinsky's abstract art and the combination of the senses, even synaesthesia, that this involved. This is preceded by a short, historical reminder of the 'kinaesthetic intellect'. Then we turn, in chapter 3, to the art most obviously and directly expressive of the movement sense, dance, and, in the light of the impact of Isadora Duncan in Russia, sketch in the origins of free dance and, most specifically, a distinctively Russian tradition of what was, and still is, called musical movement. All this activity was closely related to a search for 'higher sensitivity' through a re-creation of Hellenic values. The next chapter then takes up the movement that is gesture and language, first in the mobile body and language of the poet Andrei Bely. We take space to argue for what we claim is the creative union of Duncan with the 'peasant poet', Sergei Esenin, and for the significance of dance movement to the poetry of the Futurist avant-garde. The modernist arts in Russian flourished through a web of mutual influences. This is also evident in chapter 5, where we show the place of dance and movement exercises in Georgy Gurdjieff's esoteric circle, which owed much to what Aleksandr and Jeanne Salzmann brought from the theatre and from Dalcrozian rhythmics. Aleksandr Salzmann's lighting changed the space, more deeply 'the presence', that actor and spectator experienced, and 'presence' is what embodied movement was thought to achieve. In the last two chapters, we make explicit what is implicit throughout, the world of practices of thinking with the body. This leads to recognition of the importance of popular dances, enthusiastically taken up, we argue, by artists like Mayakovsky, to an account of the way biomechanics passed from being a medical science into Meyerhold's theatre and to Shklovsky's experiments with breaking the automatism of conventional language. In conclusion, we come back to the issue of the sixth sense, to kinaesthesia as central to sensuous and affective knowledge, most especially 'knowledge how'.

The interest focuses on dance but goes well beyond dance. For example, a modern Russian researcher on synaesthesia, Bulat Galeev, argued that 'the muscular feeling of a person and the perception of heaviness' is responsible for 'lexical synaesthesia' in commonplace phrases like 'heavy condition', 'stunning hum', 'high and low sounds', 'light music', 'sad rhythm of a march' and 'fine taste'.[55] Certainly, in the twentieth century it became attractive to speak about 'kinaesthetic pleasure' and 'muscular joy'. The American critic John Martin considered that kinaesthetic pleasure from muscular experience of another person, thanks to this experience itself, lies at the base of 'aesthetic satisfaction which results from contact with completeness of form' in the appreciation of performance art.[56] This directs us to the arts where the muscles of movement give delight, about which Shklovsky wrote, and to the delight with which a young woman leaped through the air.

CHAPTER ONE

The Sixth Sense

Century after century – will it be soon, God? –
Under the scalpel of nature and of art
Our spirit cries, the flesh wears itself out,
Giving birth to the organ of the sixth sense.

NIKOLAI GUMILEV[1]

The senses

Everyday English language about the mind, now and for centuries
past, firmly identifies five senses – '*the* five senses': sight, hearing,
smell, taste and touch. This is a social convention, though there are
those who have thought there really are, 'naturally', precisely five
senses. It is common to cite the classical authority of Aristotle, in *De
Anima*, a text which was a mainstay of Arabic and then European
education down to the seventeenth century and even through the
eighteenth century. Aristotle dealt with the five senses in turn and
described vision as superior to the others. Yet, at the same time, he
identified touch as in some manner at the foundation of sensation
generally and not straightforwardly comparable to the other senses.
'The most basic of the senses, touch, all animals have . . . so is touch
separable from the other senses,' he wrote, implying that without
touch animals simply would not continue to preserve themselves, to
remain alive. Touch is the sense without which the animal (and

person) 'can have no other sense'.[2] Touch is primary, and the other senses share or reflect the fact that it has passive and active dimensions (contact is brought about by movement) at the same time. Then, Aristotle noted, there are different kinds of touch awareness, indeed very many. 'Touch ... has a wide range of objects'. A reference to touch may denote awareness of very different kinds of things: contact, pressure, tactual qualities, temperature, vibration, not to mention the senses of movement.[3] Indeed, one recent summary listed thirteen different types of nerve fibres running from the hand and supplying the brain with sensory (afferent) impulses.[4] Aristotle himself even wondered whether touch should be called one sense or many.

The epigraph at the opening of this chapter is from the Russian poet Nikolai Gumilev, Anna Akhmatova's first husband, who was shot by the security services in 1921. In the last year of his life, he composed 'The Sixth Sense' and voiced a longing that the age might finally come in which the body will acquire a new capacity, a special organ for 'sensing' poetry. Here poetic language ran together allusion to intuition and to an actual sense organ. Indeed, the age had come to expand beyond the traditional five senses. In the same year, 1920, the Russian Expressionist poet Ippolit Sokolov wrote that there must be between ten and fifteen senses.[5] Most obviously to a modern reader, perhaps, touch differs from the other four senses since its relations with things is not mediated by one localized organ: touch is present (though variably) all over the skin, and, if we include bodily sensations (tired muscles, stomach ache and so forth) under this heading, there is also deep touch throughout the body. 'There is no neatly circumscribed "organ" of touch, other than the dynamic human body.'[6] For this reason, Aristotle wrote that all the senses can be understood as kinds of touch. Developing such a view, we might conclude, the body is *one* sense organ. Jacques Derrida, in his study of touch, amplified the insight of Jean-Luc Nancy to this effect: 'there is no "the" sense of touch' – touch is the way in which animate beings are animate, not properly described one among five senses.[7] This is a significant suggestion, to which we shall return. Ordinary speech, however, continues to differentiate the senses.

Another ancient writer to accord touch special status was the Epicurean philosopher, Lucretius. His poem *On the Nature of Things*, rediscovered in the West in 1417 and written in Latin much admired for its elegance, presented a fully materialist worldview.[8] He explained all phenomena, including the soul, in terms of the motions of particles in a void. If all that exists are particles and motion, then the contact, the touching, of particles is the principle of change in the world, and the human sense of touch the basic source of knowledge of what exists and brings events about. Lucretius, like Aristotle, described the senses in turn, though when he came to touch, he had nothing to write that he had not implied already in describing the contact of particles. Touch just is what it is, con-*tact* (Latin, *tactus*, touch), particles touching each other. The challenge was to show how the other senses, like vision, also resulted from the contact of particles. (Lucretius thought that objects give off very fine films of particles, like a spider shedding its skin, which, moving, touch the eye.) In the seventeenth century, suitably distanced from Lucretius's distinctly non-Christian views, this way of thinking became central to the new natural philosophy, the modern science of understanding nature in terms of matter and motion. This, too, gave touch special status among the senses.

We summarize a large history. Many authors fixed on touch as the route to the most direct knowledge of what is real; indeed, touch achieved status as *the* sense through which there is knowledge of the primary, or irreducible properties of things, their massiveness, spatial dimensions, motion and resistance to us. Touch, it appeared, is the most direct, or the deepest, engagement of a living organism with 'the real', a condition of it being alive not dead. In Aristotle's words again (in a passage where he argued that no one of the four elements, earth, air, fire or water, without soul, was sufficient to be the substance of a sense organ):

> For without touch . . . [the animal body] can have no other sense, every ensouled thing being . . . a tactile body, and, while the other elements apart from earth might be sense-organs, they would all produce sensation by indirect and mediate perception, whereas touch consists, as its name suggests, in *contact* with objects. The other sense-organs seem to perceive *by* touch, but *through* something else, touch alone being thought to do so through itself. . . .
>
> It is the deprivation of this sense alone that leads to death in animals. Just as it is impossible for anything that is not an animal

to have this sense, so there is no other sense that something must have to be an animal except this one.[9]

This argument (which we are abstracting from what Aristotle wrote as a whole) has parallels in contemporary debate on the theory of knowledge. Its modern incarnation in phenomenology goes back to the work of Edmund Husserl in the first decade of the twentieth century, and it became widely spread in the second half of the century through Maurice Merleau-Ponty's *Phenomenology of Perception* (first published in 1945). For Maxine Sheets-Johnstone, who is both a biologist and a phenomenologist (and she was also, not coincidentally, a dancer), the sense of movement is simply *the sense of life*. Discussing the vexed question of the nature of consciousness, especially of the qualities of 'feels', like redness (an example of what are called *qualia*), she wrote: they are 'integral to bodily life. They are there in any movement we make . . . They are not a "mental product," but the product of animation. They are created by movement itself.'[10] Developing a similar argument, the physiologist Alain Berthoz and phenomenologist Jean-Luc Petit linked Husserl's discussion of the shaping of the world in kinaesthetic awareness to recent work on the brain's active construction of what is taken to be the world. They boldly concluded that 'on the basis of this theory, we can account for everything that exists for a subject with the meaning of being "a thing"'.[11]

Husserl took up phenomenal awareness of embodiment, or experience of life as contact and movement, as pivotal for the re-establishment of philosophy. We may think of this as a philosophical parallel, coinciding in time, to modernism in the arts, though Husserl worked without (to our knowledge) direct interaction with the arts. Husserl called for a rejection of the immediate philosophical past, judged inadequate by the high calling of his field. He sought to re-describe 'the real', and for this re-description he introduced a new technique (phenomenological reduction); and he turned to his own thinking for the authority to make statements about what is real. All awareness, he supposed, even the awareness of a philosopher thinking as intensively and as rationally as himself, is embodied. The phenomenal reality of this embodiment is given in and by kinaesthesia, the sense of being alive, moving, at each moment.

Already in the constitution of a sensed spatial something . . . we have a formation of a hidden, analytically exhibitable [demonstrable], constitutive synthesis; it is indeed an 'appearance' which refers back to the kinaesthetic 'circumstances' to which it appertains. We are always led back further analytically and arrive finally at sense-objects in a different sense, ones which lie at the ground (constitutively understood) of all spatial objects and, consequently, of all thing-objects of material reality too.[12]

For Husserl, analysis led to kinaesthesia as the ground of awareness of things, and to awareness that awareness is in a body. Kinaesthesia is involved in every apprehension that we exist as embodied in the world: 'I am at all times in one or another kinaesthetic stance.'[13] Husserl supposed that analysis can trace the phenomenal presence ('in consciousness', as ordinary language has it) of spatial things to the kinaesthesis, the movement of an organism as part of, *in*, the world, not as a mind or some kind of internal observer looking out on the world. Kinaesthetic awareness is awareness of a particular stance or movement; and the awareness is localized. The body is the bearer of spatialized locations, beginning with the double character of touch, which is at one and the same time touching and being touched. The pattern of localization is the source of knowledge of body differentiated from and having relation to objects:

> *Given with the localization of the kinesthetic series in the relevant moving member of the Body is the fact that in all perception and perceptual exhibition (experience) the Body is involved as freely moved sense organ, as freely moved totality of sense organs,* and hence there is also given the fact that, on this original foundation, all that is thingly-real in the surrounding world of the Ego has its relation to the Body.[14]

Husserl's argument made the basis of all knowledge, that is, the character phenomena possess which analysis cannot further reduce, the spatiality of the body given by kinaesthesis. In a course of lectures in 1907, he discussed at length the 'animation' binding apprehension of the existence of a world to the world. Going through the place of the visual and tactile senses in this apprehension, he argued that these senses alone are not sufficient to give rise to awareness of spatiality. This comes, he said, from self-movement, which, understood psychologically, we know in kinaesthesia. (He self-consciously adopted the foreign word.)[15]

The importance Husserl accorded to kinaesthetic awareness passed, transformed, into the philosophy of Martin Heidegger and of later phenomenologists concerned with *Dasein*, the being that has as its being the understanding of itself as being. Being is 'being-in-the-world', and this is disclosed with being itself. As Heidegger wrote, using an expression redolent with reference to touch: 'In anything ready-to-hand the world is already "there".'[16] Subsequently, Merleau-Ponty developed this way of thought in the language of phenomenological psychology, a psychology setting out to show analytically how knowledge of self and world, that is, knowledge of embodied self in the world, originates in the facts of embodiment. The body 'is the horizon latent in all our experience and itself ever-present and anterior to every determining thought'.[17] Hence all perception involves an 'attitude' of the body, knowledge of which is given by the position and movement of the body, which is always position and movement in relation to some thing. These kinds of arguments, in the language of phenomenology, very much continue to inform the writings of those, like Petit, Ratcliffe and Sheets-Johnstone, who would find the base in awareness of movement or touch for a theory of knowledge that is also a theory of significance or meaning.

These philosophical discussions did not, and do not, describe a neutral, disinterested encounter of reflective subject and world, mediated by movement. Meaning is given *in* the perception of an event, not added on by some rational or affective judgement; movement is movement in evaluative relation to something. The relation is an 'encounter' that expresses a 'concern': 'the fact that observation is a kind of concern is just as primordial as the fact that action has *its own* kind of sight'.[18] This is well reflected in ordinary language usage, which makes clear that 'contact with', 'movement towards', 'movement away from', 'touching the heart' and so on, in the inexhaustible richness of language, are not simply spatial but qualitative, moral and aesthetic, expressions.

Relations of touch and movement, as well as of gesture, with ourselves, with other people and with things, relations embedded in a vast range of culturally variable practices, embody moral as well as material stances. As Ratcliffe wrote: 'To make touch with the world is to be "in touch" with it, but it is about significant contact rather than just physical contact; the latter is an abstraction from the richness of tactual experience.'[19] The embodied relations known in touch and kinaesthesia *are* the animated expression of the ethical stance. This is a very significant point. Husserl's life-work, indeed, was a response to what he called 'the crisis of the sciences as expression of the radical life-crisis of European humanity'.[20] The crisis, which he and many other intellectuals and artists experienced, came with the massive expansion of the authority of the sciences (humanistic as well as natural). The 'crisis' was that this success appeared to rely on a positivist theory of knowledge, a form of knowledge revealing facts but leaving values without rational foundation. Phenomenology was a commitment to supply that foundation by grounding knowledge in the animated, living being that is 'in touch with' a world, a world of concerned relations, a world 'ready-to-hand'. In however abstract a manner, the philosophy expressed the sensibility informing much modernist endeavour in the arts. To leap into the air, to take to flight, expressed joy, confidence in the body – it expressed 'spirit', as people say – the *value*, the *being*, not just the fact, of being in movement.

Hence, as we discuss in the chapters to follow, the significance of movement to the Russian modernists: in movement they sought to recreate the world – not only personal worlds, but the very possibilities of being-in-the-world. As young and idealistic dancers well understood, the leap into the air was a leap into a higher existence. In the 1920s, our Russian dancer would not have read Husserl, but she had her own answer, in performance, to the 'crisis' which drove the philosopher's life-work.

The arts and philosophy, together with physiological science, advanced new techniques to arrive at and express 'the real'. By drawing attention to the history of the muscular sense, we draw attention to the prior existence of an appropriate sensory, kinaesthetic language for what was found to be 'the real'. It was appropriate language because discussions of touch, and more particularly of the movement sense, had recognized the double character, the *relation*, given in the senses, of moving to being moved (or of touching to being touched), self to other and 'the I' to the world. It was the language of embodied, not alienated, being.

To find a way through these complex matters, we turn to the history of what we call, in the title of our book, the sixth sense: the history of the sense (or senses) of movement. There is a lot to be learned. The stance of the body at every moment, in sleep or in the most violent activity, in passive states as in voluntary efforts, requires the co-ordinated activity of the moveable structures of the body. Such co-ordination requires something very like knowledge, conscious or unconscious, of the state the body is in and the state the person wishes to be in. Such knowledge is made possible by the existence of a system of sensory and motor nerves, linked in co-ordinated circuits, so that an organism is constantly up to date about what, in terms of posture and movement, it is doing. Where there is conscious awareness of posture and movement, we refer to kinaesthesia, which, speaking loosely, we may call a sixth sense.

The actual phrase 'the sixth sense' has, in fact, been used in a number of different ways. The historical search embodied in the *Oxford English Dictionary* uncovered usages referring to sexual feeling and to the remarkable sense of the bat, quite unknown to humans, and to repeated speculation that there are one or more senses going beyond what is normal in this material world. The use of the phrase to signal special sensory power is confirmed by an internet search, which will first throw up a US film from 1999 about paranormal or psychic powers. In the film, a young boy, disturbingly, sees and talks to the dead. Incidentally, the title of the film says something important about reference to a sense: reference is not to a passive reception (though it sometimes is), but to an active capacity. In this regard, the film's use of the phrase approaches a further, quite widespread use, in which 'the sixth sense' describes an ability 'to sense', not through 'the senses' but, rather, through a power in the mind itself. This is sense understood as a kind of intuition. Intuition itself has been conceived among other things as a potential in each and every person's mind, or as an esoteric gift found only in a small elite or in people of genius. Reference to the intuition of women and poets was, of course, once – and, as it may be, still is – a commonplace of folk (or everyday) psychology.

In addition to such usage (and this brings us to our subject), reference to the sixth sense denotes the sense (or senses) of movement. Before about 1800, authors did not clearly distinguish this sense from the sense (or senses) of touch. There was appreciation that touch involves more than mere surface contact, and there was even reference to 'dark feeling', but there was no precise specification of new 'extra' senses.[21] Indeed, it is still common practice to use 'touch' to cover the whole range of both tactile and movement senses, and there may be good reasons for this (as Matthew Ratcliffe argued, for one) in the integrated way that tactile and movement senses discriminate bodily self and other bodies and tell us about their most fundamental sensory characteristics.[22] Our usage denotes a sense that, unlike intuition or psychical knowledge, is very definitely embodied. All the same, as we shall see, language about the movement sense has at times (as in Gumilev's lines) approached language about intuition and even approached the 'aesthetic sense' or a sense for poetry.

A very significant part of the history is about belief that the sense of movement goes beyond, or goes higher (or deeper), than the traditional five senses permit. It has been held up as the sense through which we know the 'really' real. This has coloured belief about the sense of movement with a noumenal aura, the kind of aura that surrounds reference to 'life'. To round out the picture, we may mention in passing that, in Buddhist thought, it is possible to describe the mind and the objects towards which it is directed, that is, thoughts, as the sixth sense: 'we feel that we perceive our thoughts with our mind just as we perceive a visible object with our eye.'[23] This, however, lies outside the usage we discuss (whatever the possible value of Buddhist thought for cognitive neuroscience). Lastly, we recall a joke from Soviet times: 'All people have five senses, but a Soviet person has one more. The sixth is a sense of deep satisfaction.'

Muscular feeling and kinaesthesia

Words are not passive labels but actors in shaping the world.

To our knowledge, description of the sense of movement as 'the sixth sense' dates from anatomy lectures that Charles Bell gave to medical students in London in the 1810s. There may be earlier usages, but Bell's marks the entry of the phrase into science. Certainly, his concern with the sense of muscular movement was preceded by interest in the sense of balance and vertigo (an interest in what, in retrospect, has been called the first sixth sense to be discovered after Aristotle drew up his list of five senses).[24] Bell, for his part, wrote:

There are five organs peculiarly adapted to convey sensations to the mind; or as I am more inclined to say, to rouse the faculties of the mind by exercising the internal organs of the senses in the brain . . . If I were willing to break in upon the received opinions in an elementary book, I would say that there was a sixth sense, the most important of all, the sense of motion; for it is by a sense of motion that we know many of the qualities of outward things, as their distance, shape, resistance, and weight.[25]

Two things are noteworthy. First, Bell felt he was innovating, going against received opinion in naming a sixth sense; and second, in spite of this, he considered the new sense 'the most important'. In a brief description of the senses, he elaborated on what he thought this importance was, and he made it clear that he was referring to a sense of movement, not to tactile qualities. The sense was important, he held, because it reveals the fundamental, or primary, qualities of bodies (solidity, extension and motion), through muscular movement and through sensing resistance to it. This, he implied, lies at the heart of sensing difference between self and other. This primary knowledge is not the result of simple contact.

But it appears to me that these qualities of hardness, softness, solidity, figure, extension and motion, would be known to us, although we had no nerves in our finger ends at all! These qualities belong to what I would call the muscular sense, that conception of distance which we acquire by moving our body or our members, by pressing upon an object and feeling the resistance it occasions.[26]

Here Bell referred to 'the muscular sense'. If he innovated by summoning up a sixth sense, he shared with predecessors and contemporaries the reference to 'the muscular sense' or 'muscular feeling' (*Muskelsinn* or *Muskelgefühl, sens musculaire*). Over the half-century from about 1780 to 1830, a number of intellectually significant authors – including Destutt de Tracy in France, Erasmus Darwin in England and Johann G. Steinbuch in Germany – made large claims on behalf of this sense, large claims because they linked the sense to the most basic knowledge of what is real. The fundamental sensory knowledge to which they pointed was the sense of activity, or movement, opposed to resistance. A number of authors made such knowledge the basis for a person's very awareness of self and world.[27]

Bell, more than other authors at this time, related the sense to specific empirical knowledge of the nervous system. Believing in a sixth sense, he made observations linking the brain and the muscles in a kind of circle: he proposed that efferent, motor nerves carry impulses from the centre to the periphery and cause muscle contraction, and afferent, sensory nerves carry impulses from the periphery to the centre, enabling the mind to sense that a muscular contraction has occurred. This laid the basis for description of the structural-functional relations of the embodied control of posture and movement. Just as the brain informs the muscles when to contract, the muscles inform the brain when they are contracted. Bell's work, announced to the Royal Society of London in 1826, was cited a century later by physiologists as the foundational study of the empirical science of co-ordinated movement. Bell was 'the first to definitely postulate the existence of a muscular sense of a physiological parity with the other senses'.[28]

After the work of Destutt de Tracy and then Thomas Brown in mental philosophy, Steinbuch in experimental psychology and Bell in nervous physiology, the muscular sense became a defined interest and area of research. This happened exactly in the decades when modern, specialized, disciplinary science and philosophy developed (some historians even speak of a second 'scientific revolution' at this time), and this disciplinary activity structured subsequent research on muscular feeling. Most pertinently, physiology developed as an exemplary experimental science, establishing techniques for and standards of empirical argument about the psycho-physiology of the senses, the sixth sense included. Many contributors to research had medical backgrounds, as the opportunities for full-time 'pure' research expanded only slowly, and the clinical case study, in the vastly complex area of knowledge of body and mind, remained a highly important source of information and medium of argument. In descriptive and analytic studies of mind, the French philosopher, psychologist and diarist Maine de Biran had a special long-term influence. Transforming Tracy's work, he discerned in the feeling of volitional effort the irreducible basis of the person or soul, and he set out to show how all knowledge has to be understood as having this sense as a foundation.[29] This placed action, movement, at the heart of subjectivity and the embodied self. It was a direction of thought to be continued a century later by philosophers as diverse as Bergson, Merleau-Ponty and Sartre.

The history of the muscular sense had begun with recognition of the special heterogeneous and distributed nature of touch, and with discussion of touch as, in some way, the most fundamental of the senses. There was input due to interest in balance. Also, from early on, there was considerable debate about the relation of touch to vision, most particularly about whether it is through touch that the eye learns to perceive distance. This placed the argument about relations between the senses at the centre of research. An appreciation of the fact that the senses interact (a subject of the influential work of the psychologist J. J. Gibson on 'perceptual systems') generated its own questions.[30]

Whatever the progress of natural science, work in mental science (or mental philosophy) continued to link discussion of empirical science and the theory of knowledge. There was seemingly endless examination, from many different points of view, of the acquisition and nature of knowledge, and reference to the muscular sense had a large place in this. As a result, it became a large and diffuse topic, spread across the whole range of discussion of mind and body, sensation and knowledge and living reality in general. Moreover, if the phrase 'the muscular sense' was hardly on everyone's lips, everyday experience was experience of movement, and everyday psychology was replete with examples of the special tactile and movement skills of people without (or with much reduced) sight, of the special movements needed for craft skills, sport and the arts, indeed, for more or less everything. The acquisition of ability to play the piano, for example, was a staple of discussion of habit and learning. Everybody was familiar with people who had 'butter-fingers', or who were 'a dab hand' at something. Bell himself wrote for the educated public on the exquisite capabilities of the hand.[31] Every school child and every soldier knew about posture.[32] Women in corsets and men in high collars knew all too much about restricted movement. All the same, by the closing decades of the nineteenth century, there was also a large, specialized literature on the nature and functions of the muscular sense, a literature which, around 1900, reached general if not universal agreement that this sense is indeed, as Bell had suggested, a peripheral sense (though perhaps located more in tendons, joints and skin than in muscle itself). Many of the details still occupy researchers. In physiological psychology before 1900, however, there was a large and (at the time) seemingly unresolvable debate, with contradictory experimental and clinical evidence, about whether the sense was central, peripheral or both. That is, the science of the muscular sense circled around whether to understand the sense as based in central brain impulses (perhaps subserving the feeling of effort) or in peripheral muscles or joints (subserving awareness of movement after it has been carried out).

Writers began to substitute other words for 'muscular sense'; there was a feeling that it was just too imprecise. William James complained: 'This word is used with extreme vagueness to cover all resident sensations, whether of motion or position, in our members, and even to designate the supposed feeling of efferent discharge from the brain [that is, supposed outgoing impulses felt as effort].'[33] In these circumstances, a new word, 'kinaesthesia', was quickly taken up, to describe sensory awareness of movement. The word appeared, in 1880, in a book on the brain for a public audience, a book in E. L. Youmans's 'International Scientific Series', a major publication venture in the public spread of scientific knowledge. The author, H. Charlton Bastian, was a London neurologist, a specialist in brain and nervous disorder, who had for some time contributed to debate about the nature of the muscular sense.[34] Relying largely on clinical evidence, Bastian was firmly of the view that the sense is peripheral. His labelling of the sense as kinaesthesia signalled that he thought it a sense like other senses, even if its sense organ is distributed throughout the body. From English, the wor quickly spread to other languages and, by the end of the cent· reference to kinaesthesia as a class of sensations was common not only in scientific discussion.

The dictionary later defined kinaesthesia as 'the sense o' effort that accompanies a voluntary motion of the ⊦ definition compounded a number of topics. In the nin⸴ and in experimental psychology up to the secor twentieth century, the phenomenon of effor´ voluntary movement, was indeed integral to d' feeling. However, an increasing body of or quotation from James) thought that the fee¹' of muscular contraction and position ⸴ different things. The latter, as an auᵗ' often barely conscious, or even uncᵣ guiding, or co-ordinating, movement and posture in the light of the contracted, or relaxed, condition of the muscles. The sense guides volition but is not the sense of effort in volition. Then C. S. Sherrington, in 1906, introduced the language of 'the proprio-ceptive field'.[36] In his original usage, the term denoted the whole class of internal sensations, many of them not conscious, by means of which the body has knowledge of its own state. By contrast, he discussed the sense organs as the source of information about the world outside. With time, usage (mostly) narrowed, and scientists referred to proprioception as the system, for the most part unconscious and automatic, responsible for the co-ordination of posture and movement. This firmly located the topic of the muscular sense in physiology. In contrast, reference to kinaesthesia persisted as part of language for describing the phenomenal world, the world of the experiencing, conscious person, the psychological world.

The research and interest was international. In Russian, the term 'kinaesthesia' is relatively recent; the academic *Dictionary of the Russian Language* of 1982 did not include it. Earlier, *myshechnoe chuvstvo* (muscular feeling) was used, a translation of the German from the light hand of the nineteenth-century 'father of Russian physiology', Ivan Mikhailovich Sechenov. 'During walking,' he wrote,

> the sensory excitation is given at every step, by the contact of the foot with the surface upon which the person is walking and by the feeling of support which arises therefrom. It is also given by the sensations which are born in the contracting muscles (the so-called muscular sense).[37]

Sechenov was himself a very active and mobile man, and in his writing he almost sang of movement: 'Be it a child laughing at the sight of toys, or Garibaldi smiling when he is persecuted for his excessive love for his fatherland; a girl trembling at the first thought of love, or Newton enunciating universal laws and writing them on paper, – everywhere the final manifestation is muscular movement.'[38] The sensations of this movement, Sechenov asserted, have meaning and purpose for the movement's regulation, the accomplishment of movement.

It remains to say something about the now pervasive word 'feedback'. When approaching this, it is helpful to remember the very considerable, complex contribution of the movement of the eyeballs in vision. There is, we might say, no vision without movement. A very extensive body of research from the time of Hermann Helmholtz (and even before) in the mid-nineteenth century to the present supports this. This topic has been a key site for research on the integration of sensory impulses. Then, in the 1890s, the development of historical and aesthetic studies of the arts included a new word, 'haptic' (from the Greek word for 'I touch' or 'I touch lightly'), to describe the way in which vision includes awareness integrated with, or derived from, touch. A century later, 'haptic' became a buzz-word in intellectual commentary on the arts, commentary keen to reveal the embodied nature of the many faces of perceptual awareness (in 'contact improvisation' or other improvised dance, for example, or in appreciation of the layers of paint on a canvas). Contemporary reference to haptic sense may simply denote touch, or more especially active touch, and there is authority for this in usage by physiologists, or it may denote the place of touch *activity* in the formation of perceptions (including kinaesthetic perceptions) generally, notably visual ones. Gilles Deleuze and Félix Guattari provided a much-cited reference to the latter, and this has been a strong influence in the rebarbative language of art and film theory.[39] There is also a branch of engineering, 'haptics', concerned with information and the touch interface.

Deleuze and Guattari recalled the work of Alois Riegl on *Late Roman Art Industry*, published in 1901, in which Riegl, a German art historian, differentiated optic and haptic perception.[40] By 1901, there had been more than a decade of constructive interaction between art history and the philosophy and experimental psychology of aesthetics, a decade which historians now perceive as laying the foundations for modern discussions. The experimental psychologist Theodor Lipps developed his theory of *Einfühlung* (empathy) at this time, arguing that the aesthetic quality of a work of art depends on the extent and manner with which the art work excites the observer to perceive and take pleasure in and thus, so to speak, participate in, the way the artist constructed a performance (whether of brush-strokes or of dance movements).[41] There was a large discussion about this, which naturally involved the suggestion that what came to be called empathy may be crucial for appreciation of the plastic arts and arts of movement (including sculpture, theatre, film and dance). Indeed, the idea that kinaesthetic feeling is involved in empathy was there from the beginning of the discussion, in the work of Robert Vischer in the 1870s.[42] Following this line of thought, theorists of art claimed that people perceive not only motions of living things but movements of a so-called pure or abstract kind by imitating them subjectively and producing them as internal plans (or motor cognitions). Vernon Lee (Violet Paget, who worked independently but also studied the research of experimental psychologists) re-thought this, reflecting the work of the sculptor and critic, Adolf von Hildebrand. In her discussion of sculpture, she elaborated on the importance of empathetic touch, including the movement sense, to aesthetic appreciation. In Lee's understanding, this appreciation exhibits and reinforces the sense we have of being alive. As Carolyn Burdett commented:

> We 'realize' the relations of the shape's constituent elements because our own dynamic experience is projected into it: 'the activity we speak of is *ours*'. We attribute balance, direction, velocity, pace, rhythm, and energy to a contemplated form, Lee writes, 'but also *thrust, resistance, strain, feeling, intention, and character*'.[43]

Separately, in the voice of a self-made connoisseur, Bernhard Berenson famously announced that the painter

> can accomplish his task only as we accomplish ours, by giving tactile values to retinal impressions. His first business, therefore, is to rouse the tactile sense, for I must have the illusion of being able to touch a figure . . . before I shall take it for granted as real, and let it affect me lastingly.[44]

In such ways, reference to touch, and with it reference to movement, and what is taken to be 'real', entered into writings at the foundations of twentieth- and twenty-first-century discussion of the arts.

The description of the place of the sense of movement in artistic culture turns out to require a very broad and deep imagination. It is an imagination with considerable contemporary resonance – in the flourishingly diverse world of dance, most obviously, but also in acrobatics (skateboarding!), walking, climbing, sport and the pursuit of health; in cognitive neuroscience with its interest in the motor brain; in automated control, prosthetics and robotics. As we have briefly outlined, there is a substantial history to all of this. This history, the history of the sense of touch understood in the broadest way, is replete with figures of speech which call touch and movement senses 'the deepest' as well as 'the highest'. There is no contradiction in this. The metaphor of depth suggests that the sense of movement underlies and enters into the other senses, and that it precedes them in terms of both individual and evolutionary development (in both ontogeny and phylogeny). Our purposes, however, are not to elaborate biological or physiological knowledge and argue the empirical evidence for depth understood in this way. Rather, if we refer to 'the deepest sense', we do so to suggest that it is, in ways to be explored, the most profound – and hence 'the highest' – in cultural context. The context for our study is modernist Russia, to which we turn in the next chapter. In Russia, where in the arts and through political convulsions people invested very large hopes in transforming humans and 'raising' humanity, the ramifications of the movement sense were large indeed.

CHAPTER TWO

Search for Deeper Knowledge

And then, without fail, there appears among us a man like the rest of us in every way, but who conceals within himself the secret, inborn power of 'vision'.

VASILY KANDINSKY[1]

The kinaesthetic intellect

The Russian avant-garde set out on an anthropological, as well as artistic, adventure, a project to change human consciousness, to refound the feeling of humanity. The art it created proposed a new frame of perception, widening human possibilities. Avant-garde artists – Vasily Kandinsky, Mikhail Matiushin, Andrei Bely, Kazimir Malevich and many others – saw the task of art as being to form a new, 'higher sensitivity' or refined feeling. Artists expressed this 'higher sensitivity' as material *and* spiritual, as a unity. This, they believed, required heightened contact with 'the real', the kind of contact that the roots of the word 'contact' itself connoted, touching and being touched in animated movement. The meanings and metaphors of touching betokened belief that sensory art united the apparently opposed poles of spirit and body, of the ideal and the material, and of imagination and practice. This unity was certainly present in the case of the senses and arts of movement, in kinaesthesia and in kinesis, in sensing oneself move and in sensing others move. The power and resonance of metaphors such as 'light breath' or 'bare feet' (for the expression of unmediated contact with earth and the world) were as strong in Russian as in other languages. Moreover, there was considerable interest in using kinaesthesia for the creation of new sensations, sensations which were as yet unknown, by synthesizing them with visual feelings or by creating them in their own right. We can even go further and say that kinaesthetic sensations were important for artists in all aspects of their lives, since they danced, developed manual techniques, took part in sport and embraced.

In this chapter, we illuminate this search for a 'higher sensitivity' and the place that movement and the sense of movement had in it. As a first step, we discuss the fact of sensed movement, movement present as part of the subjective world, for the person who is herself moving and acting. We introduce the idea of the kinaesthetic intellect. The concern with touch, movement and physical action as the material of art is, for this purpose, secondary. The argument is that the subjective world of movement has its 'reason', its 'intelligence': the body has knowledge, which is 'known' in the sense of balance and movement and in gesture. It is shown to be possible for this 'intellect' to serve 'higher' aesthetic and human ends. In the second part of the chapter we turn to the story of Kandinsky's introduction of abstraction into painting in order to illustrate how, in the actual practice of a new form of art, an outstanding Russian artist drew on the sense of movement. The final section discusses the phenomenon of synaesthesia, the fusion of different sensory modalities, which, for the Russian avant-garde, was very much tied up with the search for 'the higher sensitivity'.

To introduce the notion of the kinaesthetic intellect, we turn to the life and work of the Futurists, of which there were Russian as well as Italian innovators and exponents. In Russia in 1914, in a memorable instance, Vasily Kamensky, a Leftist artist who was to welcome the Revolution, caused a scandal in Saint-Petersburg with his 'ferro-concrete poems'. His *Tango with Cows* remains famous for its performance: bringing movement into the reading. Not coincidentally, Kamensky was one of Russia's first aviators, carrying his own movement into the air.

The avant-garde world fostered artists who considered gesture to be a pre-aesthetic phenomenon; they took elements of bodily kinesis, or movement, as instruments for the artist, available to be turned into art in order to create a new sensibility. There was a precedent for this in Italy, where F. T. Marinetti proposed to create verses utilizing a kind of groping feeling. He then went further, having thought up his own art of touch. As is well known, the Italian Futurists welcomed the First World War, and Marinetti himself took part in the actual fighting. On the front, in the dark of the trenches, he recorded, he studied the recognition of things by groping, and as a result of this experience he thought up a new art, Tactilism. He brought out a manifesto for *Tactilismo*, the art of touching, in 1921, and, together with the artist Benedetta Cappa, he created a tactile tablet for 'the travelling hand'. It was necessary to prepare people for the perception of tactile art and to develop their touch feeling, and for this Cappa (who married Marinetti) made tactile 'scales' and 'panels' from materials of different textures. A person groping over them was to report sensations and even orally improvise:

> The Tactilist will announce the different tactile sensations that he experiences during the journey made by his hands. His improvisation will take the form of Words-in-Freedom, which have no fixed rhythms, prosody, or syntax. These improvisations will be succinct and to the point, and as nonhuman [as possible].

Besides his tablet for the hand, Marinetti thought up 'tactile rooms', in which the walls and floor were tactile panels, only of gigantic sizes. According to his thinking, in these rooms 'mirrors, running water, stones, metals, brushes, low-voltage wires, marble, velvet, and carpets will afford different sensations to barefooted dancers of both sexes'.[2]

In such ways, touch and kinaesthesia appeared in Futurist practices not as a picture of movement seen by viewers, but as their sensation, their feeling experience, connected to their inner, subjective worlds. That movement may at one and the same time be highly public and highly personal, self-evident as it may seem, is of the utmost importance for the theory of knowledge and of art. The automatic proprioceptive system and conscious kinaesthetic life, together, have a central place in understanding the distinction between knowledge how (or 'know-how') and knowledge that. It was, we argue, an inestimable contribution of modernist artists to bring into the highbrow cultural world, filled as it was by class-consciousness, snobbery and conservatism, an appreciation of the depth, intelligence and range of knowledge how, knowledge tacit in the body and in what the body has learned. The Russian Formalists called this knowledge *priem* (technique). The cultivation and popularity of dance in the lives of the artists, as in the lives of other people, knowledge of technique, from ballet to the dance known as 'turkey trot', expressed in vital terms an appreciation of bodily knowledge. This has an interesting cultural history in its own right, and we shall return to it in our conclusion. It is also relevant to contemporary science, where there is much attention to understanding cognition as the activity of *a person*, with a socially embedded body, not cognition as the function of a mind or a brain or a computer. There is contemporary recognition of the thought of the muscles, in addition to recognition of conceptual thought, for which tactile-kinaesthetic sensitivity, or the feeling connected with any human activity, is basic. Indeed, the human embryo, to the extent that the embryo moves, already has this capacity. Kinaesthesia, it would seem, appears first relative to the other senses; cognition involving language is post-kinaesthetic.

A movement, the Russian physiologist Nikolai Bernshtein wrote, 'reacts like a living being'.[3] With these words, he exposed the central weakness of Ivan Pavlov's 'theory of higher nervous activity': human movement cannot be reduced to unconditional or conditional stimulus-response relations; it is holistic, not mechanical. Since the 1960s, this argument, placed 'in a drawer' during the Pavlovian era in Soviet physiology, has given a large impetus to motor theories of cognition in neuroscience. Thanks to Bernshtein and others, movement became understood not as a mechanical event, but as action according to 'the movement task', indeed a solution of the task similar to an act of intelligence. Bernshtein introduced the notion that a 'model of the desired future' is necessary for the completion of an organism's movement, a presentation of the wished-for result, the biological equivalent of anticipation and foresight.[4] Bernshtein assessed such a capability as a bodily capacity, the kinaesthetic intellect. When his works became known in the West, after his death in 1966, they had a deep influence, for example, on the US psychologist Howard Gardner and on the French physiologist Alain Berthoz. Bernshtein and his followers made it possible to say that movement has not only its proper feeling but its proper *logos*, its reason. Thus our book is about the bodily-kinaesthetic *logos* of the avant-garde, the 'sixth' and, as it may be, the 'highest' of the senses.

With the kinaesthetic intellect, with the help of muscular feeling, whether conscious or unconscious, we perceive spatial relations and incorporate knowledge of them into the most elementary acts of thought and movement. Dancers are at the forefront of those who well know that thinking and muscles (in Russian, мышление and мышца, or, transliterated, *myshlenie* and *myshtsa*) are close to each other. A creator of postmodern dance in North America, Yvonne Rainer, thus presented a work which she called 'The Mind Is a Muscle'.[5] Its core piece, 'Trio A', lasts four and a half minutes and consists of a repeated series of simple, everyday movements; each part of the series has equal significance and each movement follows without interruption. The movements are completed in an unhurried fashion, under control, strongly; they proceed in real time and with real weight. The dancers do not for one moment reduce force or lose energy, displaying the same kind of endurance as long-distance runners. According to the choreographer's design, the viewer becomes, as it were, a witness to the work of reason, not of a machine but of the human dancer. The operation of thought is in this case fulfilled by means of the body.

Kinaesthesia is not only awareness that accompanies the means to regulate a person's own movement and connection with the world but, many people would claim, the basis for understanding the movement of others. Already in 1913, the dance critic Hans Brandenburg had asserted that 'the spectator can only really participate actively when the most complete and most concentrated optical impressions urge him to inner participation, provided that he also possesses a trained corporeal awareness'.[6] This built on the then much-discussed, and now revived, theory of empathy. The argument was not so much about the literal, physical imitation of movement (like a reflex shuddering at the sight of one person shaking another) as it was about the existence of a certain kind of kinaesthetic experience with cognitive content. In the 1930s, John Martin called this 'metakinesis': if kinesis is physical movement, then its mental parallel is metakinesis, the psychological phenomenon accompanying movement.[7] Without metakinesis, Martin stressed, the viewer, at the sight of a ballerina balancing on one point would receive no greater pleasure than from the contemplation of a little feather soaring in the air. (Personally, we rather think the feather might give much pleasure.) The viewers applaud the ballerina, he argued, because they recognize the force of the weight, firmly supported on the ground, as their own. Also in the 1930s, the Russian actress and researcher on dance, Lyubov Dmitrievna Mendeleeva-Blok, wrote: 'The perception of dance penetrates deeper into consciousness than the visual and oral impressions alone; with them are combined much more firmly remembered and incorporated motor impressions.'[8]

'The higher sensitivity'

Creative people at the beginning of the twentieth century, as later, were well familiar with the muscular sense, by intuition if not as an elaborated science. 'Work is possible for me only in the open air,' pronounced Andrei Bely, 'and eye and muscles participate in the work. I tap out and cry out my rhythm in the fields; with waving arms; all the sought for dynamics in the contraction of muscles.'[9] Bely (the pseudonym of Boris Nikolaevich Bugaev), to whom we shall frequently return, was a significant participant in the Symbolist direction in new art, contributing both poetry and a major novel, *Petersburg* (first appearing in book form in 1916), well known in translation as well as in Russian. He became a member of Rudolf Steiner's Anthroposophy movement and joined the emigration after the Revolution, before returning to Russia in the early 1920s.[10] Showing a similar sensibility, his fellow poet, Aleksandr Blok, proposed to listen to the music of the Revolution 'by all the body, by all the heart, by all of consciousness'.[11] Blok, whose poetry was and still is revered, was a very distinctive voice, welcoming the Revolution, if in almost apocalyptic terms.

Dance, movement and kinaesthesia became part of the avant-garde project of life-creation, consciousness of new being and the introduction of art into life. In Russia, with its autocratic tsarist system and deeply conservative religious and administrative institutions, any such project was in its nature radical, potentially revolutionary. The social and political context fostered grandiose conceptions of art, conceptions more at home in a philosophical anthropology of 'the new man' than in polite society. For this reason, inspired by Isadora Duncan – 'a contemporary Bacchante', the first swallow of that 'artistic humanity' about which Wagner and Nietzsche had dreamed – intellectuals turned to free dance as to a new religion.[12] Abandoning ballet and ball dances, the highly rule-bound disciplines of movement enjoyed by the social establishment, they were inspired by Dionysian dance. In the Russian language, there are two different words for dance: one, *tanets*, derived from the German *Tanz*, is for a formalized, controlled way of dancing; the other, *plyaska*, denotes a free and exuberant dance coming from the individual creative soul. *Plyaska*, in addition, connotes the dance of a soul of Russian character, as, famously, in the scene where Tolstoy, in *War and Peace*, portrayed Natasha dancing after the day's hunting.

The consciousness of intellectuals who, taking up dance and other practices of movement, like eurythmics and gymnastics, opened up to their own embodiment and the embodied nature of art, changed. A number of the most famous, including the revolutionary poet Vladimir Mayakovsky, were supple and athletic, danced, engaged in sport and appeared on the stage and in films. Bely was famously agile. The stage director Vsevolod Meyerhold himself moved excellently and, teaching his actors to move, developed biomechanics (which we shall discuss in chapter 6). This was at the forefront of establishing kinaesthesia as the basis for training actors. Thus the artists of the avant-garde fully valued the semantic potential of the body to become a source of scientific and everyday metaphor and of new conceptions of movement and rhythm in art and life. They did not just value these things, but began to use them: Boris Eichenbaum wrote about 'the muscular movements of history', while Viktor Shklovsky compared art with 'the touch of a world' and Sergei Eisenstein brought into film-making the 'delight of moving bodies'.[13] As we shall see, sensibility to movement entered into the arts of writing, painting, the theatre, the circus, sport and – hugely important for the spread of the sensibility through society – the new popular dances of the twentieth century, spectacularly reshaped in street-dance and other dances of contemporary culture.

Before we turn to the new forms of dance in Russia, however, we extend the discussion of the heightening of sensibility, correlated with the widening of the forms of artistic expression, which were such prominent ideals of new art works. As we have noted, autocratic and then revolutionary conditions in Russia fostered utopian, or at least idealistic, writing about a dreamed-of and longed-for future, in which 'higher' men and women would redeem the suffering and limited spiritual, moral and aesthetic consciousness of the actual times in which people lived. Mystical traditions within the Orthodox Church, with ancient roots, fed into this, along with the deep respect accorded to the great Russian poets and writers of the nineteenth century. This idealism became part of modernist projects, most clearly perhaps in the work of one of the principal pioneers of abstraction in art, Kandinsky. As Kandinsky's painting is so well known, discussing it provides a useful entrée to the points to be made about the sense of movement, points much less familiar.

Any discussion of 'higher sensitivity' or higher feeling must acknowledge the looming shadow of Nietzsche. The main part of his brilliant, aphoristic writings first appeared in the 1880s, and they became widely known a decade or so later and had enormous impact. His work was then translated into a number of European languages, including Russian (though many Russian intellectuals, having lived or studied abroad, would have read German). For young people taking part in or attracted to artistic innovation, he was *the* philosopher, because he turned philosophy from an academic pursuit into a living practice, a practice rejecting bourgeois and conservative norms for a purer, 'higher' recognition of the forces of 'life'.[14] The medium of Nietzsche's expression – the poetry, the self-consciously exaggerated language, the intensely individualist idioms, the venomously sharp dissection of hypocrisy, cliché and falseness – set new standards for the intellectual and artistic voice.

Nietzsche's language *seduced*. Infatuated with Nietzsche, Russian intellectuals prophesied the transformation of life through art. The Symbolist poet and art historian Viacheslav Ivanov even elaborated a conception of Dionysianism which identified the roots of art in ancient Dionysian mysteries. In the Russian setting, Nietzsche's message, that there must be a 'transvaluation of values', merged with native traditions of idealist and mystical longing for 'a new man' (for whom Zarathustra became a model) as the agent of a new age for humanity. Utopian themes were common, unexceptional, in Russia, where political engagement was excluded. They appeared alike on the revolutionary Left, in anarchist circles and among the members of the conservative, finely educated elite. Very significantly, for our purposes, Nietzsche repeatedly and graphically drew on dance as a metaphor of 'transvalued' life. Dionysian dance, in his language, recaptured the wholeness of being. Body and soul are one in the dance: 'Lift up your legs, too, you fine dances: and better still, stand on your heads!'[15] Seekers after 'higher' things drew the obvious conclusion. Through dance, they would both embrace life and reach a deeper understanding of what life means: to dance is to be alive, to be alive is to dance.

The hope that a special, higher sense, not the intellect, would open the secrets of the world is often to be glimpsed in the writings of poets and philosophers. The younger contemporary of the Symbolist poets, Iakov Golosóvker, a translator into Russian of Sappho and of Nietzsche, wrote about 'a discovery that will shock'. This discovery, which 'existed of old in the intellectual experience of the ancient philosophers, soon, like lightning, will strike in the very system of our knowledge and in our consciousness'.[16] In such contexts, there was talk about inner sensitivity, which we liken to a sixth sense, and about mystical perception. We point to the way that muscular feeling, kinaesthesia, became the empirically verified, scientifically validated and artistically exemplified embodiment of this 'higher sensitivity'. Reference to kinaesthetic sense thus encompassed both body and spirit, signalling the wholeness of the person and the unification of the temporal and the eternal. Golosovker himself related to this 'higher sensitivity' through what he took to be the work of perception, work fulfilling a cognitive function. The work of perception-creative imagination is, he proposed, completed unconsciously, bypassing the conscious intellect. 'The code of inner senses is not yet declared. It is perceived by us only dimly and at the edge of uncertainty, and it agitates rather than calms us: the spirit disturbs the body, the body the spirit.' When this code becomes clear, our external senses will have to yield place, and we will give priority not to the external apparatus but to our inner senses which biologists and philosophers have not yet fully understood.[17] Then, the poet believed, unmediated knowledge of the spirit, or 'the absolute of the creative imagination', will become accessible.

These beliefs stemmed from Theosophy and other kinds of mysticism popular with the early twentieth-century philosophical and artistic intelligentsia. The Polish-born eurythmist, Jeanne Salzmann, for example, argued that 'experiencing a pure sensation within the physical body can lead to a spiritual experience. We penetrate the world of vibrations, of fine substances.' She continued: 'We begin to see the poverty of all our feelings and the need for a feeling that is more pure, more penetrating.'[18] She was a student of both Emile Jaques-Dalcroze, the Swiss musician and music educator, and Georgy Gurdjieff, the Russian-Armenian mystic. 'A world of vibrations': such phrases, along with words summoning-up the aura of rhythm, were a mainstay of reflective commentary on new art forms. If obviously associated with music and hearing, vibration and rhythm were equally qualities felt in the body, the sensation of which, there was precedent to consider, was 'deep' or 'primitive'. This is hardly in need of exemplification in our age of amplified electronic beat. But it was well understood also in the nineteenth century that the arts of gesture, rhetoric and poetry deployed rhythmic patterns. In the lines of Stéphane Mallarmé, rhythm itself had become the subject, creating a kind of abstract poetry. Mallarmé also radically re-thought typeface and the space of the printed page, thus relating the word to space and to eye movement in innovative use of the senses in art. The language of vibrations was also a feature of the writings of those, like the Theosophists (led by Madame Blavatsky) and Anthroposophists (the followers of Rudolf Steiner), who strained after universal understanding, to be achieved by bringing the vibrations of the human soul into harmony with the vibrations of the cosmos.

In the decades before and after 1900, the language of energy, force, vibration and rhythm had a large place in the overlapping ways of thought of science and esoteric or mystical belief of people looking for something beyond material existence, something speaking to a longing for purpose and guidance in the universe. The vogue for spiritualism, found at all levels in society, spoke to this: members of the Royal Society of London, such as William Crookes and Oliver Lodge, searched for forces beyond those already known to science, while the bereaved used the force of mediums to commune with the dead. Physics before Einstein (who published his paper on special relativity in 1905) was preoccupied with the aether, a supposed medium, filling space, transmitting the wave-like, vibratory form of light and electro-magnetic forces.[19] The Nobel Prize-winning physical chemist Wilhelm Ostwald build himself a country house near Leipzig which he named 'Haus Energie', as a sign that it would be a place where physical and human spiritual forces united in one worldview. (This worldview was called 'Monism', which Ostwald took over from the evolutionary biologist Ernst Haeckel, who had a very wide audience, including Isadora Duncan.) Subjective knowledge, in the form of phenomenal awareness of force (the quality experienced in the effort to move and in the resistance to movement), was implicit in these beliefs and hopes. The whole language of 'the forces of nature', as well as belief in the causal activity of spirit, was dependent on the perceptual dimension. In moving, it then seemed, a person had unmediated awareness of participation in the movement of the world. This sensibility, we suggest, was open to a range of interpretations, from those of a physicist formulating thermodynamics, to the esotericist communing naked, dancing, with the trees of the forest – as dancers, including Rudolf Laban, did at Monte Verità in the Swiss Ticino.

The idea that the underlying energy of spiritual and natural forces is, in essence, one and the same has a long history (which included strands of Newtonian science) in European culture. It was also prevalent in a number of cultures from around the world (for example, it informed the Melanesian category of *mana*). In nineteenth-century Europe, the idea reappeared with a secular and materialist colouration in the natural philosophy of energy and of evolution, and it did so in ways that included a body of commentary about the relation of forces to the senses of effort, movement and resistance. As a result, when modernist artists took up the language of vibrations, they took up a language resonant with imagination for the place, known through sensitivity to movement or rhythm, of the individual soul in the cosmos. Under the hugely disruptive conditions of modernity, the (at times extremely rapid) spread of industrialization and urbanization, and manifest transformation of the landscape by new technology (the railways of the 1840s, the electricity and telephone lines at the end of the century) and by many miles of bourgeois and slum housing, it was a natural and much-taken step to look for hope and healing in the restoration of connection between human movement and the movement of nature. New art forms often participated in this, sometimes by re-imagining the harmony of energies that the Ancient Greeks were supposed to have possessed, sometimes by seeking in the aesthetic qualities of line, colour, form and rhythm themselves the qualities expressive of a deeper truth or harmony. Duncan's dance exemplified the former, Kandinsky's abstract art the latter.

It might be thought possible to understand these concerns with the harmonies of nature, spirit and art to have been culturally and politically reactionary, a throwback to earlier ages rather than modern. This, however, imposes an ideal of what modernism should have been, influenced by later anti-humanist formalism in aesthetic theory, rather than attending to what artists actually thought and did. Many Russian modernists were profoundly idealist, and they sought in subjective experience of force, intrinsic to muscular feeling, ordered in vibrations and rhythm, an expressive route to 'higher sensitivity' and a deeper life. They looked to art *to perform* kinaesthetic feeling. This was certainly true among many of the dancers discussed in the next chapter, and it was clearly true for Kandinsky. Artists strained for connections between colour, sound and form, trying not only to open new artistic metaphors and thoughts but also to shape new sensitivity. Their purpose was to transform, even to redeem, their lives and the life of the world.

Kandinsky vividly recalled the sensual delight he had as a thirteen- or fourteen-year-old boy squeezing oil paint from tubes:

> One squeeze of the fingers, and out came these strange beings, one after the other, which one calls colors – exultant, solemn, brooding, dreamy, self-absorbed, deeply serious, with roguish exuberance, with a sigh of release, with a deep sound of mourning, with defiant power and resistance, with submissive suppleness and devotion, with obstinate self-control, with sensitive, precarious balance.[20]

As Dee Reynolds argued, citing this passage, one can see at work the imagination of an artist who would, from 'inner necessity', have the colours of the palette dictate the form of painting. Kandinsky also referred to colours showing 'power and resistance' and 'balance' – 'precarious', like a tight-rope walker – metaphors taken from the sensed movement of the body. For Kandinsky, 'everything "dead" trembled'; everything dead was alive, and the sign of this aliveness was movement. Thus, when he created abstract paintings, line and colour literally animated the picture: a successful picture 'vibrates'. As he succinctly concluded: 'movement is life, life is movement'.[21] If empathy with 'dead' colour paralleled the aesthetic theory of Lipps, sensibility in relation to movement, and balance, implicitly gave voice to accounts of kinaesthesia. Kandinsky also intended colour and line on the plane of his pictures to create movement, to draw the spectator inside the painting and make the spectator's imagination move backwards and forwards in the dimension of depth and across the surface, from side to side and up and down. The artist himself did not just appreciate movement in painting but took upon himself the task of giving movement to the spectator. This, in Kandinsky's cosmos, was tantamount to giving 'life'. He retrospectively attributed inspiration for these beliefs to the carved wooden ornamentation of peasant houses, which 'moved' him while travelling in the northern Russian province of Vologda: 'They taught me to move within the picture, to live in the picture.'[22]

The mission of the artist, Kandinsky believed, was to open people's eyes wider, to intensify sound, to free and develop all the senses. In the future, the ruder feelings, such as fear, joy and sorrow, will attract people less and less; the artist will wake up finer senses that now have no name. His colleague in Russia, the composer and artist Mikhail Matiushin, introduced an understanding of 'widened perception' as the affective equivalent of 'widened consciousness', the term used in Theosophy.[23] Matiushin, with his wife, Elena Guro, was a key figure in a Futurist group in Saint-Petersburg just before the First World War, and he was preoccupied by the search for what he called 'the fourth dimension'. Both Kandinsky and Matiushin were fond of speaking about 'the inner sound', 'the fine subject', which must change the substance of art, art which in its portrayal of objective subjects had become too 'material'. They both also described vibrations as the source of contemplative works of art. Kandinsky understood music, which gives birth to vibrations and hence to pure movement in the listener, as the model form of abstract art. If music or painting excludes instrumentality, he argued, then it turns into abstract existence, pure sound, and gives rise not to banal joy or sadness, but to complex spiritual vibrations. Borrowing such language from Theosophy and Anthroposophy, they represented the transfer of 'vibrations' from artist to viewer, through music or painting, as a psycho-physiological process, spiritual and material at one and the same time. From music and painting, the understanding extended into the worlds of theatre and dance. Mikhail Chekov, a famous actor (and nephew of the writer), said that

the actor's body can be an optimum value for him only when motivated by an unceasing flow of artistic impulses; only then can it be more refined, flexible, expressive and, most vital of all, sensitive and responsive to the subtleties which constitute the creative artist's inner life. For the actor's body must be molded and re-created from within.[24]

This, we would add, brought the play of an actor close to dance.

When, in 1914, the young poet Mayakovsky set out finally to free art, that is, to detach art from bourgeois investment in the subject matter of art as common-sense realism, he recommended dance as the means: 'From the painting of camels, the animals loaded for the transportation "of the common sense of the subject", we must make a herd of cheerful bare-footed girls turn around in a passionate and clear dance.'[25] By that time, he had had the chance to view and picture a number of new dance forms. The new dance positioned itself in opposition to ballet, by underlining the absence of pictorial representation and sentimentality. Dancers changed the old language of feelings, of joys and fears, into terms evocative of natural science. Like scientists, they spoke about vibrations, space, dynamism, force and energy. In Duncan's words, creating a dance she always awaited a push, coming from the centre or source in the body: 'when I had learned to concentrate with all my force on this one Centre, I found that thereafter when I listened to music the rays and vibrations of the music streamed to this one fount of light within me.'[26]

Kandinsky appropriately recognized the reform of artistic movement born in Duncan's dance when she turned to 'Greek dance' and achieved 'free' dance, which was dance – very importantly – without a subject. Like Duncan, he considered the language of classical ballet obsolete. The ballet of the nineteenth century, without fail, conveyed feeling and told a tale. Ballet, which served 'only as the expression of material feelings (love, fear, etc.)', Kandinsky considered, 'is today understood by only a few, and still loses its clarity', and it is clearly unfit for the future. It is, he went on, necessary to change to abstract movement; only then 'will we soon be able to sense the inner value of every movement and inner beauty will replace outer beauty'.[27] He then drew on his vision of the inner movement of the living cosmos: 'Absolutely simple movement for an unknown purpose, in itself, already produces meaningful, secret and creative impressions. And this exactly, in as much as its mysterious external, practical purpose remains. Then its influence is the influence of a pure sound.'[28] According to the artist's conviction, this principle must, and will, underlie the construction of new dance, dance that stresses the inner value of movement. New dance uses every meaning, all the inner thought of movement in time and space, not in narrative. Kandinsky anticipated that the search for the abstract meaning of movement, either separate from music or in combination with it, would lead to the creation of a new kind of dance – 'new ballet'.

In the 1920s, Kandinsky made sketches of the Expressionist dancer Gret Palucca. In one of them, he captured her figure in the midst of a jump, with arms and legs spread out to the sides to form a geometrical figure, a five-pointed star, shining in the air. 'In dance the whole body, in modern dance every finger, draws lines with a very vivid expression . . . the dancer's entire body, right down to the fingertips, is at every moment a continuous linear composition.'[29] By contrast, his colleague, the architect and participant in the avant-garde, Iakov Chernikhov, in 'linear compositions' sought to impose his own character on living dynamism, to give 'a condition to our graphical solutions, when the impression of motion, striving, displacement, rocking, instability and some form of participating vibrations, is experienced'. His graphical constructions 'transfer to a stronger and finer form striving, motion, vibration, that is, something "living", inherent to life'.[30]

Artists intended the new dance, together with music and abstract painting, to form a staged composition, as Kandinsky called his variant of the total work of art, his vision of *das Gesamtkunstwerk*. In was in this context that artists questioned the meaning for art of muscular movement, kinaesthesia. The specialist experimental and clinical literature about the biological character of kinaesthesia little, if at all, informed the artists' knowledge. As a sixth sense, kinaesthesia therefore remained, in Russian creative work, close to intuition and the mental capacities thought sensitive to mysterious and hidden forces of spiritual and cosmic being. Kinaesthetic sensibility was thus a natural candidate, along with intuition and imagination, to become the route to 'higher sensitivity'. There was also a good deal of contemporary appreciation of the place of kinaesthesia in synaesthesia, the fusion of sensations from different senses, and of the potential of synaesthetic art forms also to foster 'the higher sensitivity'.

Kinaesthesia and synaesthesia

The project to create a new 'synthesized' sensitivity by combining several kinds of senses is at least in part attributable to Richard Wagner and his idea of 'the synthesis of art'. By creating 'the total work of art', Wagner wanted to return art to what he supposed was its ancient power, with the strength of myth. Ancient Greek tragedy, with its unity of music, song and drama, served for him as the prototype of *das Gesamtkunstwerk*, to which he hoped to give birth in his operas. The artists of the avant-garde took over and, in different ways, modernized the Wagnerian idea. With this in the background, in Germany the founders of the Bauhaus created works crossing the borders of different arts within the sphere of buildings and objects in daily life. From this developed much of the modern understanding of design. In Moscow, after the Revolution, the Institute of Art Culture (INKhUK) similarly came into existence, in part for the study of 'synthesized art'.

The avant-garde interest in uniting the arts, like the interest in synaesthesia, uniting the senses, presupposed that a synthesis of the various arts differs qualitatively from a simple sum.[31] Just as a chemical synthesis gives rise to qualitatively new properties, the synthesis of separate arts, or of sensations, it was believed, creates a completely new work and another sensitivity. As the new sensitivity was thought to be higher than any one of the individual sensory feelings from which it had been created, it appeared the means to approach nearer to the world of the extra-sensory, the intangible and the invisible. Such belief connected avant-garde artists to the Wagnerian project: the return of art to its other-worldly, transcendental purpose, engendering the capacity 'to see', to be at one with being and with myth. Thus the idea of the synthesis of art, and of synaesthesia, which a modern researcher, Bulat Galeev, has called 'synaesthetic alchemy', was part of the striving of Symbolists 'to grasp in ruptured words the misty entrance of other worlds', as Aleksandr Blok wrote.[32] This project, to open the way to a 'higher sensitivity' and to sensory consciousness of symbols, went back at least to Baudelaire's poem, 'Correspondances' (1857). Rimbaud had responded with his poem, 'Voyelles', about the coloured perception of vowel sounds, and artistic interest in this continued for a long time.[33] The composer Aleksandr Scriabin created an electric circuit with different-coloured light bulbs, which illuminated in response to his own composition. This can still to be seen in the house where he lived in Moscow. The Expressionist poet Ippolit Sokolov, who promoted a radical idea of the human machine in the 1920s, referred specifically to the sixth sense, citing 'the coloured sound of A. Rimbaud, or the lighted scents of Baudelaire, or the tasting sounds of Huysmans'.[34]

Synaesthesia certainly interested scientists, especially those engaged in studying visual perception. We need to note only that there was intensive experimental and theoretical discussion of colour and of spatial perception in the second half of the nineteenth century, and this research included a detailed examination of the manner in which the sense of movement of the eyeballs fuses retinal sensations and thus makes possible visual cognition (which the physiologist Hermann Helmholtz considered involves 'unconscious inference'). Such work implicated a kind of synaesthesia of movement and visual sense in normal vision. By contrast, other research focused on exceptional forms of synaesthesia, treating them as if they were pathological. This made a language of 'perverted sensibility' available to critics of the works of the avant-garde. When Velimir (Viktor Vladimirovich) Khlebnikov, an early and (in Russia) influential poet and playwright taking both Futurist and Symbolist directions, talked of 'the blue colour of the cornflower . . . ceaselessly changing, passing through a region of rupture, mysterious to us, to people, turning into the sound of the cry of a cuckoo or the cry of a child', one commentator dismissed this as 'foggy explanations of *the phenomenon of synaesthesia*'. This sacrificed Khlebnikov's intent, since he described not simply a combination of sensations, but a strategy to achieve closeness to 'another world' through a 'region of rupture' mysterious to people.[35] If, following Galeev, we call the correspondences Baudelaire drew between sensations 'vertically' or 'deeply' connected, in contrast to the 'horizontal' connections habitual in perception, then we have to recognize that the Symbolists did not strive to set up 'horizontal' connections.[36] For them, sensory correspondences were valuable precisely because they opened up the radiance of the symbol, the 'vertical' measure, the way into the depths and heights, the sensations of another world. Yet, remembering the gender associations of vertical and horizontal (coming together in the cross), familiar to someone like Kandinsky, the vertical understood as male, the horizontal as female, we may be wary of such language.

Kandinsky carried out experiments with sensory synthesis of different kinds (contemporary psychologists would speak of 'different modalities') in 1910 in Munich. In this project, he joined with the Ukrainian-born composer Thomas von Hartmann and a dancer, later well known, but then only starting out, Alexander Sakharoff. 'I myself had the opportunity of carrying out some small experiments abroad with a young musician and a dancer,' Kandinsky noted.

> From several of my watercolors, the musician would choose one that appeared to him to have the clearest musical form. In the absence of the dancer, he would play this watercolor. Then the dancer would appear, and having been played this musical composition, he would dance it and then find the watercolor he had danced.[37]

Already in the years 1908–09, Kandinsky had thought of adding the language of movement to the language of music and colour. In his abstract ballet, *Yellow Sound*, geometrical figures decorated in different colours moved around the stage to the music, also composed by Hartmann. It was proposed to stage a performance in the Munich Artistic Theatre, but the project remained unrealized. Much later however, in 1928, Kandinsky succeeded in presenting in Dessau, in the Bauhaus theatre, another abstract ballet, to the music of Mussorgsky's *Pictures in an Exhibition*. It had no subject in the conventional way, and it did not reproduce the themes of 'Pictures in an Exhibition'. Abstract figures in the ballet, performers dressed in abstract costumes, danced, moved in different directions, came together, then moved away from each other. Earlier than this, in the Belorussian town of Vitebsk, the group UNOVIS had shown a Suprematist ballet. Its author was Malevich's student, Nina Kogan, and the personages wore the black square, the red square and the circle. The performers, dressed in Suprematist costumes, moved these figures about the stage. The figures pictured a cross, then a star, then an arc.[38]

In the same year, in 1920, in Moscow, Kandinsky's initiative resulted in the creation of the Institute of Art Culture. One of its first research projects was to interrogate the synthesis of sensations. Kandinsky himself composed the questionnaire, and he included questions about synaesthesia that took it for granted that synthetic effects include the sense of movement:

How, for example, how does a triangle appear to you – doesn't it seem to you that it moves, where, doesn't it seem to you more sharp-minded than the square; isn't the sensation from a triangle similar to the sensation from a lemon, and even more similar to the song of a canary? And in a triangle or circle, which geometrical form is similar to vulgarity, to talent, to fine weather?

Do you consider it possible to express some of your feelings graphically, that is, with some straight or bent lines or some geometrical figures? . . . Try to do this and occupy yourself with such exercises.

How does colour act on you: yellow, blue, red? Which of them acts more strongly, and is it pleasant or unpleasant? Is there something unbearable for you in these colours? Especially enchanting? Which of them seems to you strong, dense, active, moving (to which side), flat, deep, unruly, stable?[39]

As the language of the questionnaire shows, the reduction of art to abstract elements and their combinations was not, for Kandinsky, the reduction of perception. On the contrary, it proposed a new horizon of sensitivity, or, as the Theosophists (with whom Kandinsky was in sympathetic contact) said, 'widened consciousness' and 'widened perception'. The sense of movement was built into the whole project, bridging psycho-physiological and intuitive perception.

The State Institute of Art Culture (GINKhUK) was established in Petrograd (the Russianized name for Saint-Petersburg once war had been declared with Germany) at the same time as the Moscow INKhUK. It also carried out research in connection with Kandinsky's many parallel projects. Matiushin, who was the guardian of the idea of 'the widened look', headed the section on 'Organic Culture' in GINKhUK. He held that every artist, if not in general every person, is obliged to develop a 'higher sensitivity'. A really observant person sees not only with the eyes but with the organs of the body, doing this directly without adaptation, in the way, for example, that people born blind perceive the world. Matiushin understood the precious quality of the dispersed look of dreamers, poets and artists: only they can grasp the universe as a single and indivisible whole. He himself began to practise such a dispersed, widened perception of the world, which turned out to be over-flowing and all-embracing. His co-workers experimented with vision 'at the back of the head' and with 'widening' this vision to 360 degrees, for example, by drawing an unknown landscape when blindfolded. Matiushin called his theory *zor-ved*, which abbreviated *zrenie-vedanie* (sight-knowledge), and, possibly playing with the words 'sight-vision', suggesting that *vedat'* (to know) has a larger part than *videt'* (to see). In the theory and practice of *zor-ved*, movement had a large role:

> The energy of colour and form immeasurably rises in movement. From a still body, the eye, widely energetic, receives the maximum of colour. In forceful movement of the body, the eye can receive all the intensity of the colour-form. These outcomes, coming from a deeply experienced [witnessed] threefold dimensionality, may set up the beginning and basis of a fourth perpendicular [that is, a new dimension of sense].[40]

Somewhat later, there were similar experiments in Russian science on the development of unusual sensitivity and the formation of new organs of sense. The Soviet psychologist A. N. Leont'ev, using trial subjects, studied the differentiation of colour with the help of the palm of the hand, not the eye, thereby exploring the ability 'to see' with the skin. These experiments took place in the Institute of Psychology in Moscow and in the Khar'kov Pedagogical Institute during the years 1936–39. In a way, this was the most radical practical widening of perception. The key to the possession of such a wonderful skill, in Leont'ev's opinion, was, indeed, activity: experimental subjects began to differentiate colour only under conditions that produced micro-movements of the hand. Leont'ev, with his students, carried out one further series of such experiments, on the training of high-pitched hearing, and they found that the main condition for the successful differentiation of relatively high sounds was inner song, active participation of the muscles of the larynx.[41] Research appeared to show the intimate role of movement sense in wider perceptual possibilities.

In the mid-1920s, Matiushin's students and co-workers, Boris Ender and his sister Maria Ender, of the Section of Organic Culture in GINKhUK, began to lead the classes in a Petrograd dance studio, Heptachor. We shall discuss this studio in the next chapter, but here we make the point that the Enders taught the students drawing and colouring, and also 'widened perception'. Their purpose was to intensify the colour and spatial senses of the dancers. In the words of the founder of Heptachor, Stefanida Rudneva, 'our students studied to find the dynamic axis, the tension and stress, in the form of branches of different species of trees: at first with the appearance of geometrical straight lines, then with the volume of the form of the branches'. The students acquired the skill of perceiving space not only in front of them but also around them, taking a circular view 'widened' to 360 degrees. Together with Boris Ender, the students similarly created tension based on 'the tactile feeling for space'. This tension helped to achieve freer movement and reciprocity with partners, making it possible 'to wield together separate bodies into one collective, inseparable whole which moves'.[42] The experiments on spatial perception were done with the eyes shut. One task was to come up to the wall, stopping at a precise distance (not further than a metre away); another was to gather in the centre of the room without bumping into other people. Alternatively, a person was required to go towards the wall, passing between other people without touching them. Yet another task was to take a position exactly in the middle between two other persons; doing this, Rudneva reported a vivid and unique sensation of an equal attraction from both sides.[43]

When Boris Ender moved to Moscow, Maria Ender began to lead the activity in Heptachor in Petrograd. Moreover, all the Ender brothers and sisters – Boris, Maria, Georgii and Kseniia – had taken part in performances which Matiushin arranged in his house on Peschanaya Street. Here, in the winter of 1921, Matiushin decided to demonstrate in performance 'different systems for the understanding of volume in the artistic treatment of the human body'. The first picture exhibited 'the one-dimensional line of the understanding of volume in Egypt'. Kseniya Ender performed, imitating a fresco depicting a priestess: 'With slow movements, with severe turns in the flat plane, the woman's figure of the priestess approached the god and began to dance ceremoniously, all the time severely restraining movement in one plane.'[44] In her 'Sketches of Individual Movement (Dependent on the Straight Body)', Maria Ender later consolidated the results of research on the axis of movement which Boris had carried out with Heptachor.

Maria Ender's own experiments in the studio touched on sounds and movements. The results of this were then recreated in watercolour and pencil paintings and drawings by a member of

Heptachor, Natalia Enman. She drew different interpretations of the sounds the dancers had differentiated. She annotated her sketches: 'The sound of trees "made deciduous" from strong wind', 'The blow on a frying-pan', and 'The sound of groats being poured'.[45] After experiments with sound perceptions, the students began, analogously to 'widening of vision', to speak about the 'widening of hearing', achieving a fuller perception of music through movement. They also tried 'to transpose into movement' the colour of sound, the sound timbre of different instruments and the human voice, and they experimented with 'the sound content of foreign, often not understood speech'.[46]

In 1926, Maria and Boris Ender, together with Heptachor, carried out a series of experiments on the interaction between the colour of a material (sand, linoleum, fabric and glass) and 'tactile impressions (with eyes closed)'. In other trials, participants were asked to sense the quality of movement, saying, for example, whether it was quick or slow, straight or curving. Interesting images were created, which Enman recorded for the dancers in her drawings and annotations: 'Enclosed space. Space broken into pieces by corners, quiet, quick chop.' They even tried to unite taste sensations with movement. Earlier, in quite another setting, Rainer Maria Rilke (*The Sonnets to Orpheus*) had exclaimed:

A little music, a stamping, a humming: –
here are the warm, mute maidens, coming
to dance the taste of experienced fruit.
Dance the orange. Who can forget it.[47]

Unfortunately, Heptachor could not carry out experiments with the taste of the orange, as Rilke had imagined in his sonnet, as the fruit was simply not on sale.

'Out with prejudices!' This was Iakov Golosovker's call in his book about the imaginative Absolute. 'It is time for science to anatomize "the mystical", in order to read through its sub-text, using its favoured methods, and not to decide in advance that in front of us is either the ill or the refined display of spirit, reflected with symbolic language.' But if the radical avant-garde saw in synaesthesia an objective window to another world, it faced conservative scientific critics who continued to see a defect, a pathological perception. Such scientific 'pre-judgements', Golosovker considered, 'are based on belief in an abyss separating two isolated substances, "matter" and "spirit". But there is no such abyss and also no such substances.'[48] The demonstration of the participation in synaesthetic perception of kinaesthetic sensations, 'widening perception', we have argued, showed exactly this: the embodied nature of spirit and the spiritual nature of embodiment. That there is 'no abyss' between matter and spirit was witnessed also in other experiments undertaken by avant-garde artists, experiments with expressive movement or 'the speaking body'. This work, as we now show, had great influence and value.

CHAPTER THREE

Expression in Dance

The Dance-Foot had hardly gone, when the devotees of the new Dionysus began to sing: 'raise higher your dithyrambic legs!'
DMITRY MEREZHKOVSKY[1]

The new dance

Nietzsche, sometimes known as the dancing philosopher, gave philosophical direction, and indeed spiritual purpose, to free individual display of creativity as dance. He made 'light feet' the metaphor of the spirit: 'And although there are swamps and thick afflictions on earth, he who has light feet runs even across mud and dances as upon swept ice.'[2]

Having seen Isadora Duncan dance, the eccentric Russian philosopher Vasily Rozanov contrasted her spirit and directness with the tired, utilitarian expression, as he saw it, of an earlier generation of writers on art. Literary critics, in an intense response to the conditions of life in Russia, had demanded that art be judged as a social and moral act. Rozanov, however, also claimed that there was Russian precedent for the spirit in what Duncan accomplished. 'How good that this Duncan, with her hips, sends everything, all these Chernyshevskys and Dobrolyubovs to the devil. However, [the poets] Briusov and Bely had already sent them there.'[3] One could not find better words to connect the *bouleversement* Duncan brought about in dance and the Nietzschean 'transvaluation of values' pursued by the Symbolists in Russia, as elsewhere in Europe.

The unbinding of the body and the freeing of consciousness partnered each other. Duncan, on the stage and in life, fought with circumstances – moral injunctions and taboos – reforming not only stage costume, even going so far as wanting to perform completely naked, but also the form of life, preaching emancipation and refusing the bonds of marriage. When she came to Russia, first in 1904 and then returning several times, the Symbolist poets and artists, seeing in Duncan an individualist and pioneering dancer par excellence, became her grateful public. For Aleksandr Blok, she was the symbol of 'the Eternal Feminine', 'the Well-Favoured Woman'; on the wall of his room, together with the *Mona Lisa* and the contemporary painter Nesterov's *Madonna*, he hung 'a large head of Isadora Duncan'.[4] A fellow poet, Sergei Gorodetsky, compared Blok's room with a cell and with a chapel, finding there the same impression of purity and prayerfulness.[5]

As the psychologist of art, Rudolf Arnheim, stated sixty years ago, dance is 'the art of the muscle sense'.[6] This chapter shows just how true this was for the introduction of modern dance in Russia. It is not necessary to tell once again the story of modern dance, to which Duncan, and the Russians whom she inspired, contributed. But it is important to recognize that the kinaesthetic sense, as we have already begun to show, also played a part in the life and work of artists whose primary medium was not dance. Like 'the light-footed dancer', Zarathustra, Andrei Bely, the poet, professed himself to be a tight-rope dancer who balances above the abyss.[7] A well-known silhouette by F. A. Golovin pictures him walking firmly in a straight line, as if on a wire, keeping balance with his arms. Mikhail Chekov saw Bely actually going along the parapet of a balcony high above the ground.[8] For other intellectuals who, unlike Bely, did not have a motor talent from childhood, the achievement of 'the opening' of the body occurred in adulthood. This happened, with notable consequences, to Prince Sergei Mikhailovich Volkonsky, the Director of the Imperial Stage. He had often criticized the theatre of his time for the absence of musicality. One fine day, seeking this very musicality, in Hellerau near Dresden, he looked in on the school of rhythmics of the Swiss composer and pedagogue, Emile Jaques-Dalcroze. It was a decisive event in Volkonsky's life; personal kinaesthetic experience turned his life around. In Petersburg, at his own expense, he opened the Courses of Rhythmic Gymnastics, and he printed a bulletin, *Pages of the Courses of Rhythmic Gymnastics*, taking Dalcroze's words as an epigraph: 'The comprehension of rhythmical gymnastics is a matter of personal experience.'[9] The Prince was not alone. Lyubov Dmitrievna Mendeleeva-Blok, the daughter of the renowned chemist Mendeleev and the wife of the poet Aleksandr Blok, lived through a similar change of life, measuring out for herself the role of a Bacchante. As a teenager, she was ashamed of her appearance, but, moving, she soon began with love 'to sense her wakened young body', and as a result, when she saw Duncan, she 'encountered Duncan with ecstasy, as for a person long anticipated and known in feeling'.[10]

Movement, gymnastics and *plyaska* (inspired dance, or dance with spirit, which we express with the Russian word to distance it from just any kind of dance) opened the body from a new direction, a direction 'that speaks'. The arts met in dance. 'Music, the art of time, and plastic art, the art of space, find this meeting-place in the moving material of the human body,' wrote Volkonsky. In movement, 'a person portrays externally what has woken in him internally'.[11] *Plyaska* heals the person who feels divided by reason and emotion, spirit and body, volition and duty. Even in the highly disciplined form taken by Dalcrozian rhythmics, *plyaska* brought Volkonsky the highest gift of his life, 'the quietening of that perpetual dissension which reigns between our "I wish" and "I may", the meeting of imagination with reason; thought, illuminating the play of the imagination, and with its images helping thought; the ethically-real justification of aesthetic-idealist attractions; and, last, the final blending of all in one "beautiful person"'.[12] Finally, *plyaska* reconciled a person with the world, harmonized her or him with the cosmos. When this happened, the poet Maksimilian Voloshin believed, the cosmic and the physiological, feeling and logic, reason and knowledge flow together. The world, splintered by the cut-glass mirror of our perceptions, receives its eternal subject-object wholeness.[13]

The Symbolists, who had such a large and impressive presence in Russia, as elsewhere in the early modernist avant-garde, along with those who, like them, sought wholesale change in humanity, believed that the experience of bodily movement, and especially rhythmical musical movement, amounted to finding a new meaning of life. Dance, people grasped, had the capacity to turn over the soul. But how, in practice, with what forms of dance, to realize this turning-over? How, under the influence of affective kinaesthetic experience, would a new vision of the world arise and give form to a new wholeness? How to fulfil the desire for 'conversion' (sometimes called, using Greek roots, *metanoia*), for a mental or spiritual metamorphosis, for transformation of meaning?

Nietzsche's metaphors of dance, the extensive, if not systematic, reference to the importance of rhythm, movement and dance in the writings of innovative artists like Rimbaud (who recognized that rhythmic poetic forms were spatial, like dance) and Cézanne (who, it has been said, choreographed his thought in painting), along with innovations in dance performance itself, suggest that dance may be a key, perhaps even the key, to a more satisfactory comprehension of modernism as a conceptual category.[14] Mallarmé's conception of the unifying art form of poetry was that it would be *performance*, like dance, in space and time. Dee Reynolds considered 'that the art of dance, which takes place in real as well as virtual time and space [in movement and in imagination], in many ways provides a paradigm for the kind of spatio-temporal interactions which these poets and painters wished to exploit'. This in turn prompted the tentative suggestion that 'dance, even more than the music, is the prototype of the avant-garde art work'.[15]

Our own argument points in a similar direction. The language of movement, used in connection with all the senses, criss-crosses the achievement of new art forms. All historians of modernism have observed this. They have not, however, always followed through to the conclusion that this makes the artistic medium specifically attentive to movement, dance, of pivotal significance. Speaking of the Russians, we consider artists who clearly and explicitly did see this at the time. Going further, we may say that historians of modernism have paid insufficient attention to the actual sense of movement, kinaesthesia, and to the rich ways in which there was a substantial interest in this topic before and after 1900. All the same, just as we think it conceptually ill-advised to pick out one sense as the sense 'of an age', it may be inappropriate to name any one medium (whether music, dance or anything else) as the prototype of modernism. We may expect particular artists, followed by their scholarly devotees, to elevate one medium, the artist's own, to a dominant position, but this is another matter. Modernism is, when all is said and done, a family name, and there is no necessity for all the different members of the family to have any one particular feature, however widely characteristic it may be, in common.

There is, nevertheless, much to say on dance, and much to be done to identify the place it had in the transformation of culture in general and of the lives of many men and women in particular.

The Russian Hellenes

Educated Europeans frequently mythologized the achievements of the Ancient Greeks. Certainly, this was for the grandeur and beauty of their arts, their philosophy and their language. Nevertheless, Nietzsche, and those who followed him, found something beyond this: a wholeness, a genius in knowing how to live. Imagination for the Greek way of life spoke to those who sought to rise above contemporary materialism to 'the higher sensitivity'.

> Oh those Greeks! They knew how to live. What is required for that is to stop courageously at the surface, the fold, the skin, to adore appearance, to believe in forms, tones, words . . . Are we not, precisely in this respect, Greeks? Adorers of forms, of tones, of words? And therefore – *artists*?[16]

In 1918, barely a year into the Revolution, the poet Osip Mandelstam declared: 'Above us is a barbarian sky, and all the same we are Hellenes.'[17] He did not stand idly by, but went to work in Narkompros (the People's Commissariat of Enlightenment) in order to bring Dalcrozian rhythmics into the curriculum of higher education generally. In the opinion of Volkonsky, Mandelstam and people who thought like them, rhythmics was the best means available to achieve a new Greek *orkhēstra*, to give birth to a person in movement, rhythmical, expressive, capable of becoming a participant in a theatrical collective. To bring this about, the philologist Viacheslav Ivanov, the theatre reformer Vsevolod Meyerhold and other intellectuals began to co-operate with the new political power. In a short time, the Commissariat of Enlightenment turned into the headquarters for the realization of a grandiose project, a New Birth, a Third Renaissance. (The first was the Italian Renaissance, the second the German age of Goethe, the third was to be the new, Slavic age.) This was, indeed, a vision that the professor of Antiquity in Petersburg, Faddei Frantsevich Zelinsky (Tadeusz Stefan Zieliński), who was of Polish origins, had already proposed at the turn of the century.

In 1910, a group of young people, led by Professor Zelinsky, set out on a journey from Petersburg to Odessa, and from there by steamer to Piraeus in Greece. On the steamer were students of Saint-Petersburg University and students of the Higher Women's Courses, the Bestuzhevskie Courses, where Zelinsky himself was a professor, and of the Raevskie Courses. These Courses made higher education available to women that was formally denied to them in universities. Meyerhold, who was collecting material for staging *Oedipus the King*, joined the excursion. He recalled how well the students on the Courses sang folk songs on the boat, how Zelinsky sat in the bow surrounded by his students, how they took off their scarves and decorated ropes with them, and how the wind played with these coloured flags above the head of the teacher. And the teacher talked about how the Athenians returned from Tauris and Colchas to the shores of their homeland and looked into the distance, anticipating the moment when the golden spear of Athena, crowning the Acropolis, would shine in the sun. The professor led his charges not to an alien ruin but to 'the hearth of home'. Each European, he considered, had at least 'two homelands: one is the country by the name of which we call ourselves, the other is Antiquity'.[18]

When Zelinsky proclaimed the coming New Birth, he envisaged it as a return to the spiritual home. The turn to Ancient Greece, he believed, had already twice saved Europe from barbarism and religious fanaticism, and, it was his hope, would save it again from contemporary 're-barbarization'. It was necessary to return to the distinctive light of Antiquity, to its joyful world-feeling and presentation of moral law not yet muddied by the Christian understanding of sin. The Petersburg 'tower' of Viacheslav Ivanov, the upper-floor apartment where poets met, and the Paris studio of Raymond Duncan, Isadora's brother, were two of many other attempts to give birth to a living Antiquity. The studio of dance, 'Heptachor', on which we shall focus, a group founded by followers of Zelinsky on the Bestuzhevskie Courses, was one more such attempt. Zelinsky and Duncan became two 'saints' of the religion of dance to which the students committed themselves.

Contemporaries considered Zelinsky not only saintly through the study of Antiquity, but almost a priest of ancient religion.

Students from all the faculties, including the natural sciences, came to listen to his inspirational lectures, 'as if one breathes with the scent of the boundless sea'.[19] The professor judged feeling the main and best thing in religiosity: universal, ecumenical religious feeling is the real kernel of religion, and all the rest is only parables. Zelinsky was a man of deep faith, not in established Christianity, but in his own religion, which he called 'Ancient Greek' or 'Hellene'. Ancient religion, in Zelinsky's understanding, not only sustained cosmological, moral and eschatological beliefs, beliefs also characteristic of Christianity, but had an indisputable advantage owing to its universalism, or, speaking in Dostoevsky's words from his famous speech on Pushkin, 'capacity for universal sympathy'.[20] Universalism guaranteed the religious tolerance of the Ancient Greeks, their inclination to recognize their own gods in other divine incarnations, rather than to fight with them. In Orthodox Russia, this was radical and liberating.

Another advantage of 'the religion of Antiquity' was that it propagated joy. It is, Zelinsky considered, the only religion of joy, beauty and fullness of life. To practise the religion is thus easy, since a person does it joyfully and not out of guilt, obligation or duty. A contemporary person, he held, someone who is prepared to bow down fully before the three-in-one ideal of beauty, goodness and truth will turn to this religion. Beauty – significantly for the arts – comes first: 'The physical beauty of the Hellenic gods is the first step to revelation . . . The second and third is goodness and truth.' It follows that beauty should be understood in a special way. For Zelinsky, 'the beauty of unmoving form is only one of the two forms of the revelation of godliness'; the other comes from movement. Zelinsky emphasized that the Hellenic Muses exist as a unity of three – poetry, music and *plyaska* – with the latter taking the lead. All three are united with godliness, but predominant 'in this trinity is *plyaska*'. *Plyaska* is the bridge which unites 'Bacchai in deer-skins', with godlike wisdom, and which serves for the transmission of moral community. Dance, he concluded, 'may much more deeply furrow our soul than a very attractive word poem could do'.[21]

Unsurprisingly, Zelinsky responded ecstatically to the appearance in Russia of the first 'Dionysian' dancer, Isadora Duncan. At one of her performances, on 22 January 1913 in the Theatre of Musical Drama, he even delivered an introductory word which (taking a Russian custom to an extreme) stretched into a whole lecture. To the accompaniment of the Russian Musical Society Orchestra and the Musical Drama Choir, Duncan was to perform a fragment from Gluck's *Iphigénie en Aulide*. The professor discoursed about Iphigenia and explained Duncan's dances, which even the most educated viewers received as 'something unusual, poetic, incomprehensible'. In conclusion, he declared the dancer 'his inspirational partner in the task of the renaissance of Antiquity'.[22] In a newspaper comment, the critic Andrei Levinson, with well-known irony, wrote that Zelinsky's presentation 'brought to the last performance of Miss Duncan the character of exceptional creativity':

> Prof. Zelinsky, a master of refined, educated and expressive ... speech, expounded Duncan's art as the authentic renaissance 'of the idea of the antique *orkhēstra*', having pointed out the likeness of her attempt to the creativity of Friedrich Nietzsche, Böcklin and Richard Wagner. . . . The correspondence of the dances of Miss Duncan to the idea of the antique *orkhēstra*, which was by no means elucidated by the lecturer, he justified by way of a psychological analysis of Euripides's 'Iphigenia'.[23]

This enthusiasm led Zelinsky to support his followers from the Bestuzhevskie Courses when they, in imitation of Duncan, took up with 'free dance'. Stefanida Rudneva, Natalia Enman, Natalia Ped'kova, Kamilla and Il'za Trever, Ekaterina Tsinzerling and Julia Tikhomirova got together and moved to the accompaniment of a grand piano, their own singing or 'internal music'. Sometimes they met in a school, where a relative of one of them was the Head:

> In the hall, after lessons, we hung the windows and walls with white curtains. It was dark, and a candle burned only on the piano, lighting the sheet music. We listened to the music and moved in the dark, in order not to see oneself or the others. . . . The rough, constrained parts of the body sometimes began to liberate themselves, and muscles, absorbing the melody, corrected themselves and began to move evenly.[24]

The girls spent almost all their free time in musical improvisation. Finally, the day came, Natalia Ped'kova recalled, when it was time to bring into the light the composition which, until then, had been created in the dark:

The spectators were Heptachor themselves, and St[efanida] Dm[itrievna] Rudneva performed. She presented a lullaby but didn't picture the rocking. The movement of her body found its plastic expression and the melody sang in the movement of her arms. It was a fully completed musical-movement composition. It was 'Heptachor'.[25]

In fact, Zelinsky was only later to think up the name of the studio, from the Greek, επτά (seven), to match the number of participants, and χορόσ (circular or group dance).

If Zelinsky's male students set up an intellectual circle, 'The Union of the Third Renaissance' (of which the Bakhtin brothers, Mikhail and Nikolai, were members), his female students responded to his call to renew the ancient *chorea* or dance-*plyaska*. The professor encouraged the neophytes of 'the *plyaska* religion', though he saw how far they were from the Hellenic ideal and believed that 'to the ancient Hellenes these attempts would have produced to a degree the same impression as when people born dumb begin to speak to us with exercises in articulate speech'.[26] Yet neither Duncan nor Heptachor occupied themselves with the precise reconstruction of the antique *orkhēstra*. Their ambition went much further: they dreamed of restoring to humanity an illuminated, joyful, dancing 'feeling for life'. In the charter of Heptachor, which was never at the time made public, they wrote:

Only the creative feeling for life gives to a man inner strength and freedom, gives to him excellence. And meanwhile, only in rare minutes of illumination does contemporary man grasp such a feeling, creative and harmonious, for life. How to prolong these moments? How to act so that life always declares itself unified, alive, speaking to us? One of the few ways to such feeling for life lies through dance.[27]

To separate itself from other schools and dance studios, Heptachor called itself a 'studio of *plyaska*'.

Faithful to the ideas of their mentor and friendship to Antiquity, as they understood it, the members of the studio lived communally. From their very first meeting, Stenya (diminutive for Stefanida) Rudneva and Natalia Enman had begun 'to dream about the organization of a group of friends, animated by one idea and by

FIGURE 2 *Heptachor Studio in the 1920s.*

FIGURE 3 *Stefanida Rudneva. 'The Wings', mid-1920s.*

FIGURE 4 *Stefanida Rudneva and Natalia Ped'kova. A study to 'Dance of the Skomorokhi' by Nikolai Rimsky-Korsakov, mid-1920s.*

unified dreams – about some kind of commune that constructs a new, unprecedented life'.[28] They formed, in the words of one contemporary, 'a small commune of Amazons of science and art'. 'If someone in Heptachor got married, her friends lived through a deep wave of anxiety. Was it possible for a husband to be included in the distinctive life? On the birth of Rudneva's son, Nikon, he became the son of all Heptachor.'[29] Their 'Hellas on the banks of the Neva [Petersburg's river]' continued to exist to the middle of the

1930s. It gave a practical beginning to 'musical movement' which, through succeeding generations of followers, has come down to the present. During the Stalinist winter, some of the women maintained ideals and technique by teaching children. Then, with the Khrushchev 'thaw', elements of studio teaching reappeared.

In the hungry post-Revolution years, the professor still gave courses in Petersburg University, including one on the 'Bacchai' of Euripides. But, according to one of his auditors, 'Dionysus was deaf to the calls of the Bacchai, their stomachs were empty and they feared police raids'.[30] In 1921, Zelinsky left for Warsaw. Later, Heptachor received a letter in which their old teacher informed them that he was going blind, like Homer, and that for him 'the outer world had gone dark, but he had begun to hear more the voice of the inner world'.[31] Three years before Zelinsky left, however, another project, in which Heptachor took a vital part, began in pursuit of the utopia of a new Renaissance.

'Ach, the devil take it, again they're dancing here!'

We recount the story of the first decade of Heptachor in some colour in order to do justice to the richness of what these young women achieved, but also because musical movement exemplifies the place that dance had in linking the arts, and in linking the avant-garde with new hopes for teaching and performance in the immediate post-Revolution years. The life and art of the young women (and, at times, a few men) in Heptachor was a kinaesthetic life and art, integrated with other changes in the arts.

For Zelinsky, the rebirth of Antiquity meant the saving of European civilization from 'a new barbarism'. His ideal included a restoration of the culture, so valued in Antiquity, of theatrical performance and mastery of oratory. Hoping to correct contemporary over-emphasis on the written word, Zelinsky and his colleagues therefore created the Institute of the Living Word. At its opening, the professor complained that from the time of Antiquity, 'the word killed gesture, and writing killed the word'. He put forward the means to bring it back life, to return to the syncretic nature the word had possessed in the ancient theatre, the *living* word, the expressive word realized in drama, the plastic arts and dance. Founded in 1918 and continuing in existence until 1924, the Institute of the Living Word was one of the brightest episodes in the post-Revolution life of the humanities in Petrograd. It became the first scholarly and educational institution to turn upside down the conventional hierarchy of the spoken and written word and to subordinate the bookish word to the word sounded, sung and danced.

A number of like-minded people joined Zelinsky in this project. The most important were Vsevolod Nikolaevich Vsevolodsky-Gerngross, who became the Head of the Institute, and Yury Erastovich Ozarovsky, the teacher of the living word in the Drama Courses at the Petersburg Theatre School (and Gerngross's teacher). Ozarovsky began and Gerngross continued to revive the art of declamation, restoring words in order to achieve the syncretic unity of poetry, music and gesture which existed in the ancient theatre. A number of theatre directors, including Ozarovsky, Gerngross, Volkonsky and Meyerhold, basing themselves on Antiquity, judged that gesture, movement, historically and naturally precedes the word, though the word gives the gesture definition. The effective word does not predetermine movement, but completes it. Ozarovsky argued that declamation is the more expressive the more it involves mime and gesture, because the expressive timbre of the voice grows out of movement. And conversely: the voice of a familiar person evokes in imagination mimicry of the person's gesticulation. Declamation, consequently, uses, in full, 'the living, that is, moving . . . mimetic sound of the music of human speech'.[32]

Ozarovsky was called 'the director-archaeologist' because of his passion for the archaic roots of the theatre. He wrote:

The theatre grew from the religious dithyrambs of the Dionysian cult. There, in blessed Hellas, amidst the sacred fumes, in the prayerful crowd of orgiasts, frenzied and drunk from passion, groans and wails of the soul were torn out, which opened eyes to the truth of ecstatic revelations. There, in these groans and wails, was created the music of the soul, the first sounds and tones of free (since without purpose and aimless) musical words.

It was necessary, Ozarovsky considered, to return performance and musicality to readings on the stage, so that art would not be 'torn from its undoubted homeland: thought and emotion – music and mime'.[33] Members of his family shared his interests: his sister, the actress Olga Erastovna, collected folklore; his son, Nikolai, contributed to the written book, *Music of the Living Word*; his wife, Dar'ia Mikhailovna Musina-Pushkina, helped to create a theatre. The married couple founded the theatre called Stil' (Style), which in its productions devoted significant attention to movement on the stage. Duncan was at their home. Dar'ia Musina-Pushkina had studied expressive movement in Paris, and in the Institute of the Living Word she taught 'plastic expression according to [François] Delsarte'. (This was a system of teaching declamation and singing, going back to the 1840s, based on systematized movements held to be expressive of inner emotion.) In 1920, when it was already determined that Ozarovsky would have to leave the country, Musina opened 'The Delsarte Studio of United Art' in Petrograd. She herself led expressive gesture, and the daughter of her first husband, Tamara Glebova, taught the popular Duncan dance, or 'natural' dance. Also in the Institute of the Living Word, Gerngross opened an experimental theatre, in which he adopted the practice of the *orkhēstra*, the art of the ancient *chorus* and its movement that 'respected plastic melody'.[34]

The Bolshevik People's Commissar of Enlightenment, A. V. Lunacharsky, supported the creation of the Institute of the Living Word, arguing, in part, that the new republic needed trained orators and that in a democracy everybody should be able to express their opinion. He assigned the Institute the task of teaching expressive movement in order 'to widen and develop the individual means to express personal feeling, to influence others and to improvise'. Lunacharsky similarly recommended the inclusion 'of didactics and the psychology of the crowd and of auditors', along with a course 'of mime and gesture'.[35] It turned to be not a simple matter to organize this last course. In part, this was because there was argument about which system, Delsarte's or Jaques-Dalcroze's, to use as a foundation. The choice fell on rhythmics, in which 'movement of the body respects a law, to seek which one follows not feeling but sound; the taker of the course must therefore study exercises in mime in order to co-ordinate movement of the body with musical rhythm'.[36] The choice of a teacher for mime and gesture also turned out to be difficult, but there was finally agreement to appoint the movement artist and budding actress Ada Korvin, who had studied with Dalcroze in Hellerau.

Rhythmics was already being taught in the Institute of the Living Word by January 1919. One student, Irina Odoevtseva, recalled: 'A hungry, cold, snowy January. But what interest, what happiness! In the Living Word, lectures were mixed with practical activity and rhythmical gymnastics according to Dalcroze's method.'[37] The spring of 1919 saw the introduction of not one but three courses in the theatrical section of the Institute: one obligatory, rhythmical gymnastics according to Dalcroze's method, and two optional courses, plastic expression according to the method of Delsarte (taught by Musina) and musical movement and dance, led by Heptachor.

When the Institute was relocated to Tsarskoe Selo, the old tsar's palace outside Petrograd, the teachers came there from the city, stayed overnight and, in the summer, they perhaps danced outside in the park as well as inside in the palace. In the autumn of 1919, the Institute moved back to the city, to the site of the former Pavlovsky Women's Institute. Here a sequence of exhibition evenings took place, with demonstrations of various systems. There were points of both difference and similarity between Dalcrozian 'plastic movement', Heptachor's 'musical movement' and Delsarte's system.

The members of Heptachor rejected choreography as a preliminary step for staging dances; their presentations grew as improvisation based on music. The group believed that bodily movements should spring up from music spontaneously, in an unmediated way. *Plyaska* is a direct and simple-hearted response to music, that is, an improvisation. Further, through improvisation, Heptachor served Antiquity. At the beginning, the students made plastic stage-presentations of ancient myths, but later they began to experiment with movement 'under the sound of singing words', and in this way they addressed Gerngross's project 'to co-ordinate movement with declamation'.[38] Heptachor broke connections with Dalcrozian rhythmics, considering that it involved a too-literal, mechanical following of music, but retained connections with Delsarte's system, successfully taking up the latter's ideas about the significance of the body's centre of gravity and the wholeness of movement.

In 1920 or 1921, the Institute of the Living Word moved again, this time to the former building of the Northern Credit Society (next to the Aleksandrinsky Theatre), which had a public hall with fine acoustics. (The building is now a bank again, but is open to view.) The Institute gave concerts for a large public, and in the spring of 1921 there was also a 'conference of workers in movement' in which teachers were able to present, explain and compare their systems.[39] In the public hall, turned into an amphitheatre, Vsevolodsky-Gerngross's Experimental Theatre gave its first performances, including *The Sunken Bell*, Gerhard Hauptmann's play, conceived as the struggle of Christianity and paganism. A chorus of 'elves and sylphs' danced to the scansion, '*smeytes', veytes'* [laugh, twist], all ahead – there it is, there it is, the round dance'. The students of Heptachor, who moved better, played the elves and fairies, and they froze terribly at the show: 'All the audience in the hall sat in fur coats, but we played in light, semi-transparent tunics.'[40]

Gerngross showed interest in every way in the work of Heptachor, which, he thought, trained students for the *orkhēstra* and prepared actors for the ancient *chorus*. Initially, he required all the students of his theatre studio to take part in this activity. This involved material support: he immediately took several students into work and saved them from hunger and cold. The teachers were provided with enhanced rations – true, based on black dried bread and heads of herrings – and the Institute was relatively well heated. In November 1921, he brought from Moscow tickets for Duncan's performance in the Bol'shoi Theatre, and he sent Rudneva and her partner, Wolf Bulvanker, on a work trip, with free transport, so that they could see their idol. With time, however, the general enthusiasm of his students for movement began to irritate him. One day, the sisters Evelina and Emma Tsil'derman (whose married name was Fisch and who, under this name, much later took part in the revival of teaching musical movement) found a pianist and, in a free moment, occupied themselves with dance. 'Going along the nearby corridor and having heard the grand piano playing, [Gerngross] half-opened the door, but having seen that we again occupied ourselves [with musical movement], said: "*Ach, the devil take it, again they're dancing here*", and banged the door.'[41]

A conflict developed in the third year of Heptachor's teaching. In part, the studio members themselves provoked it, having declared to Gerngross that they would not allow 'unprepared students' to take part in public performances, to which the Director often enough sent them. Gerngross had no option: in order to continue to receive precious rations, it was necessary for him to give an account of the Institute which included concerts. So he forced the students working with Heptachor to make a choice: the theatre or musical movement. In the autumn of 1922, the people in Heptachor left the Institute. 'It was a heavy crash,' Rudneva recognized; 'we lost not only a splendid site for performances and a practice room; we lost an already prepared young group, with the large repertoire put together with them ... (And besides that, the "scholars'" food, potatoes.)'[42] Rudneva did not say anything about the fact that the exit threatened Gerngross's experiment with the rebirth of the *orkhēstra* in the theatre. Together with the teachers, the Institute lost thirteen or fourteen students who had become members of Heptachor. Up to April 1923, however, the members of Heptachor still considered themselves co-workers. But then the Institute of the Living Word was cut from the Commissariat budget and moved under the jurisdiction of the Russian Academy of Art Sciences; in the winter of 1924–25, it was finally eliminated.

The experiment, within the walls of one institution, to enliven the word demonstrated that *logos* and *musikē* are not opposed to each other but unite in 'the logic of the thought-feeling' (Ozarovsky's term).[43] The logic of this arose from the music or melody of speech, from the timbre of the voice and from mime and gesture. Gesture, in Delsarte's words, is 'the direct instrument of the heart; the unmediated manifestation of feeling, the expression of that which in words is lost'.[44] Gesture receives meaning if it is connected without mediation to music and feeling. Rudneva spoke convincingly about this. At the same time, Andrei Bely wrote about 'inner music', from which the word is born or by which it is newly 'animated'. One of his lectures at Proletkul't, a post-revolutionary political project of the avant-garde in Moscow, was called 'The Living Word', giving voice to a parallel with what his Petrograd colleagues were doing.[45] He considered that 'inner music', a synonym of feeling, is expressed at first in gestures and only afterwards becomes 'the inner word', the meaning of which comes from music and movement.[46] Bely, like the founders of the Institute of the Living Word, in reflections and initiatives appealed not to the rational image of the world turning around *logos*, but to another world, in the centre of which, as Nietzsche had put it, elevating music, there is 'the primordial contradiction and primordial pain in the heart of the primal unity'.[47] The logic of the *chorea*-dance, 'the new meaning of the sounds of words, the sunshine of their reasoning', is distinct from rational logic.[48] During the period of Heptachor's activity in the Institute of the Living Word, when rations of herrings and dried bread were given out, these surprising people found 'the sunshine of reasoning': thought-feeling in *plyaska*, and *logos*-reason in music.

Looking back to ancient times and looking forward to 'higher sensitivity', Heptachor brought together new techniques and expression of movement and dance. Assuredly, there were, later, more famous forms of new dance. At the end of 1923, Gerngross himself undertook a project with a dancer of 'The Young Ballet', Georgii Balanchivadze, in which the future choreographer, George Balanchine, made his debut as the stager of plastic movement. Together they prepared a performance, to accompany Aleksandr Blok's poem, 'Twelve', without music and only to the declamation of a *chorus*, perceived as a vocal part, a musical-rhythmic beginning for a dancing-mime event.[49] If later less well known, the work of musical movement did not exist in a world by itself, or on the margins of other kinds of innovations usually seen to belong to modernism. It interacted with and contributed to the rethinking of staging and movement in the theatre, and to the relation of the word to movement in the dramatic and poetic arts. Moreover, in Russia, there was no possibility that it could have been cut off from radical political and social change. The colour of the historical detail reveals the new art of kinaesthesia to have been at one and the same time collective and personal, objective and subjective, embodied and the elevation of the spirit. For all the deference accorded to Ancient Greece, the new art was a transformation of life for the future.

CHAPTER FOUR

Speaking Movement

I saw eurythmics – a dancer of sounds . . . In it, the tongue of tongues.

ANDREI BELY[1]

The perfect language: Andrei Bely on gesture

The current prominence of the body in the arts and in practices for well-being in daily life hardly needs to be stressed. Some time ago, the emphasis spread from the performative arts, the arts of movement (theatre, film, mime, dance, the circus, gymnastics), to academic culture. Even in literary studies, there are writings dedicated to the 'embodiment' of literature, the 'pragmatics' of written utterances and the 'behavioural' character or 'performativity' of creation. Much of this has been prompted by the way avant-garde artistic productions pose a central problem of interpretation. Avant-garde art has often been performative art, in which the realization of the art just at a particular moment *is* the art. As Nikita Sirotkin wrote, avant-garde art 'opposes tradition . . . [and] relativizes the boundary between interior and exterior, making the external internal, and vice versa'.[2] It is art fully committed to rejecting dualism of mind and body, and to the elevation of the former over the latter in terms of aesthetic and ethical value, followed by social preference and status for mental over bodily cognition and capability. It is art that embraces gesture as the unity of mental meaning and bodily movement. Indeed, to mention gesture is to point towards a view of communication and language as originating from, or having a basic structural form in, movement. As has been said, 'gesture is an action that helps to *create* the narrative space that is shared in the communicative situation'.[3] As a result, this chapter turns from the dance of the body to the dance of language and poetry. Sharing kinaesthetic experience, and sharing performative techniques based on kinaesthetic knowledge, the dance of the body and the dance of language have the same roots. For the poet Andrei Bely, the body and the language were simply the life of one and the same person.

As it happened, one day a friend of Bely's said that at his place, at night, rats danced along the corridor. Bely became heated: 'They dance, how do they dance? Ah, how interesting it is that rats dance! I have to see them, you cannot even imagine how important it is.'[4] And Bely spent the whole night, starting at ten in the evening, at a partly open door watching the rats.

Dance interested Bely in many different manifestations. He knew, better than other people because of his agility, that a person achieves meaning through movement or rhythm, the acts which Bely called 'rhythmical gesture'. Lack of movement, stasis, became his personal enemy, and the greatest insult which he could hurl at official philosophy was to call conceptual thought 'static'.[5] Bely himself, as a living person, embodied thought in movement. When one reads his writing, as Mikhail Osorgin commented,

> One sees Bely, his gestures, his stops, the searches for words, the underlinings, the double underlinings, and the wide illuminated smile: he found it! And once again, twice, three times, there is a going down, losing lines and air, a splash, and again he swims up to the surface with a new catch and the latest result: 'we move, we progress'.[6]

'In the whole way he held himself there was something always ready for a spring, for a dive and perhaps for a flight,' Fedor Stepun, who knew him well, wrote. 'He didn't simply go into an enclosed place but, somehow specially diving with his head and shoulders, either flew, or burst or danced into it.'[7] Bely's body and his language formed a whole. One has to 'dive' for meaning, he claimed, to acquire the skill arbitrarily to change the rhythm of movement, to turn it around, and to jump over a gap, and this is the craft of the muscles. This was not simply the style of exposition but the acrobatic dance of his thought. 'What the lecturer says is for him ... a trampoline. Look, his thought runs away, pushes off, and it already circles on the flying trapeze on its own questions in the high cupola of his singular "I".'[8]

Memoirists wrote about Bely as about a 'dancing' or 'flying' person:

[Bely] 'dances' – his gestures circle, flow, saunter, conclude, bring you to a new thought. But, well, he rises on tiptoe, and in a moment, just as suddenly, he stands on his knees or, glancing at you from below, springs into a squat. If you are not an experienced sharer of his presence, you lose him for a time, and, finding him, you will not know whether you should stand or also be on your knees. But Bely is already on the divan, has sat in the corner, having folded one leg under himself. He already runs, tacking agilely between the tables and chairs.[9]

FIGURE 5 *Fedor Golovin. 'M. F. Kokoshkina, Andrei Bely and F. F. Kokoshkin'. Paper, Indian ink. 1917.*

Once, when deathly ill, Bely suffered as much from the impossibility of moving as from the illness: 'I am in essence a peripatetic philosopher; and I cannot sit and cannot even stand in the process of thinking; no, I'm not a "Stoic": "*Stoa*" is not for me; I'm a follower of Heraclites.'[10] For Symbolists like Bely, 'the very understanding of the Heraclitean *logos* was . . . the understanding of rhythm, the law of change, and not the static forms or norms of judgment'.[11]

In this worldview, the principal role in the act of meaning-formation, or semiosis, belonged to the symbol. Bely provided an example. While still a child, frightened by the purple lid of a box, he hid the lid in the shadows in order to see only its colour. Playing, the little boy said to himself, 'something purple':

> 'something' is the experience; the purple spot is a form of expression; the two taken together . . . is a symbol – it is a third thing. Having constructed it, I overcome two worlds (the chaotic condition of fearfulness, and the object of the external world given to me); both worlds are not actual; there is a *third* world; and I am tied into this third world, given neither to the soul nor to the external object.[12]

The symbol ('something purple') is thus concrete and sensuous. In the creative act of cognition, it is a changing of sensitive experience which has the ability to transform meaning. 'In symbolization,' Bely explained, 'we underlined the process of establishing new qualities.'[13] Experience as a student of chemistry, seeing 'the chemical birth of new properties of a substance in the productions of our laboratory', provided him with a model for the birth 'of the third world', the world of new qualities or symbols.[14] He transferred the miracle of chemical change to the world of ideas.

Rhythm, however, appeared in Bely's childhood before the symbol. Lying in his bed, the little Boris Bugaev heard his mother play on the grand piano; this awoke his consciousness and filled it with rhythms. The boy perceived sound kinaesthetically. In music, 'all is clear' to him, 'and all free: fly as you wish, up, down, to the right, to the left, in this sounding space'.[15] His father was a mathematician, and when the son was a little older, he learned about his father's theory of number and measure under the name of 'arhythmologia'. In 1909, as an adult and a poet, Bely organized a

Rhythmic Seminar and, together with the participants, prepared a *Text-Book of Rhythm*. In the words of Mikhail Chekhov, 'by way of calculations, researching versification, he penetrated to the soul of the poet and heard how he spoke – the pulse and breathing of Pushkin, Tyutchev and Fet at the moment of their creativity'.[16]

If rhythm was one of Bely's first impressions, then eurythmics was his passion as an adult. The boy was motor gifted from early childhood, and he became conscious of his unusual dexterity when a new governess began to take him to a German gymnastic society.

> And for two years, still before going to the *gymnasium* [classical high school], I marched and jumped and stretched on the 'parallel bars' (subsequently, as an older boy, I showed off with different tricks on the trapeze, ran with speed, sprang high, with the ability to move with a lighted lamp on my head and crawl on four chairs placed next to each other).[17]

When Bely came to Anthroposophy, his kinaesthetic experience was further concentrated. At this stage of his life, he began to work as a wood carver on the construction of the anthroposophical temple, the Johannes Baum or Goetheanum, in Dornach (Switzerland). In a letter, Bely confessed:

> I never worked physically in my life, but now, it turns out, I can cut fully in wood . . . One goes out in the morning to work, one returns towards night: the body aches, the hands are finished, but blood pulses with some kind of unprecedented rhythm, and this new pulsation of the blood gives to one . . . a life-affirmative song, hope and joy.[18]

Anthroposophical eurythmics, the art of movement in a group that he himself took up and even passed to others, also produced a strong impression.

Bely's own motor, kinaesthetic giftedness, was the sister of his dynamic and flexible thinking. Zarathustra – a dancer with light feet – was his brother by birth. Rudolf Steiner also appeared to him to be a Nietzschean dancer with light feet, 'not a man, but himself rhythm': 'he came slowly from the passage, greeted me and went round a row of chairs, but it seemed to me he floats'.[19] After Steiner separated from the Theosophists and created his Anthroposophical Society, he and those who supported him used theatrical practices to create their own rituals. In 1910, Germany, and especially Munich, became the centre for experiments in expressive movement and new dance. There, it seems that Steiner was familiar with Dalcrozian rhythmics and with new experimental dance (*Ausdruckstanz*). Besides this, his comrade-in-arms and wife, Maria Iakovlevna Sivers, had learned art drama and declamation, first in Petersburg and then in the Paris Conservatory of the Arts, and she substantially assisted in creating anthroposophical theatre. One day, after a lecture on the opening phrases of the Gospel of St John, Steiner asked his follower, Margarita Sabashnikova, whether she could dance through these phrases. Sabashnikova did not take this up, but another woman, the young Lori Smits, had the courage. She undertook 'to dance the words', and thus arose eurythmics.[20]

The eurythmicists created their own repertoire of movements: level gliding on half-tiptoe, as if to fly above the earth, free waves made by the arms, and statuesque, noble poses. Long, many-layered tunics from streaming fabric, with wide-winged sleeves, emphasized and prolonged the movement. Running to and fro on the stage, the eurythmicists traced geometrical figures with symbolic meaning, while their arms pictured sound-letters: 'A variety of forms of consciousness fly, like many circling wings; and with arcs of arms we begin to reason, with spirals of scarves to explore the world.' Bely himself, even before he became acquainted with eurythmics, had pondered over and written a lot about 'the rhythmical gesture', 'the sound-form' and 'the ornament'. However, it is perfectly possible that dancers, Duncanists and eurythmicists, in light tunics and with scarves, suggested to him the graphic gesture which he loved, the spiral. 'Spirals are the constitution of worlds and every day the universe expresses a cosmic dance in the harmony of a living sphere.'[21]

The word 'eurythmia' was ancient. In Plato, 'eurythmia' expressed the determination of the whole of life by correct rhythm, by a kind of universal image of time. Vitruvius used the word to denote the proportionality of parts, the attractive look and the beauty, which correlates with the demand of vision. Following in his footsteps, Vincent de Beauvais wrote that 'architecture consists of order, disposition, eurythmy, symmetry and beauty'.[22] Steiner, in turn, defined eurythmia as 'visible speech, visible song'.[23] According to his calculation, the correspondence between breathing (eighteen breaths a minute) and the pulse (seventy-two beats a minute) is exactly 1:4, and this is one of the principal musical times. The bodily-musical rhythm flows into movement, dance and eurythmia – and action: rhythm is drawn into waves of the circulation of the blood from the heart, finding itself in finitude as will.[24] Steiner placed great hopes on eurythmia for the creation of 'the new man' whose physiology and constitution would be permeated by music.

Bely, like Steiner, wrote about how, in the future, men and women will change physically thanks to the flowing together of sound, gesture and meaning. The thought, which at the moment takes place 'in one part of the body under the bone of the forehead', will spread all over the body. 'My whole body overflows with thought,' Bely wrote. But the idea that it is possible 'to record' sound 'in lines', 'to dance' them, 'to build form in them', evidently ripened long before he shared this view with Steiner and Sivers. In *Glossolalia*, he discussed theurgical (divine or magical) words and the importance for them of physical movement and plastic gestures. He also compared the tongue as a physical organ with a dancer: 'The whole movement of the tongue in the cavity of our mouth, is the gesture of an armless dancer, which envies the air, like a gauze, a dancing scarf.'[25] The motion of a tongue-dancer – 'speech mimicry' – creates a new meaning before the appearance of words: 'here thought flows in the heart; but the heart with arm-wings speaks without words; and the doubled arms speak.' If one thinks over the movements of 'mimetic dance', opens their inner form, then the dance surpasses usual speech. And then the tongue, 'an armless dancer', 'having created arms for itself, with the arms splits apart the grave; and it comes out from its dark cave, the cavity of our mouth'. Man finds the means to create the living word as a being from 'fine flesh', as if the word were human: 'From heat and sound we create language. And our words will sometime become, like us, human.'[26]

At the end of the 1910s, Bely experienced disappointment with Anthroposophy. This was closely connected with a personal drama, separation from his wife, Asia Turgeneva. He bitterly complained that 'eurythmic art took away my wife (this is a fact)', and he criticized 'the paradise fields of Anthroposophy in which the eurythmic female dance saviours forget, for the ceremonial dance, husbands, children, her people'. As a consequence, in Berlin at the beginning of the 1920s, he was often seen in cafés dancing the foxtrot. Bely himself called this episode 'a flight ... from "*the paradises of anthro[posophical] society* into ... *Variety*, where eurythmicists don't dance, but, simply, people do, though "*half-naked*"; and this is more open than eurythmic curves ... I ran away from the mystical bodily-dancings of a woman to the highly, openly real bodily-movements of Variety girls.' Music was to Bely 'the way of consecration', but he came to prefer 'a good jazz band to the bells of Parsifal'.[27] To Russian emigrants in Berlin after the Revolution, shy and embarrassed at dancing new dances in public, the foxtrotting Bely appeared strange and even terrible. One observer thought he showed 'a distorted reflection of his true character' in reaction against events in Dornach. But who can say what exactly Bely experienced dancing and improvising light-footed dance? Another observer saw him at the centre of respectful attention.[28]

When Bely was mentally reconciled with Steiner and had returned to Anthroposophy, and to Russia, he was very active in eurythmics, in particular in association with Mikhail Chekhov and the actors of the Moscow Art Theatre. The actress Maria Knebel recalled:

> Bely (and after him Chekhov) was taken with the idea that each letter and word, and each sound in music, has its plastic expression. Consequently, it is possible 'to calculate' plastic verse, prose and music. Bely, with the fixation characteristic of him, drew us into this search. ... We sought the plastic expression of every letter, studied 'the grammar' of gestures, transferred from the letter to the syllable, then to the phrase and to the sentence. Having trained, we made difficult enough exercises. We 'read' with gestures the poems of Pushkin, the sonnets of Shakespeare and the chorus from 'Faust', and one day independently prepared verses of Mayakovsky, which Bely much loved.[29]

Chekhov grasped from Bely the thought that the body of the actor must develop under the influence of impulses of the soul. Bodily movement and narrative, or story, meet, according to Chekhov, in 'the psychological gesture'.[30] What he called 'the psychological gesture', we call the dance-word. Bely, precisely, gave the dance-word the principal role in his linguistic utopia, the idea of the 'tongue of tongues'. There was no discussion of kinaesthesia as a psycho-physiological phenomenon in this, but the modalities of the movement sense occupied the prime place in the phenomenal awareness presupposed by the discussion.

Eurythmics developed in the midst of Europe at war, when peoples – or, as was said in the past in Russian – 'tongues', went to war against each other. The word demonstrated its lack of strength and the brotherhood of peoples-tongues was destroyed. Switzerland turned out to be an oasis, a refuge for many Europeans, a place of meeting of many peoples-tongues. And there eurythmics appeared: dance, uniting gesture, word and sound, came to the help of the word. In the fourth year of the war, in the autumn of 1917, Bely described a cosmic 'tongue of tongues' which could put an end to the war. The young Bely had given the role 'of a tongue which unites' to music; later he filled this role with dance and gesture.[31] He had the vision, recreating Christian mythology, that in its second coming, the word would be perfected and universal, general and understandable to all people without exception. In a perfected language, expressiveness would correspond to substance and the name of a thing to its essence. In just such a language God spoke to Adam.[32] The Bible, however, said nothing about whether God's language had been verbal or gestural. It might have been that God spoke to Adam in the language of dance, through dance-words. Bely himself, it turned out, was ready to create the perfect language. The daughter of Vyacheslav Ivanov, Lidiia, recalled how, as a guest with them, Bely taught her five-year old brother, Dima, his letters: 'Having spread his legs widely and having placed his arms akimbo, Bely very clearly mimicked the letter "Ф", and then with corresponding movement of long arms the letter "У".'[33]

The art of the nursery is not great art. All the same, Bely, relating to his own childhood, linked the linguistic sign and the movement of the body. The child learned that his body, in precise, delineated symbolic performance, constituted his relation with others. Kinaesthetic sensation was the living, phenomenal content of the (social) relation. Cognition of language was at one and the same time mental and bodily – a *person's* (not a brain's or a mind's) cognition. Later, when he became a master of Symbolist prose and had a vision of a universal language based on movement, or gesture, Bely learned how to put the same movements into poetry. The play in the nursery was a microcosm of culture.

Bely attracted his young comrade in poetry, Sergei Esenin, to his project to create a universal language. At Tsarskoe Selo outside

Petrograd, in the autumn of 1917, Esenin and Bely often met and talked. Under the influence of these meetings, Esenin wrote a tract about art, *The Keys of Maria*. In this he thought over and expounded a scheme of letters formed into poses, as Bely had done in his *Glossolalia*. If Bely wrote the Latin alphabet ('for the gesture "b", taking a step back, having inclined the head downwards, I raise my arm above it, leaving under a covering'),[34] then Esenin did the same for the Cyrillic alphabet. The letter 'Б' appeared to him to be a crouching man whose lifted arms draw the arch of heaven. Further, 'the navel is the knot of the human being; the man has put his hands down on the spot from where everything began, and produced the letter Б'.[35] In *The Keys of Maria* and other work on poetics from the years 1918 to 1920, Esenin, developing Bely's theme, wrote about plasticity, 'the modelling of word and form', their 'current' and 'fluidity' and about characteristic verbal 'ornament'. His fundamental terms were 'line' and 'ornament', 'song' and 'melody', and 'dance' and 'gesture'.[36]

It is as if Esenin's early work on poetics anticipated his later meeting with Duncan. In his phrase, the sound of words began to appear to him to be palpable and not only plastic, thus anticipating the expressive movement of which she was the mistress. As the poet Maksimilian Voloshin said, 'Isadora Duncan dances everything that other people say, sing, write, play and draw.'[37]

The dance-word: the creative union of Esenin and Duncan

There is a recollection (there is no way of knowing its accuracy) of Esenin's meeting with Duncan:

'You're an Imaginist!'
    She understood but, having raised 'the blue spray' of her eyes on him, said, puzzled:
    '*Pa-chem-u?*' [Why?]
    'Because in your art the *obraz* [image] is the main thing.'
    'Was ist "*obrass*"?' Isadora turned to me.
    I translated.
    Esenin began to laugh, then tried to explain to her in a variety of languages without a verb.

'Image', he said, making a sharp negative gesture with his arm, 'is not Mariengof [the Imaginist poet]! Image is Isadora!' He extended a finger to her side.[38]

It seems that no one has thought seriously about this anecdote, in which, in a way, there is much truth. Memoirs, biographies and histories of belles-lettres describe Duncan's and Esenin's relationship in the genre of a romance, not for the depth of contact in their art. Nevertheless, the meeting turned out to be fateful for both, artistically as well as personally. If, speaking in different languages, it was difficult for them to associate, Duncan and Esenin understood each other excellently as artists. Without judging the intimate side of their relationship, we shall think about the way they might have been interesting to each other as artists. Duncan already had experience of a creative partner, having worked with the artist and director Edward Gordon Craig (and it was through her that Craig, in tsarist times, received the invitation to do the scenography at a performance of *Hamlet* at the Moscow Art Theatre (1911–12)). We want to show that there was a sharing of the movement sense between Duncan's dance and Esenin's lyric poetry. This modality of sensory awareness underlay different forms of the arts, and it made it possible for the two artists to share something artistically in common and to provide mutual support.

Esenin and Duncan lived almost all the time, in private as in public life, within a theatrical frame, often bordering on provocation and scandal. Indeed, it is thanks to Esenin that the word 'scandalist' became accepted into Russian. It is not surprising that, from the very beginning, the story of their meeting gave rise to myths. Thus, we read, with the words *zolotaia golova* (Golden Head), allegedly using the only Russian words she knew, Duncan seized hold of Esenin's head, drew it to her and kissed him on the lips.[39] Was this not the kiss impressed by Salome on the dead lips of John the Baptist? Fear of the woman-destroyer also sounds in stories about how Isadora performed 'the apache dance', fashionable at the time, with a scarf in place of a partner, and in the finale she threw the scarf on the floor and trampled on it. All the same, Duncan never performed the role of Salome in public.

Not all memoirists, however, gave way to myth. Varlam Shalamov, a writer and journalist, later famous as a recorder of the Gulag, came to Moscow in 1923, when Esenin and Isadora were still together; two years later he was present at the funeral after the suicide of the poet. Disputing the opinion of those who had seen in Duncan only a 'rich woman' seducing the 'peasant poet', he wrote that what she possessed 'was wealth of the soul'. In Esenin's

> very short path to the summit of art, Isadora Duncan, an enthusiast, revolutionary member of the intelligentsia, who had come to serve the Soviet people, played a large and very positive role. (This is a claim opposed to the usual picture.) She introduced Esenin not to the circle of people in great art but to the circle of his ideas, his air.[40]

They met on 3 October 1921, on Esenin's twenty-sixth birthday. By then, he had for some time borne the glory of renown as a rebellious poet. On that day he met a sister in spirit, a revolutionary in art, in the image of life, dress and love. Duncan had come without fear to Soviet Russia because she believed that the government would grant her 'a free school and a free theatre'. Having come, she wrote, inspired: 'Farewell Old World. Welcome New World!'[41] Russia was not terra incognita for Duncan. In Russia she was held in such high regard that she was called 'almost the only woman to whom . . . we attach . . . the epithet, genius'.[42] She appeared the incarnation of Dionysian dance, and her dance was a real reform in art. Meyerhold called Duncan's dance the leading example of the ennobling influence of movement.[43] Esenin could not have failed to know what Duncan meant for his fellow-workers, and therefore, having heard she was in Moscow, he rushed to see her.

The first condition of creative contact is sensitivity to the interests and activities of the other person. In 1918, well before meeting Duncan, Esenin contributed to a film scenario, *Zovushshie zori* (The Call of the Dawn). In one episode, the events in the film were to take place in a temple for the proletariat with a large hall where workers exercised by doing rhythmic gymnastics. Another episode included workers' festivities on green meadows by a lake, in which workers danced around the Statue of Liberty.[44] For Esenin, dance was therefore part of the revolutionary scenery. He was ready to meet Duncan.

Isadora Duncan knew literature well and loved poetry – her mother read Shakespeare, Keats and Burns to the children. Duncan herself was not a bad producer of literature: while still a small girl, she 'published' a domestic newspaper, and she wrote articles, an autobiography, free verse and letters which were in love with rhythmic-sounding prose. To Elizabeth Styrskaya she showed 'verses, written by her in English and translated into Russian, filled with the same inspiration as her speech'.[45] But Duncan's dance was more expressive than her words. As her contemporaries recognized, she possessed an exceptional capacity for pantomime, in its root sense. She was called 'the tsarina of the gesture'.[46] Preparing to show her dance, 'The International', in the Bol'shoi Theatre, she promised:

> You will 'see' the word. See in my gesture – hand, shoulder, back and face – you will see the word. Gesture is dumb words! It is speaking silence. I want to read by gesture with my body all the lines of 'The International'.[47]

Duncan herself recalled that she first sensed the force of inner gesture when she observed the performance of the great tragic actress, Eleonora Duse. In one of her spectacles, Duse stood unmoving, but she created in the viewer, Duncan recounted, the full impression that she grew and became an even more significant presence. After the performance, Duncan said to herself: 'When I can come out on the stage and stand unmoving, as Eleonora Duse stood this evening, and in this way depict the colossal force of dynamic movement, then I will become the greatest female dancer in the world.'[48] In this she was brilliantly successful. In 'The Ride of the Valkyries', 'the great mimetic actress [Duncan], almost not moving, had the ability with magic strength of gesture to summon up the impression of a whole crowd of warrior Amazons of Valhalla, striving forward'.[49] The audience even saw what was not on the stage, 'the double-headed eagle' (the tsarist symbol) which, in her 'Slavic March', Duncan seized and threw down, or 'the heavy shaft of a huge standard in the force of a strongly blowing wind' to the music of Tchaikovsky's 'Sixth Symphony'.[50] The Imaginist Anatoly Mariengof (mentioned by Esenin in his first meeting with Duncan), who was absolutely not charmed by Duncan, all the same recognized her as a great actress:

> It is apparent that 'The Slavic March', God-like and human-like, these sounds of great, mighty pride and terror, not only violins,

cellos, flutes, kettledrums and drums can play, but also a woman's torso, neck, head, hair, arms and legs. Even with suspicious little dimples alongside knees and elbows. The breasts which have become weighty, and the belly which has become fat, and the eyes with the fine lines of creases, and the dumb red mouth, and the crooked nose, as it were, which divides the round face, can play it. Yes, they can play splendidly, if they belong to a great actress.[51]

Contemporaries like Rudolf Laban believed that Duncan returned to contemporary men and women the feeling of the poetry of movement.[52] Her dance was considered full of 'lyricism' and was compared with 'verse forms or small poems, loaded with emotion and meaning'.[53]

What gave 'lyricism' to Duncan's dance? (It must be remembered that the only surviving filmed sequence of her dance lasts less than a minute.) Possibly, first, there was its difference from classical dance, the refusal of balletic mimesis and *pas* or steps, and the rejection of the conventions of stage presentation. Deviating from the customary rules and norms, free dance approached verse, and with this created, in Baudelaire's words, 'the miracle of a poetic prose without rhyme, supple and rough enough to adapt itself to the lyric movement of the soul, to the undulations of reverie, to the sudden starts of consciousness'.[54] Free verse has a special closeness to free dance. Compared to metrical verse, at this time free verse appeared 'shaky'. The metre played a subordinate role, and yet rhythm carried the poetic form. According to Bely, 'metre is a mechanism, but rhythm is the organism of poetry'.[55] In contrast to a metric poem, with its single form, a poem with changing rhythm comes closer to music, and it may be thought of as proto-music. Bely proposed, in poetry, to get rid of 'excessive extremes and fancy images, sounds and rhythms which are not coordinated around the singing soul-lyric, the melody'.[56] Rhythm and intonation, endlessly changing, like dance, may better express the deep meaning of verse forms than words do with their lexical meaning.

Insofar as the freedom of the modernist artist lay in improvisation and individually spaced accentuations of rhythm, Duncan fully realized freedom in her dance. Before her, the canvas for dance was considered to be music, which presented formal parameters of tempi and metrical rhythm and which the movement of the dancer had to follow. Jaques-Dalcroze had created his rhythmics precisely according to this formula, as exercise to prepare for the exact reproduction of the tempi and rhythmic frame of musical works. Duncan, by contrast, considered rhythmics mechanical, rejected the blind following of tempi and rhythm, and never reduced her dance 'to the level of musical illustration'.[57] Her movement in no way recalled 'dancing algebraic formulae'.[58] Her dance was always passionate; improvising, she felt free to express her own emotions, within the mould of music, but nevertheless still with her personal feelings.

Duncan conducted herself in relation to Antiquity just as freely, though with tact. At a time when she had not had enough experience, she had wanted to present Aeschylus's tragedy, *The Supplicants*, in Greece with a real chorus, which would have sung and danced. If one accepted, as she did, that poetry began from legs and arms beating out a rhythm, then it was possible to read poetry as if it were its own kind of dance or as instructions for creating sounds and gestures. To a degree, therefore, she had at first thought it possible to reconstruct the movements encoded in the poems of Homer or in ancient tragedies and comedies. Duncan had hired dozens of Greek boys for the chorus, and in order to find the music she had listened to Byzantine hymns and consulted with a Greek priest. She had tried to found the movements on what was conserved of vase and carved depictions. Soon enough, however, she had understood that the whole task was too difficult for her. From then on, she affirmed that she strove to communicate the spirit but not the letter of ancient dance.

Esenin, a lover of *chastushki* (two or four line rhymes of humorous verse sung to a simple tune) and *Kamarinskaia* (a folk dance), would at first glance seem to have been distant from the spirit of Antiquity that Duncan tried to revive in dance. Yet, as concerns rhythmic structure, the *chastushka* is nothing other than a hexameter. To create a glittering *chastushka* is as difficult as to write a good sonnet. Its rhythmical structure is complicated and refined; it contains 'artfully combined long and short, and sometimes contracted lines, pauses of different intonation and structural length, and constant and inverted accentuations'.[59] The art of the *chastushka* is the art of arranging emotional, meaning-forming accentuations with the help of intonation and gesture. In other words, a *chastushka* rhythm is not, finally, metrical, but dictated by expressive intonation, and this intonation can be connected with dancing movement. Esenin grasped this connection well, and not only in relation to *chastushki*, which he sang, accompanying himself on the accordion, and, possibly, dancing a little. His readings of his own verses were distinguished by artistry and expressiveness, and also accompanied with gesture.

There was a circle of discussion and mutual influence among 'the Scythians' (a name taken from the ancient inhabitants of the lands north of the Black Sea), a close-knit society of poets at the time. Their ideas can be found in Bely's article, 'Aaron's Crosier', Nikolai Klyuev's verse cycle, 'Earth and Iron' and Esenin's tract, *The Keys of Maria*. One of the themes discussed was the plasticity of the sounding word, visualized in 'gesture', 'line' and 'ornament'. If Bely inclined towards theatrical metaphor ('rhythmical' or 'gestural intonation'), then Klyuev inclined towards musical metaphor ('song', 'line') and Esenin towards plastic metaphor ('ornament'), though their vocabularies overlapped. Bely wrote about 'picturing the sounds of words in the ornament of a line' and about ornament as 'the flesh of our thoughts'.[60] The phrase 'ornament of bodily movements' led him to recall Duncan's dancing.

At the beginning of 1918, Esenin, at Bely's invitation, attended meetings of the Anthroposophical Society, and in this way witnessed the activities of the Moscow eurythmic circle. Margarita Sabashnikova led the latter, and one day she performed the second chapter of St Luke's Gospel:

> Tall, slim, covered with a white, shining mantle, which was spread open by her movements, she turned into a white flame. Her arms, together with the chorus standing behind the eurythmicists sang vowels, and all her figure trembled and moved just like the flame of a hot candle. But this was not without order, a candle trembling by chance, hot in the wind. It was music, song, filled with higher Meaning. Her face, slightly lifted upwards, free from any emotion, reflected a face in prayer or meditation. And all the body was in full harmony with what was developing around its attire, around what clothed it, which moved together with it in a united sound of the great words: 'Glory to God in the Highest and on earth, peace.'[61]

In this way, Esenin saw the flowing and streaming movements of the eurythmicists. Shortly thereafter, Bely called Esenin's poetry 'streaming, eurythmic words'.[62] Esenin himself, with his friend Mariengof, wrote an Imaginist manifesto in which the friends proclaimed two paths for verbal art: 'the attire of everything flowing in a cold, fine form', and 'eternal animation, that is, a turn to the transformation of fossilized into spirited flesh'.[63]

Esenin's task, as his biographers put it, 'was to lead the image, the word into movement'.[64] The striving to give dynamic life to works of art and to find artistic means to represent this was, of course, not specific to Esenin. The Italian Futurists had been one of the earlier groups to set out this project, and it was the Russian Futurist, Vadim Shershenevich, in February 1914, in an article, 'The Dotted Line of Futurism', who wrote that the artist 'wants to convey all the simultaneity of one moment'. Esenin, however, called Futurism 'half-stupid' because it did not understand the meaning of images, including images of movement. Along with 'the Scythians', in opposition to the Futurists, he believed in connecting with the life-giving myths of nature in the past and with the mystical meaning of the way ahead. It was not given to the Futurists, Esenin declared, to see that 'the earth swims', that 'night is the time when whales go down for food to the sea depths' and 'the day is the time for the continuation of the journey by sea'.[65]

When Esenin discussed 'the organic image', he may have known Duncan's ideas, formulated by her in the article-manifesto, 'The Dance of the Future', two Russian translations of which had come out between 1906 and 1908. Duncan wrote about her understanding of 'the organic' in dance:

> If we seek the real source of the dance, if we go to nature, we find that the dance of the future is the dance of the past, the dance of eternity, and has been and always will be the same.
>
> The movement of waves, of winds, of the earth is ever the same lasting harmony. We do not stand on the beach and inquire of the ocean what was its movement in the past and what will be its movement in the future. We realize that the movement peculiar to its nature is eternal to its nature. . . .
>
> Through this human medium, the movement of all nature runs also through us, is transmitted to us from the dancer.[66]

Free dance, from its birth, nourished the ideals and images of nature: growth, light and the wave. It shared the background for this in Goethe, Romanticism and *Naturphilosophie* (romantic philosophy of nature on idealist principles) with Steiner and Anthroposophy. The forms of the Goetheanum and the movements of eurythmics followed cosmic lines and, by this means, like free dance, were intended to bring elevated spiritual mediation.

In thoughts about the organic image, Esenin and Duncan were thus on one side, in opposition to the Futurists on the other. The Futurists almost refused to depict the naked body, because it was Nature, and instead they hymned the geometrical and mechanical wonder of the machine. In the 'Futurist Manifesto of Dance', Marinetti looked down on Duncan for 'feelings of desperate nostalgia, of spasmodic sensuality and cheerfulness, childishly feminine'.[67] Duncan's followers were criticized for sentimentality, called 'milk-blooded Hellenes', and their 'wave-image movements' were considered 'amorphous' and 'sugary'.[68] When 'machine dances' became popular in the 1920s, circus eccentricity – 'aggressive movement, gymnastic step, dangerous spring, slap in the face and box on the ears' – took the place of 'the thoughtful immobility, ecstasy and dreams' of the Duncanists.[69] The new choreography, modelled on machine production, discredited the dance of bare-footed women as women's protest against mechanistic civilization. Dance borrowed movements from the city, the factory and the machine. Duncan ignored the criticism, but Esenin, following Klyuev and Bely, responded and, to repeat, called Futurism 'sub-stupid'. He answered the Futurists and proletarian poets with lyric images taken from peasant culture, opposing 'the red-maned colt' to the steam engine.[70]

Both sides of the argument, we would note, nevertheless took *movement* to be at the base of what they articulated in aesthetic terms. It is not that one side of the argument was modernist and the other not, though, clearly, Futurism was modern in a way that Duncan dance was not, given that the latter looked back to Antiquity and to Romanticism. Each side broke with predecessors, in their respective mediums, for not recognizing the dynamism that would give life to the modern age. An interpretation of modernism in kinaesthetic terms has place for both.

One day, Duncan and Esenin together conceived of a performance in the manner of an ancient tragedy. She was to dance, he to present a Greek chorus. Duncan outlined it with passion, explaining to Esenin the role of the chorus in ancient Greek theatre. With a bold line, drawn around the amphitheatre, she enclosed the orchestra and, having placed in the centre of it her black circle, wrote under it 'Poet'. Then she quickly drew from the point many spreading rays, in the direction of the audience.[71]

Duncan, in love, schemed for Esenin to go with her to Petrograd. In fact, the project for a joint performance remained unrealized. Yet, even after his separation from Duncan, Esenin, reflecting on all the nine muses, called only one by name – the muse of dance, Terpsichore.[72] In the union of these two artists, poetry and dance, the word and plastic art, achieved a special closeness, a closeness so intimate that it was possible to think of one muse as the common inspiration. She was the voice of movement.

Word plasticity: the *budetliane* and the bare-footed

Esenin and the Russian Futurists swapped insults, yet they shared a fascination with movement in artistic expression, if in different ways. To the Futurists, or the *budetliane* (literally, those of the future), as we shall now call them, as they are sometimes called in Russian, to distinguish them from the Italians, the underlying difference was an appreciation of the plasticity of the word – the mobility of sound, the capacity to shape speech and language on the page. Mallarmé, in his poetry, had great influence with his experiments with typefaces, the distribution of the words on the page and the look of facing pages. In Russia, there were subsequently many examples of the visualization of verse. Vladimir Khlebnikov's poem, 'Razin', which has the drawings of Petr Miturich added to the right side of the page like a mirrored reflection of the strophe of the poem, is a well-known example. The poem, a palindrome (which can be read backwards as well as forwards), is designed to be followed visually. The text and drawing in 'Razin' are not simply combined with each other but form a new whole, a structure or gestalt. Similarly, when Aleksei Kruchenykh showed Khlebnikov the sketches of his poem, 'A Game in Hell', the latter suddenly 'sat down and began to add, above, below and around, his own lines to mine', composing a palindrome.[73]

Such techniques of visualization change the reader's relation with a text as a self-sufficient object into something that demands completion of the construction.[74] The visual additions to the verse create a new whole, which oversteps the text. This new wholeness, in addition to being visual, may be aural, through the uttering or singing of verse, or kinaesthetic, through dancing or gestural performance. Further, the enlargement of the text may involve all these things at once, bringing into existence something similar to the Wagnerian synthesis of art or to 'the synthetic theatre' of the Russian *budetliane.*

Yet historians of the arts have not written about the novelty that the *budetliane* brought into art in terms of theatricality, performativity and revision of the borders of production. In the previous chapter there was discussion of the belief that ancient theatre had achieved a syncretic unity, conserved, some people maintained, in folklore and the dance culture of the people. This would seem to have put the scholars of Antiquity who made this claim, like Ivanov, Innokenty Annensky and Zelinsky, at the opposite pole of culture to the Futurists. But in fact it was not like this. The *budetliane* actively took part in discussions about Antiquity; for example, the avant-gardist Khlebnikov frequented Ivanov's 'Academy of Verse', where Annensky and Zelinsky gave lectures. This 'Academy of Verse' was a group of young poets and writers which began to gather at Ivanov's home in Petersburg in May 1909, to discuss questions of form, to take part in 'theoretical and practical researches on metre', and so on.[75] For their part, the *budetliane* took a lively interest in ideas about the Dionysian cult, the dance-*chorea* and the syncretic character of the word. Two decades later, the classicist O. M. Freidenberg, in her doctoral dissertation, covertly cited the poets (when it was hardly possible to do so openly), referring to 'splashing', the sound-act, as poets understood it, at the basis of words: 'The most ancient Zeus in Didona prophesies on the rustling of the leaves of the oak, on the *splashing* of water . . . Every verbal utterance is sung or recited. Bodily movement and mimicry are turned into the kinaesthetic part of a rite; dancing and pantomime exist alongside.' The meaning 'of the small formulations, which are sung and danced', Freidenberg wrote, 'is not their factual content, but the semantics of their pronunciation, their existence in themselves, as the factual content only repeats the act *of the word as such*'.[76]

Freidenberg used the very phrase with which Kruchenykh, in 'The Declaration of the Word as Such', announcing the poetic freedom of the word from meaning, called on 'singing, splashing, dancing, the throwing out of awkward constructions, oblivion, the learning of a part'. This declaration led to the formation of a group of poets who took part in the discussions and adopted the name *zaumniki* (literally, 'those who are unintelligible' or produce 'nonsense'), implying that they set out to free the word from meaning, so that the word could act independently ('splashing' and so forth). The practice of *zaum'* (nonsense) was thus close to giving the word a syncretic life: '*Zaum'* is the original form (historically and individually) of poetry. At first, there is the rhythmical-musical wave, the proto-sound.'[77] This sought meaning in the audible and kinaesthetic sensory world rather than in conventional semantic discourse. Both the scholars of Antiquity and the *budetliane* made the semantics of the word dependent on its sound, on its aural, acoustic and moving, kinaesthetic character, on *singing, splashing and dancing*.

The Futurists generally freed the word from its former logical, grammatical and syntactic ties with the help of discussions of this ancient context. Marinetti's *parole in libertà* (utterance in freedom) and Kamensky's 'free-word poems' recalled the actual quality of performance. Kamensky, for instance, criticized the Symbolist manner of reading as 'monotonous', 'with some kind of mystical-rhythmic soughing at the ends of the lines'. He characterized his own declamation with kinaesthetic metaphors: 'we, shrill guys, read, that is, press the words, absolutely differently, like weight-lifters.'[78] Kamensky's 'ferro-concrete poems', which N. I. Khardzhiev considered analogous to Apollinaire's 'simultaneous verses' and the Italian Futurists' free-word poems, were not to be read but to be performed, and the performance was to include movement. Reinforced-concrete building material had appeared not long before, and it was associated not with harshness and brutality but, on the contrary, with flexibility and plasticity. At first, people looked on concrete as a material close to wood, on account of its plasticity: cement was poured into a wooden mould and afterwards retained the impression of this structure. Indeed, for these reasons the second

FIGURE 6 *Vasily Kamensky.* Tango with Cows. Ferro-concrete Poems, *1914.*

Goetheanum, after the first, wooden construction burned down, the cathedral of Steiner's 'organic' project, was made from reinforced concrete. It may be that Kamensky called his poems 'ferro-concrete' because they were well-structured, or because they were made from a kind of carcass filled with the plastic 'cement' of poetic content.

The textual record of the poetry of the *budetliane* is of idiosyncratic instructions or scenarios for performance. Il'ya Zdanevich, for example, proposed to write an 'orchestrated poem' and verse partitas, and he tried to record his own declamation on the phonograph.[79] 'The words in freedom' approached articulated-sung-danced words – incantations and rituals.

FIGURE 7 'An Embarrassing Situation.' Amongst bare-footed dancers there is a new trend to illustrate poetry with dances.

The Futurist (recites):

Te ge ne
riu ri
le liu
be

The dancer: O Lord! What gestures can illustrate this poem!

In spite of the fact that the macho Marinetti considered Duncan's dances sentimental, he loved the society of bare-footed performers. It was similar with the poets in Russia. The actress Alisa Koonen, playing in the Kamerny (or Chamber) Theatre in Moscow inspired Kamensky to write the poem 'The Bare-footed Girl':

Girls bare-footed –
Oh, poetic possibilities –
Like the Northern Lights –
Which crown
The nights of my loneliness.

All the girls bare-footed –
All in the world –
All my loved brides.

Kamensky not only imagined how 'on their toes they sing while drinking / singers bare-footed', but he invited the dancers to appear at the evenings he orchestrated with the actresses Sofia Mel'nikova, Ol'ga Glebova and Vera de Bosset.[80] When, for the first anniversary of the October Revolution in Moscow, he staged his *Sten'ka Razin*, for the role of Princess Meiran, at Kamensky's demand, Alisa Koonen was not just 'invited' but, given the Civil War conditions, 'mobilized'.

In 1917, Kamensky, 'the pilot-aviator of flesh and soul', set out on tour around Russia in the company of two like-minded people.[81] One Ekaterinburg newspaper reported: 'already for several days strange people, who shock with their external appearance, have been walking on the streets of our town. Without caps, lightly, sometimes unusually and oddly clothed, they do not incline towards the usual stereotype set up for everyone.'[82] This trio was 'the king of the Futurists' Kamensky, 'the Russian yogi' Vladimir Goldschmidt and 'an ash-haired girl in an original costume, with black patterns on her matt forehead', a 'bare-footed female Futurist'. Kamensky declaimed his 'ferro-concrete poems', the yogi talked about 'the sunny joys of the body', demonstrated *asana* yoga and broke wooden name-plates over his gilded head, and the bare-footed girl, Elena Buchinskaya, performed 'word-plastic dances' to the verses of Kamensky and other contemporary poets.[83]

Apparently, the idea of poetic-plastic performance originated earlier with the *budetliane*. When Duncan came to Russia at the beginning of 1913, the rumour went around that she would dance the Futurists' verses. Duncan in fact did not do this, but Buchinskaya did. She came out on the stage bare-footed, with a free, long *chiton* or eastern garb, with her arms exposed to the shoulders. She read, standing on her knees, accompanying the reading with flexible movements of her arms. Buchinskaya later repeated her performance in the 'Café of Poets' in Moscow. A witness recalled: 'Here is the garlanded muse, and, between the ferro-concrete poems and an address about spiritual loneliness, a theatrically-dressed woman draws in the air the letters of an Assyrian choreography.'[84] A regular frequenter of the 'Café of Poets', N. N. Zakharov-Menskii described 'word-plasticity' as a special genre:

> As Elena Buchinskaya performed with word-plasticity, so there was the same plasticity with reading the verses of the Futurists and the humorist Teffi. Especially memorable was Buchinskaya's realization of Vasily Kamensky's 'Swan'; we listened to this piece with bated breath, as the actress carried out the piece with so much feeling, with so much mysterious and touching, with movements which recalled the realization of Saint-Saens' 'Dying Swan'.[85]

Kamensky also had his own rich experience of performance: as is well known, he appeared in the circus arena and tried out in the troupe of the director Meyerhold. One day, Kamensky came to an exhibition in Mikhailova's Petrograd salon with two mouse-traps on a rope, containing live mice, thrown over his shoulder. He 'sang a *chastushka*, spoke humorous catch-phrases and accompanied himself with beats of a ladle on a pan . . . [People] started up from him in horror, but he triumphantly went around the hall.' This was his 'moving exhibition', and Kamensky actually presented himself as 'an exponent of synthesis'.[86] Thus he was well able to appreciate Buchinskaya's word-plasticity, and, possibly, he borrowed something for his own public appearances from her. 'You perform, clearly with talent, the word-plasticity of my verses', he wrote in dedication.[87] His fellow avant-garde poet, Vladimir Goldschmidt similarly dedicated poetry with a title full of meaning to Buchinskaya, 'Funerals of My Love', with the inscription: 'I give into the possession of the most talented girl in the world, ELENA BUCHINSKAYA.'[88]

These poets also took an interest in pre-First World War film, in which Buchinskaya acted. S. D. Spassky recalled how at the shooting of the film, *Not for Money Born*, walking in early spring, Buchinskaya threw off her shoes and ran on the warm thawed patches of ground.[89] In her role, she had to dance on a table-cloth:

in order not to break from the rhythm, she read Kamensky's verses. When the public in the 'Café of Poets' had dispersed and only her friends remained, she sometimes danced naked. Later, she joined the emigration, and in the 1920s and 1930s, Helena Buczyńska (as her name was spelled in Polish) appeared in Warsaw cabaret, showed talent as a comic actress, played many parts in the theatre and cinema, and wrote plays.

In 1919, by which time neither the 'Café of Poets' nor Buchinskaya remained in Moscow, a new group of poets and artists, the Imaginists, contemptuously christened the *budetliane* 'bare-footed artists' (with the implication that they were 'simple'). By an irony of fate, the first of the Imaginists, Sergei Esenin, a couple of years later met with the first of the bare-footed, Isadora Duncan. Kazimir Malevich forewarned his fellow artists in vain 'to be careful with the grape juice: you know that for Dionysus it gives life, but for you, death'.[90] The juice of Dionysus, full of the spirit of *plyaska*, embodied in the movement of the bare-footed women, continued to nurse the poets. The Dionysians from Ivanov's 'Tower', the Futurists, and the Imaginists all saw in *plyaska* a pledge that a person could become free.

At one time, Russian Futurism appeared to the historian V. F. Markov to be 'an imperfect and disorganized manifestation of a clear aesthetic idea, that of poetry growing directly from language'.[91] He disdainfully called Kamensky 'a showman', introducing a contrast and creating a conflict between the 'serious' linguistic experimentation of the *budetliane* and the playful, 'unserious' side of their poetry. We have looked again at this history. It is necessary, at long last, to value the role of free dance and of the creative union of the poets and the bare-footed performers. It was definitely not by chance that, on the path that we know culminated in the modernist focus on 'the word as such', the Futurists opened their poetry to *singing, splashing and dancing*. The poet and painter Elena Guro wrote, shortly before she died young in 1913: 'To all the poets, creators of future signs: walk barefoot while the earth is summery. Our feet are innocent and simple-hearted, inexperienced and admiring. . . . The earth talks to bare feet.'[92]

CHAPTER FIVE

By 'the Fourth Way'

Why must there be a struggle between spirit and body?
Surely there may be reconciliation?

S. M. VOLKONSKY[1]

The mystic arts

Describing theatrical technique at the beginning of the 1920s, Sergei Eisenstein simply observed: 'Everyone raves about yoga.'[2] It is well known that twentieth-century theatre experimented with esoteric or quasi-esoteric conceptions. Konstantin Stanislavsky took up yoga and rhythmics (and indeed invited rhythmicists to lead activity with the actors of the Moscow Art Theatre); Mikhail Chekov, eurythmics; Peter Brook and Jerzy Grotovsky, Georgy Gurdjieff's system. In all these systems of body techniques, the accent on the individual body and movement, and on sensing that movement, turned out to be especially valuable for the theatre. Indeed, a range of very different people came to the idea that kinaesthesia helps the actor, not necessarily through conscious volition, to attain the condition of 'presence', to concentrate on the 'here and now', and in that way not so much to play a role but to live on the stage, to sense being authentic and real in the role. This ideal was summoned up with substantial help from physical activity, experienced kinaesthetically.

In the years on either side of the Revolution, Gurdjieff, drawing on yoga, practised exercises that strained, then freed, the muscles, as well as exercises to concentrate attention. With the experience of movement exercises in mind, the eurythmist Jeanne de Salzmann, who, as we shall see, was largely responsible for the creation of Gurdjieff's 'sacred movements', identified cognition with experience: 'The Fourth Way is a way of understanding that is to be lived.'[3] We look again at this 'way of understanding' in order to illuminate the place of movement in at least one branch of esoteric modernism. This chapter takes the story of kinaesthesia along what some have known as a mystical path. The first part of the story goes through innovations in stage lighting, opening up a new account of the importance of light in creating dynamic effects, that is, in creating experience of movement. In the following chapter, we return to the mainstream of Russian theatre.

The seeker and mystic Petr Dem'yanovich Ouspensky, in 1911, published his book, *Tertium Organum* (The Third Organon), a new canon of thought. (The first was the medieval collection of Aristotle's texts, the second, the *Novum Organum* of Francis Bacon.) He wrote:

> And the future belongs not to *man* but to *superman*, who is already born and lives among us.
>
> A higher race is rapidly arising from the bulk of humanity, and it is arising through its own peculiar understanding of the world and of life . . . And not only is this race coming, but it is already here.
>
> Men approaching the transition to this new race are already beginning to recognize one another; watchwords, signs and countersigns are already being established.[4]

One such 'watchword' was 'India', or, collectively, 'the East'. Unlike the West, which had taken the road of external, material progress, the East, Europeans thought or imagined, had taken the way of human self-knowledge and fulfilment. Belief that Indian culture implicated a higher step in the spiritual development of humanity was widespread across Europe, and it accompanied enthusiasm for yoga, Buddhism, Theosophy and Anthroposophy.

The interest was especially vibrant in artistic circles. The composer Aleksandr Scriabin, for example, worked on a *mysteria* that included proposals for an instrument of light, 'Luce', and for the final performance to take place on the banks of the Ganges.

Stanislavsky studied yoga, and his method of acting drew on an understanding of *prāna* (breath of life), 'ray-emission and ray-perception', 'the freeing of the muscles', 'the sternum' (connected to breathing) and 'higher consciousness'.[5] Jaques-Dalcroze selected as an emblem for his Institute of Rhythmics in Hellerau the yin-yang sign of balance and harmony of opposites. With the help of music and rhythm, he dreamed of educating a 'new race' of people with unbounded consciousness of their possibilities. Dalcroze saw in rhythm the co-ordinated beginning of the unification of body and soul, the means to achieve a single, harmonious whole.[6] In Russia, the main propagandist of rhythm, as we have discussed, was Prince Sergei Volkonsky. When, in the autumn of 1912, he opened the Rhythmic Courses, a filial of Dalcroze's Institute, and in the following spring began to publish *Pages of the Courses of Rhythmic Gymnastics*, he used the same emblem on the cover of his journal.

The coming of war closed the Institute in Hellerau and the Courses in Petersburg. It also caused Ouspensky to return from a journey through India and Ceylon. In one of the Moscow newspapers, he then read about a ballet, *Struggle of the Magicians*, in which an alleged Indian intended to present, with a display of Eastern magic, the miracles of the fakirs and holy dances. So, in the spring of 1915, Ouspensky made the acquaintance of the author of the idea of the ballet, Georgy Gurdjieff (Gyurdzhiev). Gurdjieff said that his ballet was not a 'mystery', but rather a drama or pantomime with song, music and dances. He proposed including dances of different peoples – Ossetian, gypsy, Arab, Georgian, Persian, Indian – and scenes that would picture schools of white and black magicians and the struggle between them, as well as student movement exercises.

It is thus clear that, by this time, Gurdjieff had thought-up the system of exercises which continued to be a fundamental part of the esoteric group he subsequently directed. The exercises were similar to those practised in yoga, Sufism and other spiritual traditions of the East. He placed the same hope in the movements, called 'holy movements' or 'holy dances', as Dalcroze placed in rhythm, the hope that they would open a new path for humanity. Gurdjieff called his path 'the Fourth Way', counting the first 'the way of the fakir', the fulfilment of the body, the second 'the way of the monk', the way of belief and asceticism, and the third 'the way of yoga', the way of knowledge and reason.[7] Although Gurdjieff thus positioned the Fourth Way separately from yoga, and though his movements had different gymnastics and rhythm, it had much in common with yoga and rhythmics. We shall follow the history of Gurdjieff's Institute of Harmonic Development, which opened a little later in Tiflis (as Tbilisi, Georgia, was called in the Russian Empire), and trace the thread that stretches from there directly back to Dalcroze.

In spite of war, or perhaps because of it, people placed hope in the healing power of art, in art that would re-establish broken ties and re-create wholeness. In this spirit, in 1916, the Kamerny (Chamber) Theatre in Moscow premiered *Phamira Kithared*, after the play by Innokenty Annensky. The deep, tragic, aesthetic performance, according to the critics, was one of the best of the season. Aleksandra Ekster's decorations and costumes, in the Cubist-Futurist manner, attracted special notice. The critics also praised with one accord the sketches of the costumes, shown at the exhibition of the group, 'The Jack of Diamonds', for their theatricality and dynamism. Ekster prepared an album of her drawings, which she entitled, 'Break, Movement, Weight'. Both the critics' language and Ekster's work thus took for granted the place in staging of kinaesthetic perception. But the year 1917 came and the album did not appear; there simply was not the material means.[8]

Aleksandr Tairov, the director, saw in the play an expression of Dionysian and Apollonian themes. Thinking about how to stage the themes, he conceived of them in contrasting rhythms, the kinaesthetic representation of which would give the play form:

> In front of me, with the construction of the maquette, two rhythmic tasks, which should run together, arose at the same time. It was necessary, on the one hand, to create a construction for the low and satirical moments of the spectacle; on the other hand, the stormy inter-weavings that inspired and ripened Phamira's loveless tragedy, required for their plastic development a completely different construction, based on the precise and even flow of the Apollonian rhythm, in opposition to the Dionysian rhythm of the first.[9]

For this reason, he created two completely different styles for the performance, Cubist decoration and costumes in *style moderne*. Tairov demanded a clash, dynamism, even in the decoration. With significant consequences for the history of the stage, he also tackled the problem of achieving dynamic movements with the active participation of light in the events. Alisa Koonen recalled that when 'working with Ekster on the construction of "Phamira Kithared", Tairov thought a lot about how the spectacle had to be lighted. He said that the very construction of the piece, its unusualness and the inspiring atmosphere of the verses, demanded special lighting.'[10] Light was required not only to enhance the dramatic effect but also to follow the author's own stage directions. Annensky had prefaced every scene with a special description, summoning-up qualities that would serve at one and the same time as instruction and symbolic image: 'Scene One. Pale-cold', 'Scene III. Still crimson rays', 'Scene IV. Light blue enamel' and so on.[11] To transmit such dynamic effects, the colour and light needed to be of an absolutely special kind.

Tairov had always counted light as a full participant in a spectacle. Accordingly, he went to great lengths to bring a young lighting artist from Hellerau to Moscow, Alexandre de Salzmann, who had recently succeeded in turning the auditorium in Hellerau into a space 'lit with light', not just a lighted space. Audiences there had been thrilled: they had seen movement in light that was dimmed 'from azure fortissimo' to 'shaking, trembling twilight'.[12] Volkonsky gave this description:

> The Hellerau hall is something absolutely special in itself. It's strange even to use the word 'hall' applied to this 'space', to the surrounding white flatness. Above and to the sides, white canvas, nothing else; it is saturated with wax and behind it are unseen electric lamps; when they are lit, they are started with a surprisingly sustained gradualness, and one is as if immersed in a lighted bath. Never with more clearness did I feel what a deceptive thing it is to show the source of light. Light! A surprising element of nature, without which it's impossible to see but which one mustn't see. The lighting arrangement in the Hellerau 'theatre' is the handiwork of our compatriot, Salzmann. All the joy is in the fact that you don't see the source of the light, you see the being of light, if one may thus express it; it is not a lighted hall but a hall of light. The participation of light in the Hellerau musical pictures has a large part in the surprising totality with which they act on the viewer. All the four elements of this aggregate impression acted together: music, man, movement, light.[13]

The use of light in Dalcroze's and the director, Adolph Appia's, staging of Gluck's opera, *Orpheus and Eurydice*, was a special success. The whole opera was presented in 1913, with light as a full actor: the singer performed the role of Amore behind the stage, and the light 'sang' in the hall in her place. At first, on stage there was nothing besides a staircase saturated in gloom and grey curtains. In this mysterious space, the light of Amore, suddenly appearing, unexpected, made a striking impression. Volkonsky recalled:

> But there was a greater degree of unexpectedness when, after the disappearance of Amore, with a ceremonial unfolding, the last curtains in the depths [of the stage], on the very top of the staircase, suddenly draw apart. A split opens, lighted with such strength that all the rest of the stage is laden in gloom. Victorious ceremonial sounds of the orchestra mount the brow of Orpheus, waking to a new life, and, rhythmically taking step after step, with spread arms he comes out from the gloom of earthly sorrows to a light of other-worldly promises.[14]

Such a radically new staging of Gluck's opera, like no other production, brought the audience an echo of ancient mystery. All the European *beau monde*, including Diaghilev, Anna Pavlova and Nijinsky, were present at the premier. Isadora Duncan, by telegram, invited her friend Stanislavsky to come to see 'a unique, one in the world' Orpheus.[15] Paul Claudel excitedly reported that 'the milk-white' light in the spectacle creates 'an Elysian atmosphere which restores the rights of three dimensions and turns any body into a statue'.[16]

Salzmann himself asserted that light 'interests us only as the elemental form of inner experience'. The action of light is to enable reality, including movement, to be seen as it is, to disclose things, again including movement, in themselves:

> For us, then, light does something more than tell stories about the sun, moon and stars. We do not demand of it that it produce effects. Nor must it make things pretty, nor evoke moods. It must only give to colors, surfaces, lines, bodies and movements the possibility of unfolding themselves. None of these elements should act at the other's expense, least of all the lighting itself, which should function as a binding force. A 'reverberating light'– that is

what we seek. Needless to say, such light must fill all the space at hand, including both the audience's and the performers' space.[17]

In Moscow, there was unanimous agreement that Salzmann's lighting, in *Phamira*, organically connected with the artistic plan of the spectacle as a whole. He filled all the space of the stage. None of the footlights, soffit lights or spotlights took part in the lighting. The light was transparent, at one moment weightless and joyful, at another moment gloomy.[18] He distributed the light sources behind a neutral horizon, and he displaced paint by light as a means of marking-up surfaces. In 'the tonal light' used for the staircase in the spectacle, Ekster discovered that cubes and cones were more monumental, costumes were brighter and the movement of the actors was more conspicuous. The canvas backdrop 'was saturated with greatly different tints from moon-blue and orange-opal to crimson-red'.[19] Tairov, for the first time, saw objects lighted by contrast, so that the characters on the stage acquired relief and appeared especially sculptural.

Salzmann used light, first, as the medium for the aesthetic expression of soul and body as two sides of one reality, and second, to create a whole new range of ways in which to perceive the spatial and moving qualities of events on the stage, extending the kinaesthetic imagination of the actors and audience alike. The lighting 'immersed' the stage. One might say that light 'embodied' the spectator on the stage rather than communicated an object to a subject in the auditorium. No one involved picked out the kinaesthetic world for explicit or special notice; rather, they built this world into a search utilizing the sixth sense of intuition of the living, moving body, to achieve total harmony of all the arts on the stage.

The war and the impossibility of writing abroad for necessary technical parts of equipment prevented the full application of Salzmann's system. Then, when the spectacle was revived in 1919, Salzmann had abandoned Moscow. Following the Revolution, he returned with his wife to his family home in Tiflis. He was the son of a well-known architect in Georgia, the academician Albert Salzmann. The son studied painting in Moscow and Munich, where he associated with, among others, Kandinsky and Rilke, co-operated with the journals *Jugend* (Youth) and *Simplicissimus*, and worked as a theatre artist. He got to know Dalcroze, and through him met and married Jeanne Allemand-Matignon. She was one of the best students of the *maître*, and accompanied Dalcroze on all his journeys to demonstrate rhythmical gymnastics.

By the summer of 1919, Gurdjieff was also in Tiflis. The composer Thomas de Hartmann (with whom Kandinsky had worked), who had joined Gurdjieff's group, introduced Gurdjieff to the Salzmanns. This was a fateful event for all of them.

From Dalcroze to Gurdjieff

Jeanne Salzmann had a studio of rhythmic gymnastics, and the students, girls from 'the best families' in Tiflis, exercised in the spacious hall of the Salzmanns' house. The activity, in which actors from the local theatre participated, brought in a reasonable income. Using the studio as a base, the inventive Gurdjieff opened the Institute of Harmonious Development of Man and gave thought to how to stage the ballet, *Struggle of the Magicians*, which he had conceived earlier in Moscow. He wanted to present a joint evening of the studio and the Institute at the Opera Theatre. In the first half of the performance, Jeanne Salzmann's students were to show rhythmical exercises, and in the second half, they and Gurdjieff's other followers were to demonstrate the movements that he at once began to train them in. At the rehearsals, Gurdjieff shocked the girls with the absolute precision he said ritual dances demanded and with the drilling he then put them through.

The joint demonstration of rhythmical exercises according to Dalcroze's and Gurdjieff's systems took place in the theatre on 22 June 1919, the Dalcroze exercises in the first part and the chorus from the ballet, *Struggle of the Magicians*, a fragment of a *mysteria*, 'Exile', and Gurdjieff's exercises in the second.[20] It is difficult to judge whether several of these exercises were taken from mystic practices or from rhythmics. The exercise 'Stop!', for example, in which the participants, on command, suddenly halted and held their poses for an undefined time, had been used by Dalcroze, when it was called 'Hop!'. Designing the spectacle, Alexandre de Salzmann did the scenography, the costumes, the lighting and the decorations.

There is a fine testimonial of the evening which saw the creation of a number of forms of new movement within the framework of a search for unity of activity and substance:

Jeanne Matignon surrendered to imagination and presented the spectators with an incomparably greater, higher grade [of performance] than all the ballet affectation that we had seen [before] in Tiflis.

But, moreover, then the bead-like Chopin . . . Why not replace it with a neurasthenic drum! . . .

Gurdjieff starts motion with a push of the will, sharp straight movement.

A finely rehearsed mass movement of the students, a simultaneous throwing-up of hands, then arms, then legs; ideal lack of restraint of these movements, and straightness, brought the public the impression of stunned relaxation. . . .

It was completely unimportant to us to know [according to the information of the composer Hartmann] that Gurdjieff studied the holy dances of the East. That is his business! It's necessary simply to walk on one's head and in the air! The rest will fall in place.[21]

From that time, the Salzmanns placed themselves and all that they knew how to do at the full disposal of Gurdjieff. When in the autumn of 1920, faced by the advance of the Red Army, Gurdjieff transferred his Institute of Harmonious Development to Constantinople, the Salzmanns followed him. Gurdjieff gave lectures on philosophy, the history of religion and psychology, his wife, Iulia Ostrovskaya, led 'plastic gymnastics' and Jeanne Salzmann taught 'harmonious rhythms', apparently some kind of synthesis of Dalcroze's and Gurdjieff's systems of movements.

Gurdjieff's group exercises conveyed to viewers a strong impression of the group's disciplined, well-co-ordinated, fine-working mechanism. This was very similar to what spectators saw in performances of the rhythmicists, where they were struck by the precision of 'the harmoniously organized mass'.[22] Dalcroze, in theatrical performances, wanted *la foule-artiste* (the artist of the people) to take the central place and 'display in movements, gestures and poses his sensations and experiences'; at the same time, however, he sought 'the orchestration of movements' of the mass of performers.[23] He called this correlation of mass and soloists 'polyrhythmic'. Having moved to Europe, Gurdjieff, with the help of Jeanne Salzmann, tried to recreate part of the former Rhythmic Institute at the location of Dalcroze's school in Hellerau (which in 1925 moved to Vienna), though he did not succeed.

A rhythmicist with great experience and elevated musical culture, Jeanne Salzmann notably influenced the teaching of 'holy movements', for which Hartmann wrote music, in Gurdjieff's tightly controlled circle. Thus, one of the most difficult exercises, in which the arms, head and legs had to move in different tempi, derived, through her, from Dalcroze. It is said, however, that, encouraging her capacity for dance, Gurdjieff at the same time made an end of her own artistic career. Moreover, in 1930, he finally drove Alexandre de Salzmann out of his group. Madame de Salzmann, as those around her respectfully came to call her in France, stayed as Gurdjieff's posthumous representative, living to be more than a hundred. She had two children, a daughter, with Salzmann, and a son with Gurdjieff. The son (Michel Salzmann) became a well-known psychiatrist and, until his death, led the Gurdjieff movement.

In published notes and conversations with students, Madame de Salzmann did not recall Dalcroze. Sometimes she quoted Gurdjieff, but for the most part she spoke about the foundation of her own experience, and in this it is possible to discern the influence of the rhythmic gymnastics that she had studied in her youth. One of her declarations about rhythm, for instance, bears the impression of argument with Dalcroze, and particularly with his intention to divide the body and isolate different parts of it so that each could move with its own rhythm. Madame de Salzmann opposed this: 'I am "in a rhythm" – what does it mean? Not that one part is one rhythm and another in another, nor that I do one position in the rhythm but not the next. The energy is everywhere the same.'[24] On other questions, for example, on the unity of soul and body, she agreed with both Dalcroze and Gurdjieff. Touch, she insisted, is the means by which to feel the being of the body in unity with the energy of the world.

I need to see that what is lacking is a connection with my body. Without a connection I am caught in thoughts or changing emotions that give way to fantasy . . . I have to feel the body on the earth, the ground. I do this by sensation – sensing its weight, its mass, and, more important, sensing that there is a force inside, and energy. Through sensation I need to feel a connection with my body so deep it becomes like a communion.[25]

In effect, she put into words the significance of the yin-yang emblem that Dalcroze had placed above the entrance to his Institute. The unity, or harmony, of soul and body is *in the energy of movement.* 'If we could truly perceive their meaning and speak their language, the Movements would reveal to us another level of understanding', Madame de Salzmann declared.[26]

Dalcroze and Gurdjieff, by contrast, agreed in valuing movement not for itself but for demanding the special concentration of attention. In order to strengthen attention, they devised a number of rhythmic exercises that required beating out different rhythms at the same time: for example, the head, two beats in a bar, the arms, three, the legs, four. Dalcroze's students achieved this virtuosity. He justifiably affirmed that rhythmic gymnastics educate decisiveness and harden the will – 'where there is a will, there is a way', we might say. One observer, Sergei Mamontov, having seen a performance, excitedly wrote that on receiving a task, the dancers 'strain with concentration, even frown, but almost always come out victorious from all the difficulties posed'.[27] Dalcroze's adherents enthusiastically endorsed the skills of full control over the body, and critics, with equal vehemence, who convicted rhythmics of formalism, mechanism and absence of emotional feeling, disliked them.

Having come to the Russian capitals – Petersburg and Moscow – just at the time when Volkonsky unleashed a storm of propaganda on behalf of rhythmics, Gurdjieff most likely heard about the practice, and perhaps he saw demonstrations. Nevertheless, his own exercises, which, according to Ouspensky, he began to lead in 1916, differed from both gymnastics and rhythmics. In particular, he created movements that brought his exercises closer to yoga. A participant at Prieuré, Gurdjieff's centre in France in the late 1920s, Charles Stanley Nott, recorded this experience:

> The movements and dances were extremely interesting. I did not find them difficult in the way some people did, but, as with everything else that I had acquired in ordinary life, I had to begin over again and forget what I had learned. It took me a long time to learn to sense and feel each movement, gesture, posture. Such a simple thing it seemed, 'to sense', but being English, brought up

on physical drill and army training, I had to be reminded over and over again to 'sense' my body.[28]

For Nott, habituated not to sense but to strengthen the muscles and to ignore negative sensations of pain or tiredness, previous experience did not help; on the contrary, it disturbed the precise completion of Gurdjieff's tasks. It was so difficult to switch to a new way of completing movement (of responding to the kinaesthetic world) that Gurdjieff had to explain it to him in rather categorical terms:

> The first 'obligatory [exercise]' I began to do as if it were a series of physical jerks. At last Gurdjieff rebuked me severely in front of everyone, which so mortified me that I left the platform and sat down. In a few minutes he came up to me and quietly explained something. I returned to my place in the class, and from that time began to understand something of the inner meaning of the dances, and I spent every spare moment of each day for practising.[29]

In this 'inner meaning', bodily sensation and spirit fused.

Gurdjieff led a group of followers who lived communally. He wrote out orders for physical work, like prescriptions for medicine, which served the same task of unification as the exercises. He himself came from a family of craftsmen and knew excellently how to work with his hands. In his wanderings in the East, the future guru had earned a living, in part, by creating a 'universal workshop on wheels', where he repaired everything, from samovars and sewing machines to guitars and accordions.[30] Ouspensky recalled Gurdjieff sitting on the floor engaged with the repair of a carpet in his house outside Moscow. Knowing the value of physical work, Gurdjieff made it an instrument in his group. To one of his followers thirsting for immortality, he said: 'For the sake of immortality, you must work, get stronger. But now I will show you how it's necessary to work. For a beginning, let go the servant and begin to do everything yourself.' Sometimes he gave both men and women heavy physical work, for example, sawing logs. Undertaking this work, they experienced something different, their self-feeling changed, they now 'sensed themselves', 'remembered themselves', and this was with joy.[31] One purpose was to direct both the movements and the physical work so as to help a person ground herself, strengthen the 'I' and develop individuality. Gurdjieff's 'Fourth Way' lay through experiencing embodiment.

The creators of what they significantly named 'free dance' had set out on a similar road: through exercise to concentrate on sensation, to feel movement from the inside, kinaesthetically. They devoted attention not so much to exteriority and the appearance the dancer achieved as to inner sensation and feeling. They presumed that kinaesthetic perception helps to focus not on the sense of external appearance but, rather, on learning to trust inner feeling. Their language and intent came close to an argument about becoming an authentic person in one's own right. With such purposes in mind, the teacher of free dance, the American Margaret H'Doubler, for example, gave out blindfolds to her students. Also for such purposes, the Russian Duncanist, Ella Rabenek, threw out the mirror from the practice room. She also advised students to dance 'as if you sleep', possibly considering that it was thus easier to display individuality. 'Gesture,' affirmed the dancer, 'must grow of itself from each new musical beat, changing, varying, being transformed in accordance with the individuality and mood of each pupil.'[32] The Duncanists 'gropingly' came to the understanding which, a little later and with the great help of yoga, Dalcroze, Stanislavsky and Gurdjieff formulated: kinaesthetic perception is the mother of individuality. Stanislavsky said to the students of his Opera Studio: 'Dances and gymnastics don't give plasticity while there is no inner sensation of movement. It's necessary in connection with walking for energy to roll along all the vertebrae and to leave by the legs . . . Then there will be suppleness.'[33] Gurdjieff formulated the exercise, 'I am', for the integration of emotion and sensation as the substance of the personal 'I':

> In a collected state I come to the feeling 'I.' I direct it into my right arm – 'I' – and then have a sensation in my right leg – '*am*.' Thereafter, I have a feeling, right leg: sensing, left leg; feeling, left leg; sensing, left arm, feeling, left arm; sensing, right arm. I do this three times, each time feeling '*I*' and sensing '*am*'.[34]

Gurdjieff borrowed this exercise from where Stanislavsky also took it, from yoga. Stanislavsky himself brought in a rule of play-acting, which he called 'I am': 'There you have real truth, faith in your actions, the state we call "I am" . . . If you sense the truth in a play subconsciously, your faith in it will naturally follow, and the state of 'I am.'[35] Such thought has been at the centre of the twentieth-century search to achieve 'presence'.

'Presence'

Full appreciation of the modern culture of dance and movement requires doing justice to an enthusiasm for movement that is vastly wider than the interests of the avant-garde. There is sport, obviously, not to mention the worlds of the disco and of street performance. Our history, pointing in this chapter to the roots of movement culture in rhythmics, free dance and esoteric practices, tells only part of the story. Moreover, no one could simply claim that, during the course of the twentieth century, movement practices spread from the avant-garde through so-called popular culture. The latter brought its own customs and activity into the equation and was very far from being a passive recipient of what the avant-garde had thought up. For instance, just at the time when rhythmics and free dance attracted notice, quite independently the tango and African-American 'animal dances', the forerunners of the sedate foxtrot, were hugely popular.[36]

We might make one suggestion for a wider history. A century before free dance, belief in what we are calling a sixth sense widened, and what had been belief in a vaguely formulated sense of intuition, a sense on the margins of cognition, took on, in part, a delineated existence as muscular feeling and in due course became the subject of considerable, systematic psycho-physiological inquiry. The sixth sense, understood in this way, was comprehensible to a large public, and people quickly took up the notion of kinaesthesia once it had been introduced. It was hardly news that life was embodied in movement. Then, in the early twentieth century, the artistic avant-garde embraced this theme and introduced a whole range of ways of exploring movement, and the perception of movement, in new kinds of productions. All the same, the different publics of the time, caught up in the massive translocation to city life, did not have to be, and were not, taught by this route about the nature and qualities of movement. Daily movement was experienced with a new kind of self-consciousness in the crowd, pressure, strain and speed of city life. This was a leading theme of the social psychologist Georg Simmel's much cited essay, 'The Metropolis and Mental Life', of 1903.[37] To a significant extent, the kind of movement discussed in this chapter was a reaction against the excess of movement experienced in the city, rather than an influence on it.

Trying to take further such large questions, linking the arts and social change (so often, distressingly vaguely, called modernity), social theorists and anthropologists of dance and the movement arts draw in the concept of 'presence'. In the background is the belief that movement, whether in avant-garde or 'popular' arts, achieves a special and much-desired condition of embodied being, or wholeness, in the world. As we have seen, speech and writing often treat movement as a state in which divisions of mind and body, subject and object, 'high' and 'low', nature and culture, disappear. The belief is as relevant in thought about skateboarding as about rhythmics.

There is precedent for this in the principle that Madame de Salzmann formulated in her reflections: '"I am" in movement.' Thanks to movement and its perception, kinesis and kinaesthesia, she argued, a person achieves a special quality of experience of self in the world. She called this special quality 'presence', which was for her a full apprehension of kinaesthetic sensation, attention of a special quality, attention to the body's way of being.[38] Martha Graham, who so influenced the development of free dance in the United States, working in the same tradition of understanding, is supposed to have observed that movement never lies. While surely questionable as a philosophical premise, such a saying points to the reasons why 'presence', known in movement, became a pivotal category of the anthropology of dance at the beginning of the twenty-first century. The word gave modern expression to the old claim that in touch there is unmediated knowledge, 'encounter', with the world. When there is 'presence', one is 'in touch'.

In the twentieth century, the concept of 'encounter' was elaborated by the phenomenologists, following Husserl's lead. Husserl had argued that kinaesthetic feeling and haptic sense (active touch, and touch active in vision) give conscious awareness an unmediated character: we grasp being *in* the world, and we are not an observer, through sensory mediation, *of* the world. This is the theory implicit in believing that movement tells the truth. As we mentioned in the introductory chapter, there was a history to this way of thought going back to the analysis of touch in the eighteenth century. The belief was a commonplace of nineteenth-century science and philosophy. The Russian physiologist Sechenov, for example, considered the muscular sense not conditional, but direct, issuing from the root of subjectivity: in contrast to vision, 'muscular sensations . . . are purely subjective; they always reach our consciousness in the form of some kind of effort'.[39] The originators of free dance, along with esoteric practitioners like Gurdjieff, then grasped, however, that 'the unconditional', or unmediated, character of movement sensation was not just material, neutral in relation to values, but moral and indeed spiritual. They returned to language, the language of 'closeness' and 'movement with' or 'movement towards' or 'movement by', its status as intuitive expression, the expression of a sixth sense, the expression of relatedness. What Jeanne de Salzmann called 'presence', Emmanuel Levinas, in the context of philosophical ethics, referred to as 'a relationship with unity without mediation by any kind of principle or ideal'.[40] Merleau-Ponty even compared unmediated feeling-sense, which has kinaesthetic sense at its centre, with the Holy Eucharist. Experience is 'a certain way of being in the world suggested to us from some point in space, and seized and acted upon by our body, provided that it is capable of doing so, so that sensation is literally a form of communion'.[41]

Both Mikhail Bakhtin and Martin Heidegger, however differently, also described this supposed direct, unmediated connection with reality with the help of the category of presence (*nalichie* or *nalichnost'*, in Russian). According to Bakhtin, a person achieves 'presence' only in special circumstances, of which one, a principal one, is *plyaska*. (Bakhtin, we recall, was a member of the circle of Zelinsky's students in Petersburg which avidly discussed the theatre of Antiquity.)

> In dance, my exteriority, only visible by others and for others who exist, flows together with my inner, self-aware, organic activity; in *plyaska*, everything inner in me strives to come out, to combine with exteriority, and in *plyaska* I must strengthen being and join the being of others. My presence (confirmed as a value from without), my Sophia [*sofiinost'*, divine wisdom], dances in me, another dances in me.[42]

In his seminal work on *Being and Time* (1927), Heidegger invoked 'presence' in the context of an argument to restore to philosophy its concern with Being, the Being that a human has, that is, the kind of Being that has awareness of temporal Being. Heidegger identified an overlaying in the form of metaphysics in Western philosophy, and he sought to show that real 'presence' had roots in a more fundamental phenomenology of 'being with' or of being 'to hand'. This in turn was one of the starting points for Jacques Derrida's philosophy of deconstruction. He questioned the continued existence of metaphysics in Heidegger's own work, since Heidegger appeared to take for granted the condition called 'presence', rather than question its place as a term in dualistic language, 'presence-absence'. Derrida convicted the Western tradition of engaging in the metaphysics of 'presence', of privileging 'presence' over absence, building presumptions into thought. These and other discussions ensured a place for 'presence' in modern philosophical language, where it signifies the 'here and now' and, often enough, reiterates some version of the privileging of 'presence' that Derrida had set out to deconstruct.

Philosophy resonates with recent changes in performance studies. If earlier theatre studies centred around notions of image and representation, the new performance studies focus on 'the real body' and 'the real space'. The interest is no longer in fictional characters in an imagined world created by the art of acting. There is a suspicion that representation linked to so-called grand narratives instantiates power and control, and there is a hope that 'presence', on the contrary, involves immediacy, authenticity, completeness, integrity and other such values. The concept of representation is embodied by the character of a drama; the concept of 'presence' is brought to life by the actor's body.[43] In contrast with the actor's semiotic character, the actor's 'phenomenal body' depends for its impact on her or his physical attractiveness, erotic appeal and, of course, capacity to move well. Theatre, understood in this way, is inseparable from dance. One drama actor even received praise for 'how he commands the space – with an almost dancer-like freedom of movement!'.[44] The actor's ability to control space and 'magnetically' attract the attention of the spectators defines 'presence'.

One of the authors of the relatively new discipline of anthropology of the theatre, the Italian director Eugenio Barba, defined 'total presence' in terms of movement and energy; it has nothing to do with strength, being under pressure or in search of speed. The actor may be concentrated to the utmost, unmoving, but in that absence of movement, she affirms movement with all the energy in her arms, like a strained bow, ready to let go the arrow. What contemporary Western theatre refers to as 'presence', Barba wrote, Eastern culture attributes to spirits or energy. On the island of Bali, there is speech about *taksu*, 'the place of concentration of light', and it is understood that the actor is lit by a special energy, and that this energy influences the public.[45] Alexandre de Salzmann, we have argued, understood something of the energy of 'presence', 'the place of concentration of light', and used it in his stage lighting. Jeanne Salzmann understood it in rhythmic movement.

The artists of the avant-garde and the esoteric practitioners arrived at one and the same point:

> to know oneself is not to look from outside but to catch oneself in a moment of contact, a moment of fullness. In this there is no longer 'I' and 'me,' or 'I' and a Presence in me – no separation, no more duality. To know means to *Be*.[46]

In such unity, the capacity to move, the capacity to carry out precise rhythmic patterns or to improvise dance, became one with the knowledge, or feeling, of movement. As in many ancient traditions, in the East but also in the West, profound, concealed knowledge, including what has been called 'higher sensitivity', is deeply practical. To *understand* something means to *know how* to do something. This was certainly the case with *plyaska*; it remains a principle underlying modern discussion of body performance in all its forms.

Madame de Salzmann lived a very long life, long enough for there to be scientific recognition of the wisdom which Dalcroze and Gurdjieff announced to her, the wisdom to know how and to be. In the first half of the 1980s, for instance, Howard Gardner put forward a theory of multiple intelligence, arguing that intelligence has many different aspects. He called one of these aspects the bodily-kinaesthetic intelligence, a person's capacity to correct movements and handle objects.[47] Speaking about this kind of intelligence, Gardner cited the work of the Russian physiologist Nikolai Bernshtein (mentioned in the early part of chapter 2), who was one of the first to demonstrate that the direction of the body involves a special type of mind, which everyday speech denotes as agility. One of Bernshtein's students, Victor Semenovich Gurfinkel, also an eminent physiologist, illustrated this with a story. After the Second World War, Bernshtein taught the physiology of movement in the Central Institute of Physical Culture in Moscow. One day, he orally examined a female student, a sportswoman, active in diving. By way of a supplementary question, he asked the girl to give an example of cyclical movement. She answered with a silly remark: 'a dive'. Nevertheless Bernshtein gave her the highest mark: 'she knows [has the ability] to dive', he explained.[48]

Alain Berthoz and Jean-Luc Petit, in their book, *The Physiology and Phenomenology of Action*, had a chapter titled 'From the cogito to kinaesthesia'. To bring our arguments to a conclusion, in the following chapters we move in the opposite direction, from kinaesthesia to the cogito.

CHAPTER SIX

Thinking with the Body

*I walk along, waving my arms and mumbling almost
wordlessly, now shortening my steps so as not to interrupt
my mumbling, now mumbling more rapidly in time with
my steps.
So the rhythm is established and takes shape – and
rhythm is the basis of any poetic work, resounding through
the whole thing. Gradually you ease individual words free
of this dull roar.*

VLADIMIR MAYAKOVSKY[1]

Mayakovsky dances the foxtrot

There are many reasons to consider ways in which 'knowledge how'
focused on a particular activity may, in important respects, be more
significant than general 'knowledge that'. 'To live,' Bely asserted,
'means to know how . . . to create or to go beyond the limits of
everyday life.'[2] Cognition, for him, was a wide knowing that, which
included capability or knowledge how. The history of the avant-
garde points to ways in which reliance on knowledge how, capacities
made possible by the animate, kinaesthetic life of the body, reshaped
cognitive understanding. This is most clearly evident in (but not at

all restricted to) dance. Movement, dynamism and rhythm were not just themes that artists took up in poetry, painting, stage performance and theoretical manifestoes. Artists and intellectuals, like everyone else, *moved*. All animals move, to be sure. But in the early years of the twentieth century, people in the arts became self-conscious that they might move – and self-conscious about traditional forms of art in which there appeared to be rigidity or lack of movement. Hence the intensity and enthusiasm of the response to Duncan's dancing. Artists did not, however, just stand by and watch dancers, though they sometimes did. They themselves *danced*. So, in this chapter, we turn to the sense of movement in the lives of artists themselves, and quite literally to their movement. We also make the argument that in a number of cases, with Mayakovsky perhaps being the most significant, personal experience of movement, of dance, entered into the art for which the artists became well known. The artists of the avant-garde – Andrei Bely, Vsevolod Meyerhold, Alexandre and Jeanne de Salzmann, Viktor Shklovsky, Vladimir Mayakovsky and many others – had *capable bodies*.

The prophet of 'the widened outlook' of perception, Mikhail Matiushin, welcomed Mayakovsky as a soul brother. At performances of Mayakovsky's radically innovative poetry, which the poet gave in Moscow dressed in a yellow blouse, Mayakovsky appeared to swell up and to take up all the space. He also parried, imperturbably and quietly, philistine stupidity.[3] The yellow blouse was soon changed for one with black and yellow vertical stripes, identifying the wearer as a leader in rebellion against conformity. The blouse was not simply yellow but of a warm colour, yellow-orange, approaching the then fashionable 'colour of the tango'.[4] Just before the First World War, Europe indeed experienced a veritable tango boom. In the winter of 1913–14 in Russia, professional dancers appeared in cabarets and theatrical shows, and it became a hit to perform the tango in public. The habitués of cafes tangoed side by side with the professionals, and Mayakovsky, we imagine, was to be found amongst them.

For the Russian Futurists, the *budetliane*, the tango became a sign of the contemporary urban style of life, a life broken and sharp, in which technology and 'barbarian' feeling, elegance and coarseness, existed together.[5] In the Futurist cabaret, nonsense was declaimed, faces painted and the tango danced. 'We found, finally, the dance that genuinely transforms our fine contemporary life, the contemporary life of a great city,' wrote Bonch-Tomashevsky in a book dedicated to the tango. 'We actually found the rhythmical outline of the world of the factories and machines.'[6] Not all the Futurists agreed with him, however. In February 1914, for instance, Nada El'sner gave a lecture in Rostov-on-the-Don, 'The Tango Gobble-Up', where she described the dance as decadent and said that it 'breaks down culture with gesture'. Contemporary dance, she declared, is performed 'to the music of automobile horns'.[7]

One thing is clear: the *budetliane* loved dances. But did Mayakovsky, who remains the most famous radical poet of this generation, dance? It is interesting that Russian literary scholars have been reluctant even to think about this. For them, great poetry and popular dance inhabited different worlds. (Similarly, until recently, biographies of Pushkin failed to comment on the fact that he was a member of a gymnastic society: such a thing could not be relevant to the great writer.) Yet there is good historical evidence that Mayakovsky 'moved lightly and danced excellently'. Galina Katanian recalled that at a party to mark twenty years of his creative activity, the poet 'dance[d] with the blinding Polonskaia in a red dress, with Natasha, with me'. And Veronika Polonskaia remembered 'how on one of the evenings he accompanied me home by Lubianskaia Square and suddenly, to the surprise of passers-by, set out on the square to dance a mazurka, alone, such a large and awkward person, but he danced very lightly and comically at the same time'.[8]

Mayakovsky not only moved well, as can be seen in film clips that have escaped destruction, but kinaesthetic perception helped him in creation. 'I write verses with the whole of my body,' he said to the poet V. Lugovskoi. 'I stride about the room, stretch out my arms, gesticulate, straighten my shoulders. I do verses with the whole of the body.'[9] The penetrating writer Yurii Tynianov called Mayakovsky's verses 'united with the muscular will rather than speech'.[10] In his article, 'How to Do Verse' (from which we take the epigraph to this chapter), the poet emphasized the way the rhythm of verse, its energy, grows from movement, from 'the hum'. Mayakovsky did not know precisely where this 'grounding hum-rhythm' originated:

The sound of the sea, endlessly repeated, can provide my rhythm, or a servant who slams the door every morning, recurring and intertwining with itself, trailing through my consciousness; or even the rotation of the earth, which in my case, as in a shop full of visual aids, gives way to, and inextricably connects with, the whistle of a high wind.[11]

Dance melodies may also have blown this hum-rhythm. Mayakovsky frequented a café where fashionable jazz was played, and he probably danced there. Creating verses, he shortened, then lengthened, his step; this was not pacing evenly but dance.

The second decade of the twentieth century was the epoch of ragtime, music with 'torn time' and confused, syncopated accents. Half-rhythmic forms appeared in music and in poetry: Igor

FIGURE 8 *Vladimir Mayakovsky (1924).*

Stravinsky broke out with 'The Rite of Spring', while Bely created a theory that verses become better the more they change their rhythm, the more the rhythm turns from regular metre. With this history partly in mind, the fine and original scholar of poetry, A. P. Kviatkovsky, proposed a theory of rhythmology. Drawing an analogy with musical time, he distinguished a 'measured-time period' in verse which does not coincide with the traditional measures of the trochee, iambus and so on. In music, the most popular times are four-four and three-four. The first is associated with evenly measured motion, the second with waltz steps and other dances. In poetry, Kviatkovsky affirmed, word sequences correspond to musical lengths, lengths filled with pauses and the duration of uttered vowels, not only syllables. In poetry, also, the time-length is divided by numbered parts, giving three-part and four-part time (the times which were Kviatkovsky's concern).

Kviatkovsky especially admired Mayakovsky's 'revolutionary marches'. He called the poems, 'Our March' (1917) and 'Left March' (1918), the indubitable *chef-d'oeuvre* of rhythmically phrased verse. In this connection, he advanced a hypothesis that some scholars reject but which we should like to take up. Kviatkovsky argued that one should read these verses so that, while reading, one may step as to march music in four-four time. So, in 'Left March', 'the refrain "Left!" must everywhere and unchangingly coincide with the strike of the left leg, but the pause which completes the four-four time coincides with the strike of the right leg'.[12] Mayakovsky loved march rhythms, and in music he preferred 'the tense, coarse marches' of the early Sergei Prokofiev. Later, however, the argument continued, Mayakovsky's 'marches' 'appeared in great number ... [in] the much more rhythmically expressive three-four time'. A change took place in the years 1924–25. Kviatkovsky gave as examples the poems written 'with cheerful, even mischievous rhythm': 'I Go', 'Verlaine and Cézanne' and 'The Altai Ocean', all in three-four time. Why the change? Kviatkovsky suggested that the poet 'moved' a lot, that is, for a long time journeyed about Russia and abroad. This suggestion only went so far, however, and did not explain 'the mischievous rhythm' of the new verses. Discussing the poem 'About This' (about love), Kviatkovsky noted that Mayakovsky chose three-four time and a 'waltz-like' rhythm, and suggested that the main rhythm of the poem was connected with its content, a reference to the waltz, content that gave clear direction for performance:

> It's a theme that'll come
>   And demand:
>   'The Truth!'
> It's a theme that'll come
>   And order: 'Beauty!'
> And,
>   though nailed to the cross,
>   you forget your rood,
>   a waltz-tune
>   or something
>   absently tooting.[13]

Perhaps the change in the rhythm of Mayakovsky's verses was connected with his immersion in the dance craze of 'the roaring twenties'. At this time, he abandoned the rhythm of marches in favour of more dance-like rhythms reminiscent of the waltz, maxixe and foxtrot.

At the turn of the twentieth century, Europeans, having tired of the waltz, got to know Latin-American dances, the tango and the Brazilian maxixe. Mayakovsky knew the energetic maxixe very well:

> And so today
> From morning to the soul in me
> The maxixe cut out lips
> I go supporting my shaking arms
> And everywhere pipes dance on the roofs
> And with each column was thrown out four-four![14]

Following these dances, in the United States people took to the so-called animal dances: the turkey trot, the grizzly bear, the eagle crag, the rabbit's embrace, the marabou polka. They were danced to the music of African-American ragtime and jazz, to which it was impossible to sit, and the steps improvised the movements of animals. New dances appeared almost every month. Unlike the old ball-dances, dances to the syncopated strain of ragtime music allowed great freedom and improvisation. To dance the cakewalk, one-step, two-step and black-bottom appeared simpler than to tango, but the embrace of the partners was no less close and warm. For this reason, in 1914, the Vatican condemned the tango and another popular salon dance, the turkey trot, while the American Association of Teachers of Dance refused to teach any kind of dance to syncopated music.[15] The dance, based on the one-step and two-step and called the foxtrot, was related to these dances.

Brik-dance

The New Year of 1922 was met in the same way in Paris, Berlin, Petrograd and Moscow, with the foxtrot. The Russians Valentin Parnakh danced in émigré cafés in Paris and Andrei Bely foxtrotted in Berlin. In Petrograd, several dozen people greeted New Year in the mirrored dining room of the House of Art:

> All were here – from Akim Volynsky to Ida and from Lunts to Akhmatova. . . . In the mirrored hall Radlov with his partner and Otsup with Elsa danced the foxtrot, the one-step, the tango, in shiny shoes and pressed trousers. . . .
> In the hall there are four couples dancing who have miraculously borrowed from somewhere all the fashionable dances of a Europe as distant as a dream. People feast their eyes on them, stand in doorways, greedily drink in the novel syncopations of the foxtrot, and look at the figures swaying and fused together.[16]

There was a premiere in Moscow on the same New Year's Eve. The director Nikolai Foregger staged a spectacle, *Being Good to Horses*, to the motif of a poem by Mayakovsky. The activity in Foregger's post-revolutionary theatre-workshop (with the acronym Mastfor) came close to the genre of review and variety, and, as was then said, was the theatre of small forms (and for large forms, it is true, there were neither resources nor space). Mastfor put the show on in the House of Printing, in a hall of 200 seats, and it scarcely covered the production costs. Somehow, a couple central to the avant-garde world, Lilya and Osip Brik, looked in on one of the evening rehearsals. She was sometimes called 'the muse' of the avant-garde, and he was a writer and literary critic. At the beginning of the 1920s, Lilya Brik, who always loved to dance, was enthusiastic about fashionable salon

FIGURE 9 *Nikolai Foregger. Machine Dances. From* Ritm i kul'tura tantsa *(Rhythm and the Culture of Dance) (Moscow and Leningrad, 1926).*

FIGURE 9 *Continued.*

dances. Osip Brik and Mayakovsky joined her. They presented Foregger with the latest collection from abroad of pieces transcribed for the piano, *Contemporary Dances to Jazz*. Foregger then staged variety numbers, including a 'tango-apache' (a macho dance with complex backings and refined movement) to the two most fashionable songs, 'Mucky from Kentucky' and 'Mon homme'.

In *Being Good to Horses*, later in 1922, people in Russia heard for the first time the sounds of jazz, played by Parnakh's 'Eccentric Orchestra'. The poet and dancer, Parnakh, discovered jazz in Paris and, having returned in the summer of 1922 to Moscow, brought with him instruments for a jazz band, which he himself called an 'orchestra rumpus': trombone, banjo, xylophone, drums, shakers, horns, rattles, bells and cymbals.[17] The show was a success, thanks not least to the jazz and Parnakh's jazz dances.

The critics at once took up arms against Mastfor. In Petrograd, the performance of *Being Good to Horses* was nearly banned for using the phrase, 'we establish a café-chantant for the proletariat of every country'. Mayakovsky beat back the censors: 'Yes, chantant and music hall. Enough of dry, bitter-sweet [satire]. Give us dancing ideology, cheerful, impetuous music hall propaganda, sparkling revolutionary theatricality.'[18] Osip Brik justified the different style to the viewers: 'operetta, chantant, grotesque' is not only 'more technically accomplished', but is a more democratic theatrical form. If in the traditional theatre the notorious 'fourth wall', the proscenium arch, separates the actor from the audience, then in cabaret or variety the actor turns directly to the audience and often speaks with it on a topic of the day. Brik even thought up a term for the times, 'agit-hall' ('propaganda-hall'), to denote political cabaret for the masses. He wanted the proletariat to take the 'light genre' of cabaret out of the hands of 'bourgeois entrepreneurs'.[19]

On a wave of success, in the autumn of 1922, Mastfor received its own space in Moscow. The new season opened with the show *Being Even Better to Horses*, and with a programme of dance numbers. Included in the show were 'Machine Dances', and these, with other 'eccentric' dances, owed something to Parnakh. 'A Walk', 'No. 6' and 'Pastoral' were quickly established as Mastfor's crowning numbers.

Parnakh thought up his own 'eccentric dance' under the influence of jazz. In his memoirs, he described how, at the time of the war, when he was in Paris and when the majority of the café-chantant and bars were closed, he suffered without music and dance. The day the bars reopened was for him a day of celebration. Full of excitement, he jumped up on a billiard table and broke into a dance, thinking up his own previously unseen movements. In his verse, he brought in the fashionable foxtrot and marabou polka, though he himself also thought up many movements:

As if the trumpets of prophets began to be heard,
The first strike,
Foxtrot, its triumph,
A trembling dervish!
Pneumatic belly.
Marabou.
Movement of the flock.[20]

On returning to Russia, he demonstrated his 'eccentric dance' to Foregger.

After each premier, in the foyer of Mastfor there was a 'vauxhall' (named after the locality in London where there had been an entertainment park), a closed party at which theatrical-artistic Moscow came together. Always present were the Briks and Mayakovsky. Parnakh's jazz band performed and there was the premiere of the Futurist 'noise orchestra' of klaxons, rattles and saucepans. The idea of a 'noise orchestra' belonged to the Italians, Marinetti and Russolo, but in Russia it was first staged by Foregger's actors. Further, certainly, the foxtrot and shimmy were danced at the 'vauxhalls'. Parnakh himself gave lessons to Muscovites, including Ippolit Sokolov in the Laboratory-Theatre of Expressionism and Eisenstein, the future famous film director, in the theatrical studio of Proletkul't. Eisenstein, who already had the beginnings of choreographic training, studied the foxtrot with Parnakh with pleasure. As he acknowledged, from these lessons he mastered the rules of dance improvisation, dance subordinated only to rhythm and to the new freedom of movement.[21]

Parnakh, with his orchestra and choreography, also participated in Vsevolod Meyerhold's performance, *D.E.* The first part of the show featured 'positive Soviet heroes' – acrobats, sportsmen, sailors – demonstrating biomechanical exercises. The second part parodied 'the decadent West' and showed the tango, foxtrot and shimmy, choreographed by Kas'ian Goleizovsky, while Parnakh showed his own dances, 'Hieroglyphs' and 'Idol-Giraffe'. When the performance was closed for being 'decadent', Osip Brik threw himself into its defence. He was indignant: 'Why is ballet decent and foxtrot indecent?' 'In what way is Duncan naked more proper than Goleizovsky naked? It's time to discard this old-girlish approach to the theatre.'[22] Brik affirmed that, in the country of workers, dance must become 'a kind of sport to restore the physical and spiritual strength of a person after the heavy work of the day'.[23]

According to the witness of such a searching critic as Lilya Brik, Osip himself danced 'ideally'.[24] The couple established dance evenings at their home and even acquired a permanent ballroom pianist. The students of Meyerhold's theatre workshops, who already danced American tap-dance at the highest level, invited Osip Brik to head a 'club for dances' (though the club never opened). Lilya had embraced dancing, and when already an adult she had studied ballet, not to dance on the stage but to become gracious and to try out a new image on herself. She gradually took on traits of a flapper, the independent girls of the 1920s, followers of fashion, contemporary dances and automobiles. Lilya wore a dress from the celebrity dresser, Nadezhda Lamanova, and 'Mama Nadia' created for her a hat, a cloche, a detail without which it was not possible to imagine oneself in fashion. And, like a real flapper, Lilya embraced the foxtrot and other 'Nep-Man' dances, which were danced in newly opened café-chantants and cabarets. (The 'Nep-Men' were the private entrepreneurs who became legal and who flourished after Lenin ordered, in 1923, the 'new economic policy', NEP, to counter shortages.)

The epoch of the café turned out to be a short one. It declined and then fell under prohibition, tarred with 'bourgeoisism' and accused of bad taste, eroticism and vulgarity. Defenders claimed, however, that the foxtrot, like other dances of the jazz era, was free from ideology and expressed only the performers' good physical form. Foregger and Osip Brik considered the dances to be dynamic, 'in the spirit of the time', part of the utopia of that 'socialist America' into which Russia had to be turned. But even a critic sympathetic to Foregger called his Americanism 'half-mythical' and, 'for us, other'. The critic added: 'what irony! In the circumstances of the kerosene burner [literally, as a source of cooking, in the absence of electricity], to preach Americanism *only* in the dance review!'[25] Then, in 1924, the Commission for Dance, organized at the All-Russian Committee for Physical Culture (VSFK), announced a discussion about 'contemporary American dances'. Members of the Choreological Laboratory of the Russian Academy of Art Sciences, Foregger, Parnakh and others took part. There was talk about creating 'a proletarian class-based' or 'national' foxtrot. Suitable music was even found for it: the well-known dynamic melody, 'Little Apple', at one moment allegretto, metrical, at another moment, two beats, rhythmical, and at a third moment with points of syncopation belonging to the general human rhythms of contemporary times.[26] To the huge unhappiness of dance fans, the Moscow city council, with a special decree, forbad holding balls in public places. Nonetheless, the foxtrot must have continued to be danced, if at reviews and in dance squares. When, in the Academy of Art Sciences, there was a lecture with a demonstration of contemporary American dances, a record number – more than a hundred people – came to watch and listen. The presenter of the paper, Ia. N. Andronikov, demonstrated the advantages of 'American dances':

constructivism in composition, purposeful change of ornamental gesture and the correlation of all the principles of contemporary physical culture. All the same, neither the lecture nor the demonstration convinced the ossified critics.

In 1928, Maxim Gorky fell upon jazz in the party newspaper, *Pravda*, calling it 'music of fat people': 'under its rhythm, in all the splendid cabarets of "the cultured" country, fat people, cynically moving their hips, dirty and simulate the act of reproduction between a man and a woman'. The stormy petrel of the Revolution opposed 'the beauty of the minuet and the live passion of the waltz ... to the cynicism of the foxtrot and the convulsions of the Charleston'.[27] There was a need, Gorky wrote, to substitute new dances, for example, those which the Section of Dance (changing its name into the Section of Artistic Education) hastily thought up. The Section, indeed, set up 'the necessary social and scientific control' over dance education.[28]

The same disciplining of movement was evident even in the radical theatre. In the middle of the 1920s, brigades of proletarian actors, named 'the Blue Blouse', were active in workers' reviews and peasant clubs. Osip Brik and Mayakovsky were the initiators of the movement. Foregger became its director and staged numbers of 'a live newspaper', which included physical culture pyramids and 'machine dances', for which, in 1925, he earned the name 'honorary blue blousenik'. All the actors of this agit (propaganda)-theatre dressed in uniform, a blue blouse with a black skirt below the knees for women, and black trousers for men; the physical culture numbers were performed in shorts and striped T-shirts. Thus striped singlets and canvas shoes became a fashion alternative to the 'decadent' flapper.

By the middle of the 1930s, the Soviet Union had its own, new neo-bourgeois elite. In this social setting, the foxtrot no longer served as a sign of deviance but became, like the haut couture skirt, the possession of the Soviet establishment. It is highly probable that Lilya and Osip Brik, together with other partners, continued to dance the foxtrot well into the Stalin era.

So, was the enthusiasm of Mayakovsky, the Briks and their avant-garde friends for fashionable dances just a diversion from serious activity as artists and cultural leaders? We think not. Dancing united sociability and the body, improvisation and self-control, refinement and vitality, and people of the 1920s were captivated by all of this. Having fed and entertained European intellectuals at the beginning of the century, the café culture became the poetry of Mayakovsky, his friends and his lovers. With the end of NEP, this culture disappeared from Russia. Not wishing to give up the café-chantant and music hall, Mayakovsky, Foregger and Brik proposed in its place the ideologically sustainable 'agit-hall' and 'theatre of the small form'. Perhaps 'the Blue Blouse' grew in part from the wish of Mayakovsky and the Briks to dance. Moreover, we have suggested, the enthusiasm for dance entered into the change in the rhythmic structure of Mayakovsky's poetry, to which Kviatkovsky drew attention. As a result, even Mayakovsky's late 'October March' (1929) was written not in four-four but in three-four time, as if it were not a 'square' march but a dance, a foxtrot.

Mayakovsky's powerful corporeity revealed itself in both his writing and his drawings. Towards the end of his tragically curtailed life, Mayakovsky recalled his work in Okna ROSTA, the agency where he wrote and painted propaganda posters:

'We worked 16 to 18 hours a day, slept without undressing, always hungry and . . . happy! I so trained myself that, with my eyes closed, I could draw with charcoal a bourgeois, a worker with a hammer and a Red Army soldier.'

He stood to the side of the chair, having given his recollections, looking somewhere far off and far in the past, made a step towards the grey side-wing [of the stage] and, as if he had a charcoal in his hand, he held it in the air, as if drawing. Then he turns to us, he closes his eyes, continues to draw in the air, and suddenly smiles broadly:

'And, if you please, I can now!'[29]

Mayakovsky's body knew how to draw posters: it was knowledge how, embedded in his kinaesthetic and kinetic nature. He made posters, like poems, with his whole body.

Who thought up biomechanics?

The post-revolutionary cult of labour, industrial art and Constructivism, without doubt, facilitated the growth and impact of alternatives to academic knowledge. Such alternatives were also talked about earlier, in Formalist declarations on language amongst other places. Moreover, sport, dance, theatre and the circus influenced and informed them no less than the ideological directives of the Revolution or Formalist theory. Adding to the range of movement practices, in the years immediately following the Revolution, the theatre director Meyerhold introduced the system of exercises for training actors known as biomechanics. If there was a connection between the sciences and arts of movement, this is most obviously where we might expect to find it. Meyerhold's biomechanics was a system of knowledge in capability, technique, knowing how: trained by such a system, the actor possessed a kinaesthetic intellect, bodily knowledge about how to do things on the stage. Art, expertise and intellect became interdependent.

There are two biomechanics: the scientific theory of the movements of the organism and of the mechanical properties of its tissues, and the theatrical set of exercises that Meyerhold devised. As a term, 'biomechanics' first appeared at the end of the nineteenth century in German-language medicine, where it denoted the application of the laws of mechanics to the construction of the functioning organism. The term arrived in Russia at the beginning of the twentieth century thanks to the anatomist and pedagogue, P. F. Lesgaft, who came from a family of Russian Germans. In 1910, a student of Lesgaft, a doctor, G. A. Kogan, proposed to teach an introduction to biomechanics in a medical school in Petersburg and to organize a parallel practical course for orthopaedists, physiotherapists and specialists in therapeutic gymnastics – that is, for all those who might benefit from knowledge of bodily mechanics.[30] We need to state emphatically that biomechanics owed nothing to Pavlov.

How did this term arrive in the theatre? Meyerhold had always declared a special interest in plastic movement, or movement for performance. He recommended 'to the actor a new theatre . . . consisting of a whole code of techniques to know how to live, theatrically, on the stage: to bow low with a cap, as if this head-gear is strewn with pearls, and to throw over a shoulder an old ragged coat with the gesture of a hidalgo'.[31] His system of actor-training attended closely to movement on the stage, pantomime and acrobatics. At first, Meyerhold placed meaning in the study of the laws of rhythm, fencing and gymnastics, so that the actor might 'liberate himself', 'temper himself and turn himself to nature' and acquire 'the natural' movement of a beast.[32] In the years 1915–16, in the studio on Borodinskaia Street in Petersburg, the master undertook studies with the actors which he called 'Di Grasso', after the name of the Italian tragedian. Meyerhold often recalled one of the scenes which clearly illustrated Giovanni Grasso's technique: the hero stole up to the seducer of his wife and, suddenly having squeezed his Adam's apple, sprang on his chest; the seducer bent his head back, and Grasso fastened onto him by the throat.

After the Revolution, it occurred to Meyerhold to employ in the theatre the then innovative and fashionable system, NOT, the acronym of the scientific organization of labour, and to become involved with 'Taylorization of the theatre'. He wanted to goad the theatre with physical culture, having created an organization for 'the theatralization of physical culture' (abbreviated to *tefizkul't*).[33] At the same time, the director borrowed from the literary Formalists their *matériel* (equipment), though not their forms of expression. He required the new actors to relate to themselves as to pieces of equipment which it was necessary to study and to keep in good condition. The actor, Meyerhold stated, had 'not only to train his movement according to a definite system', into which entered the basics of classical dance and an introduction to acrobatics, but also needed to take up the study of his 'nervous apparatus'.[34] It was for precisely this purpose that Meyerhold turned to biomechanics, the science of movements of the living organism. The outcome, in the School of Acting Craft and in the Courses of the Craft of Stage Presentation in Petrograd, was that Dr A. P. Petrov, medical man and Olympic medallist in free-style wrestling, taught biomechanics as a valuable discipline at the point where anatomy, mechanics and medicine met.

Aleksandr Petrovich Petrov trained at the Military-Medical Academy in Petersburg and then in Heidelberg, and he followed a standard career into forensic medicine. What was not standard was that Petrov became a gymnast and sportsman at the international level and also studied medicine in connection with sport and physical culture. At the beginning of the twentieth century, it was the rider and athlete Count G. I. Ribeaupierre who set the pattern of much of the sporting life in the northern capital. Together with the wrestler Ivan Lebedev, nicknamed 'Uncle Vanya', the writer Aleksandr Kuprin and Petr Lesgaft, the count founded the Saint-Petersburg Athletic Society, which Petrov joined. In 1897, in the *manezh* (riding arena) that the count owned, they organized and directed the first championship in Russia of French (free-style, classical) wrestling. Ribeaupierre helped to bring out into the world arena many talented Russian athletes, and he took part in the formation of the Russian teams participating in their first Olympic Games and financed their journey. Petrov was selected for the Olympiad in London in 1908, where he won a silver medal. Besides this, Petrov took prizes in practically all kinds of sport: gymnastics, swimming, riding, skiing, light athletics, fencing, wrestling, boxing and cycling.

This Petrov, then, in the 1910s, not only gave a theoretical course in medical higher education but taught gymnastics to future teachers of physical culture. The Society of Physical Education, 'Bogatyr' (the collective name of the mythical heroes who carved out the lands of the Russian people) had been founded at the beginning of the century; and the Gymnastics Institute for the Preparation of Male Teachers and courses for women then followed. From 1905 to 1915, Petrov led the women's courses in pedagogic gymnastics, and he taught anatomy in the Gymnastics Institute. Besides this, he taught therapeutic gymnastics in the Psycho-Neurological Institute founded by V. M. Bekhterev. After the Revolution, Petrov trained red commanders in ju-jitsu, created a programme of physical education for new Soviet schools and, as before, did much university teaching. In the Herzen Pedagogical Institute, he not only gave theoretical courses but led a circle of 'gymnastic dancing'. One of his students recalled:

> In the Herzen Institute, Professor Petrov gave us lectures on physical education. Attendance was then optional, but Aleksandr Petrovich – he looked imposing: tall, broad-shouldered, thickset – always assembled a full audience. And besides that, I went to him in the circle of gymnastic dancing. He worked from plastic but not balletic movement. These were dances built on gymnastics and anatomy. Our demonstration performances invariably went with great success. We danced the [Hungarian] *Csárdás*, [Ukranian] *Gopak*, waltz and Tirolean dance. But none of us guessed that our professor was such a splendid sportsman.[35]

Thus, movement in sport and movement in dance, movement for teaching physical culture and movement for aesthetic pleasure, came together. Both before and after the Revolution, that coming together was not a coincidence but served national aspirations. After the Revolution, however, there was the opportunity, at least for a few years, to innovate radically in the way physical culture and avant-garde aesthetics interrelated. This can be seen in the work that Meyerhold did for mass stagings in the service of the Bolshevik state, work which was of considerable importance for his now better-known work in the theatre.

As a result of all of this, Petrov, a well-known man in Petrograd, was invited to teach actors 'gymnastics by some kind of new system'.[36] We suppose that he introduced biomechanics into Meyerhold's courses at first as a theoretical tool, side by side with anatomy and physiology, and then as a convenient foundation for his gymnastics. It was obligatory for participants in these courses to study movement. The politically oriented activity required of students, such as leading theatre studios in the Baltic Fleet or organizing mass events and travelling street performances on tram platforms and lorries, demanded the actors' thorough physical preparation. Meyerhold himself, it appears, well appreciated Petrov's gymnastic system and his understanding of biomechanics. When the director opened work in Moscow, the State Higher Directing Workshop, he taught 'biomechanics' there himself. The first information about this known to us appeared on 27 January 1921 in the *Theatre Bulletin*. A somewhat confused article appeared about 'the education of the actor on the basis of the laws of pan-technics [*sic*], of expressions . . . in physics, mechanics, music and architecture'. The author (it might have been Meyerhold's student, Konstantin Derzhavin) wrote about the actor 'as real physical material, subordinate . . . to general mechanical laws: size, metre and rhythm'.[37] Meyerhold and others affirmed that 'the roots of a new, communist staging of drama lie in the physical culture of the theatre which gradually overcomes doubtful psychological laws, with their pseudo-science, with the science, by contrast, of precise laws of movement based on biomechanics and kinetics'.[38] Biomechanics helped Meyerhold to decide what were then being discussed as vital questions: the proximity of art to life, and the verification of the *science* of art.

In 1919, N. I. Podvoisky, a member of the Revolutionary Military Council and head of Vsevobuch (the Main Directorate of General Military Education), posed the question of the 'theatralization of physical culture'. Vsevobuch was active in training recruits to the Red Army and oversaw a section of physical development and sport. Moreover, a month after the creation of Vsevobuch, in May 1918, the first military physical culture parade on Red Square took place. In the spring of 1920, however, Podvoisky had to set out for the Civil War where, on the staff of the Tenth Army, he took part in what for the Reds was the liberation of Novorossisk in the south of Russia. Meyerhold was in Novorossisk at the time. Their paths crossed, and the director ran a course for young soldiers and began to work in the political section of the army under Podvoisky's direction. When, with the end of the Civil War, the commander returned to Vsevobuch, he was accustomed to work with his former comrade-in-arms.

Podvoisky dreamed about training strong, brave and agile 'red Spartans'. On 10 October 1920, in Moscow, with his participation, the foundation stone for 'a physical culture camp' was triumphantly laid on the Sparrow Hills. The organisers planned that, besides the Red Stadium for 60,000 spectators, there would be a theatre of mass action, which Meyerhold was to direct. The theatre director at this time headed the Theatrical Section (TEO) of Narkompros (the People's Commissariat of Enlightenment) and had begun to prepare his 'Theatrical October'. For the third anniversary of the Revolution, he planned 'mass actions' with the participation of Red Army soldiers, and he counted on Vsevobuch's help. Meyerhold and Podvoisky indeed supported each other. Podvoisky called for 'the bringing together of the activity of physical culture with mass theatrical activity', while Meyerhold declared: 'It's necessary to bring closer together theatre with natural and physical culture and to create conditions for the new actor – who is to be agile and strong.'[39]

Besides two parents, in the form of Podvoisky and Meyerhold, the idea of 'theatrical physical culture' had a midwife, Ippolit Sokolov. He was mobilized in the Civil War, began to serve in Vsevobuch and made himself a specialist in physical training. With all the poetic temperament and energy of his nineteen years, he took up the project of *tefizkul't*. He considered its tasks to be the struggle with physical degeneration, working up labour gymnastics, the organization of 'mass actions' and the 'Taylorization of the artistic formation of labour demonstration'.[40] It was also Sokolov who first proposed the formation, in the former Nikitin Brothers Circus, of a

Palace of Physical Culture. This gave Meyerhold the idea of staging a mass action, 'The Taking of the Bastille', with the help of the circus and with the participation of Red Army soldiers. The Commissar of Enlightenment, Lunacharsky, gave his approval.

This project interested Meyerhold so much that, leaving TEO in the spring of 1921, he retained duties in *tefizkul't* for himself. In addition to gaining a space for his theatre laboratory, he hoped to receive rations for the students of the Theatre Courses from Vsevobuch. When making the request, Meyerhold stated that the purpose was to achieve 'a new basis for a proletarian theatre tightly connected with the principles of physical culture'. Indeed, the first course, and part of the second, involved the students in considerable physical training. The programme included 'the presentation of normal movement, gymnastics, biomechanics, gymnastic play, dance, martial movement, the strengthening of rhythmic awareness (Dalcroze system), the laws of stage movement, imaginative movement with the size and form of a stage space and pantomime'.[41] Biomechanics, understood as the scientific study of movement, here took a place in a long row of other techniques; this was to change.

It appeared realistic to set up *tefizkul't* in the old circus, and a mandate for this was even received. Meanwhile, the physical culture camp was to open on Workers' Day, 1 May. Meyerhold and Podvoisky planned a staging on Khodynskoe Field of a mass action, 'Fight and Victory', in which more than 2,000 foot soldiers, 200 cavalry, artillerists, aeroplanes, armoured cars and motorcycles, and also combined detachments of sports clubs, studios and military orchestras and choirs, were to take part. The slogan of the festival proclaimed 'the theatralization of physical culture'. Both plans, however, remained unrealized: money was not forthcoming, and the circus site was moved. All the same, those committed to *tefizkul't* continued to construct grandiose plans: the musician Evgeny Krein proposed staging an event under the title 'Spartak', to Beethoven's Fifth Symphony (Duncan was invited to participate in the performance), and Meyerhold proposed Wagner's 'Rienzi'. Nevertheless, in spite of Podvoisky's support, *tefizkul't* did not succeed in getting financed by Vsevobuch, and then, with the end of the Civil War, Vsevobuch itself was eliminated. Just at this time, however, Meyerhold finally received his own stage where, on 1 October 1922, they premiered *The Magnanimous Cuckold*.[42]

Tefizkul't was a 'mobilized' version of modernist theatrical art for the masses. To realize it depended on bringing together sport and physical culture with theatrical gesture; and, of course, it also depended on the political will to provide funding during a period of severe shortages. There was, in fact, a highly unstable relation between the visionary innovations of a few avant-garde artists dedicated to the Revolution and the realities of achieving mass organization. Nonetheless, it was a decisive time for the history of mass political spectacle in the new Soviet state, and indeed elsewhere. At this time, the kinaesthetic world of the avant-garde transformed from an individual, subjective reality, a potential domain of free dance and symbolic enactment of the spirit, into a potentially collective, manufactured reality in the service of the state. Taking this road, the movement arts recreated the position of sports generally. Sport was, as of course it still is, both the display of individual kinaesthetic perception and ability and public performance, ritual, for collective ends.

Once Meyerhold had his own theatre, biomechanics, which had appeared in the programme of the earlier acting courses as a specialist discipline, the study of the body and its movements, became the distinguishing characteristic of the theatre. Everything began to take second place to it: 'Physical culture, acrobatics, dance, rhythmics, boxing, fencing are useful tools, but they succeed in having utility when they are introduced as ancillaries to the course of "biomechanics", to the basis of technique necessary for each actor.'[43]

Seeing the success of theatrical biomechanics, A. K. Gastev, the Director of the Central Institute of Labour (TsIT), also decided to take it up in earnest. In July 1922, an article came out in *Pravda* where the Director wrote: 'in the human organism there is a motor, there is "transmission", there are shock-absorbers, there is a precision regulator and there is even a pressure gauge. All this demands study and utilization. There has to be a special science – biomechanics.' This science, Gastev added, 'cannot be narrower than "[the science of] labour", [but] it must border on sport, where strong and agile movements are at the same time light in breath and mechanically artistic'.[44] Gastev's slogan, 'the machine that works is the machinist', was very close to 'the first principle of biomechanics' formulated by Meyerhold.

From the end of the 1930s, nothing was remembered in public about theatrical biomechanics: it was, one might say, repressed together with Meyerhold, its creator. All the same, thanks to Meyerhold's students, biomechanics was kept alive. One of today's teachers, A. A. Levinsky, spoke about its meaning for the actor:

> Biomechanics may bring you into balance. Balance comes into existence through it, and literally you learn to see on an inner level and to hear yourself from the side. You learn how 'to mirror'. It contains an emotional element within certain shores. . . . And simple repetition of this form collects you, subdues and, as if limiting your freedom, maximally directs you to one side. The side of precision! . . . Biomechanics is a kind of theatrical yoga . . . But at the same time, biomechanics is attached to the fulfilment of theatrical forms. It is oriented towards the viewer.[45]

Biomechanics is a training for the actor, but it takes into consideration the viewer, and it is training not simply in movement but in movement *of expressions*. It presupposes perceptual knowledge of the body, kinaesthesia, but from a definite point of view, as material for the creation of expressive artistic form. The psychologist Rudolf Arnheim stated that for expression the dancer uses muscular tension and relaxation, balance and stability, as building material for the creation of a choreographic image. The dynamic nature of the results of movement practices, Arnheim emphasized, underlies 'the surprising correspondence between what the dancer creates by his muscular sensations and the image of the body seen by the audience'.[46] Kinaesthesia, the sixth sense, and, in the words of the director Eugenio Barba, 'muscular responsiveness', is pivotal in performance and in its reception.[47] This is the insight we have traced in the theatre to Meyerhold.

Meyerhold first became familiar with biomechanics as a science which could help to reform the theatre and take it in the direction of labour and physical culture. It also helped him to find experimental ways to establish the laws of actors' movements in the stage space. In the theatre, theoretical knowledge turned out to be practical, and to know that became to know how. When, at the beginning of the 1920s in Moscow, the director himself led 'the activity in biomechanics', he led not a scientific discipline but a practice in stage movement. The directions that he had already given to his actors in 1915–16 reappeared under a fashionable scientific label. As a result, the word 'biomechanics' received a new meaning: it became 'a system of training the actor, the aggregate of techniques and skills (gymnastics, plastic movement, acrobatics), with the help of which the actor gains the possibility creatively, precisely, as a whole and naturally to direct the mechanism of movement of his body'.[48]

It was important that the anatomist, Lesgaft, and the doctor and sportsman, Petrov, helped Meyerhold; thanks to them theatre biomechanics acquired the status of *knowledge*, though it was not in the first place written knowledge. Biomechanical exercises were brought in to teach the actor not only to relate irreproachably to her or his own body, but also *to think* with this body. Barba underlined the fact that, as part of the actor's training, biomechanics is 'a way to acquire physical intelligence'.[49] The thought of the actor or dancer appears through the technique which organizes activity, creating a definite dramaturgy. Exercises are like a box with many tools inside, which the acting body-thought can use to break itself into parts or reconstruct, in order to master the embodied means of thinking. The theatre demands a kinaesthetic intellect, an intellect stepping out from the frame with which it is usually associated, in order to distance itself from ordinary behaviour and enter a region of extraordinary behaviour for the stage.

In seeking to answer questions about the secret of the art of the dancer, the actor or the performer, and about the role of technique, Barba turned to Michael Polanyi's far from exhausted concept, tacit knowledge.[50] Tacit knowledge is hidden, implicit and 'personal' knowledge, in contrast to explicit, theoretical or formal and 'collective' knowledge. All knowledge is in some way social, or shared, knowledge. But because tacit knowledge is unspoken knowledge, it can also be highly individual and personal. This is especially the case for the knowledge underlying the capability in movement of a special dancer or actor. In conclusion, there is more to say about kinaesthesia as knowledge.

CHAPTER SEVEN

Art as Bodily Knowledge

Does he not go along like a dancer?
FRIEDRICH NIETZSCHE[1]

Technique

'And let that day be lost to us on which we did not dance once! And let that wisdom be false to us that brought no laughter with it!' said Zarathustra.[2] Nietzsche wrote about 'the joyful science'. Similarly, the Formalist and Russian Nietzschean, Viktor Shklovsky, if in a distinctive way, set out through writing 'to dance science' (in our words, using 'science', as continental Europeans do, to denote disciplined, systematic knowledge, not necessarily natural science). Certainly, he knew how to do many things: to write, to play the violin, to wrestle – and he even wore the Russian Saint-George Cross for valour in war. Lidiia Ginzburg recalled that Shklovsky was fond of telling how, in the years of emigration, working in some kind of editorial office in Berlin, he taught all the typists to write novels – 'to dance' ('after which the editorial office quickly collapsed', added Ginzburg).[3] Having made a skill or instrument from his theory of poetry and composition, Shklovsky transferred this art to the typists. Writing, for him, was almost a manual craft:

> I begin work with reading. When I read I try not to be tensed. To be precise, I do not try to memorize. Tension, to be on guard,

disturbs me. One needs to read calmly, looking the book in the eyes. . . .

I make bookmarks of various colours and width. It would be good to write the page number on the bookmarks, in case they fall out (but I don't). Then I look through the bookmarks. Make notes.

The typist (the same one who is at the moment typing this article) retypes the parts with the page number. I hang these pieces – they are very numerous – on the walls of my room.

To my regret, my room is small. And it's crowded.

It is very important to understand the quote, to turn it around, to link it to others. Pieces stay on the wall for a long time. I group them, hang them side by side, and then linking passages appear, abruptly written. Then I write a plan of the chapters, rather a detailed one, on paper sheets and put pieces pinned together in files.

I start dictating the work, numbering the inserted pieces. . . .

As if I worked on a typewriter with open type-face.[4]

The Formalists, like Shklovsky, opposed knowledge of another character, knowledge how, to the kind of knowledge that academics had created from philology. 'The Russian Formalists,' Sergei Zenkin considered, 'could serve as a model for the "*bricolage*" character of the literary criticism which improvises its notions, crafts criticism from the material of the very literature in hand.'[5]

It was not only writers who took an interest in this. Meyerhold wrote that when a violinist 'takes a difficult passage, you feel that he suddenly thinks through the musical construction to show us how he looks on the world'.[6] Becoming a virtuoso, a person becomes a thinker in her or his craft and in a worldview. Shklovsky spoke in the same way: exposing the construction of his writing, his *instrument*, the writer shows us his feeling for the world, his feeling for life.

Shklovsky often derived his terminology from movement practices. In particular, he borrowed from free wrestling for the idea of *The Hamburg Account*, his best-known, innovative and, in a way, autobiographical writing on the life of a writer in the emigrant Russian community in Germany after the Revolution. He used technique ('defamiliarization') to distance his language from the reader's expectations, thus pushing the reader, as it had pushed the writer, to a different way of perceiving and of being. The concept of *priem* (technique) in Formalist writing came from the sphere of sport. As Shklovsky argued, it was anticipated by the Greek conception of the schema, denoting 'the gymnast's anticipatory trial of movement [before actually executing a movement]'.[7] This opened up a theory of the connection between poetics, gesture and movement, linking writing to other artistic forms. The historian Yury Tsivian wrote:

> [The Formalists] Tynianov and Eichenbaum spoke to us about word techniques, Shklovsky wrote about techniques of establishing the subject and [asked] why one would not grant that art conserves favourite techniques for gestures? If it can be shown that several of the gesticulatory techniques work in different expressions of art, it may be possible to speak about a new region of knowledge, about a general poetics of motion and gesture.[8]

Shklovsky introduced his conception of technique by adopting the gesture as a model, and Tsivian then, in a kind of retrospective converse operation, thought through the gesture with the help of the idea of technique. Tsivian took the conception of technique, as the Formalists used it, and extended it to expressive gestures. Developing a similar assessment, the contemporary literary scholar Ilya Kalinin turned attention to the fact that, for the Formalists, bodily experience served as a 'distinctive plastic model for the construction of theoretical concepts'.[9]

Such an argument has contributed to the stance that we have taken in writing this book: it is necessary to speak about *the living body*, the person who moves and feels movement, as the source of meanings and techniques. Our book, in its way, by exploring kinaesthesia, confirms Shklovsky's aphorism: art must be felt.[10] (To appreciate the impact of this, one must remember that Shklovsky was a *writer*, and readers would not, at the time he wrote, have thought of 'sensing' language.)

The search to cast off habits acquired without reflection, for renewal, for a celebratory feeling for life, was the inspiration of the avant-garde. 'Life-feeling' Dionysian dance was uniquely suited for this. Shklovsky told a tale:

> There's an old story in some Greek classic . . . A certain royal prince was so impassioned with the dance at his wedding that he

threw off his clothes and began dancing naked on his hands. This enraged the bride's father, who shouted: 'Prince, you have just danced yourself out of a wedding.' To which the young man, addressing the would-be father-in-law, said: 'Your Majesty, I couldn't care less!' and went on dancing anyway, his feet up in the air.[11]

Did Shklovsky really uncover this legend in old Greek books, or did he read it in Nietzsche? In 1916, the same year in which the Society for the Study of Poetic Language (OPOIaZ) emerged in Petrograd, with Shklovsky the driving spirit, further West Mary Wigman danced not to music but to a reading of 'The Song of the Dance', passages from *Thus Spoke Zarathustra*. She also spoke about sensitivity to 'the fullness of life', 'vitality' and 'brilliance' – 'a heightened realization of life' – which the experience of dance brings.[12]

Carnivalesque striving to turn upside down, to throw off the higher and older, the prepared and the completed, to seek in the material-bodily underworld for death and new birth, about which Zelinsky's student, Bakhtin, wrote, went back to Dionysian dance.[13] An attitude of carnival was typical for OPOIaZ as it set out to free language to display its own qualities rather than serve as the slave of meaning. (It was for this that it acquired the soubriquet 'Formalism'.) Telling his tale about the royal prince, Shklovsky called on artists to make art tangible, to overcome convention (indeed, to turn convention on its head) and to leave automatic expression behind, similarly to the way dance lifts a person out of the automatism of taken-for-granted walking. Dance was to be the exit from automatism; it was to be the movement that finds new, sensitive and emotionally informed being for a person. 'Dance is movement that can be felt. Or more accurately, it is movement formed in order to be felt.'[14]

From a physiological viewpoint, there is, all the same, something absurd in the wish to destroy automatism and to feel what was formerly unfelt. Everyone knows some version of the joke about the beast with forty legs, which stops to ponder which leg to step out with and, as a result, fails to move at all. Everyone also knows about the automatic skills people acquire, for example, in learning to play a musical instrument like the violin. As the result of extended exercises, the violinist stops feeling the bow and strings and becomes able to concentrate wholly on the music. For this reason, Shklovsky's lament that people get stuck in habits and stop feeling the world, like a violinist ceasing to feel the bow and strings, appears misdirected. As to what touches the violinist, however, one can trust Shklovsky, as he himself played and knew first-hand that without making movement automatic, without the loss of conscious awareness of the strings and bow, it is impossible to play something of value.

In order to get over the apparent contradiction here, we have to go further into the understanding of automatism and the acquisition of a skill. According to the Pavlovian theory of conditional reflexes, formulated in Russia in the decades that we are discussing, the acquisition of a skill comes through the repetition, many times, of one and the same movement in response to one and the same stimulus (or, more precisely, a combination of stimuli). As a result of the repetition, Pavlov believed, nervous connections form in the brain, beaten out like well-worn paths, and a durable reflex skill forms. Contemporary critics of Pavlov exposed the weakness of this theory, though it seemed to correspond roughly to common sense and to an everyday understanding of how mastering a skill comes about. The German neurologist Kurt Goldstein and the Russian physiologist Nikolai Bernshtein argued, however, that the education of a movement skill does not take place by repetition; rather, the organism studies the purpose for which it decides on a movement task, not the means for carrying it out. The fact is that the situation in which the training of a skill occurs is a little different each time. Only the task, the purpose, the thought of the movement, remains the same, while the means of completing the movement may change. (As a consequence, educators even recommend varying the conditions of training, for example, completing a movement with the side of the body not used before.) A skill, even an automatic one, is not mechanical but a live human movement, by this means tightly connected with a person's conscious activity, and regulated by it. This kind of account was noticeably different from the understanding of the automatism of the body built upon the theory of reflex action in the nineteenth century.

In the first decades of the twentieth century, a new understanding of skill began to be available, an understanding which no longer considered a skill to be something mechanical, a habit from which consciousness had departed. There was new interest in how a person, in the process of acquiring a skill, reorganizes movements in relationship to the world. 'To get used to a hat, a car or a stick,' Merleau-Ponty later wrote, 'is to be transplanted into them, or conversely, to incorporate them into the bulk of our own body. Habit expresses our power of dilating our being-in-the-world, or changing our existence by appropriating fresh instruments.' The acquisition of a skill, to grasp movements, 'to incorporate them into ... our own body', is not at all a mechanical process. It is the capacity to carry out a movement that was formerly not natural to

FIGURE 10 *Cyclography of stroke movement. Central Institute of Labour, Moscow, 1920s.*

FIGURE 11 *Nikolai Bernshtein in the Central Institute of Labour. Moscow, mid-1920s.*

a person, formerly other, as one's own, to do it organically, to appropriate it. So, 'if habit is neither a form of knowledge nor an involuntary action what then is it?' continued Merleau-Ponty. 'It is *knowledge* which is in my hands, which is forthcoming only when *bodily effort* is made, and cannot be formulated in detachment from that effort.'[15]

Step by step, scientists began to understand the acquisition of a skill not as mechanical learning, but as 'a rearrangement and renewal of the corporeal schema'. As Merleau-Ponty wrote:

> before the formula of the new dance can incorporate certain elements of general motility, it must first have had, as it were, the stamp of movement set upon it. . . . The acquisition of a habit is indeed the grasping of a significance, but it is the motor grasping of a motor significance.[16]

There is a larger history to this, connected to the notion of 'the schema' found in the work of a number of psychologists and physiologists in the decades between the two world wars. The English psychologist Frederic Bartlett, in particular, taking the concept from the neurologist Henry Head, used it in order to name the central plan or framework built up by past 'active organisation' that makes possible a well-adapted response to a particular situation in which the organism operates as 'a unitary mass'.[17] We can see that a musician mastering the technique of playing reorganizes the scheme of movement, in the process of which she interests herself in the construction of the instrument. For this reason, for example, an organist does not have to remember all the time where to find which register on the organ:

> It is not in objective space that the organist in fact is playing. In reality his movements during rehearsal are consecratory gestures: they draw affective vectors, discover emotional sources, and create a space of expressiveness as the movements of the augur delimit the *templum* [as the movements of the Roman reader of the auguries defined the open space in which this took place].[18]

These gestures in space have less relationship to the mechanical construction of the organ than to the source of the meaning of the organist's movements – that is, the music.

When Shklovsky called for the destruction of technique or the breaking of automatism, he proposed a move from objective space to the space of the body (and writing instruments as its extension). We may use the words of Merleau-Ponty and say that he invited a person to return to 'primary actions' and, setting out from them, to seek 'a core of new significance', as occurs in dancing. He also wrote that when 'the meaning aimed at cannot be reached by the body's natural means . . . it must then build itself an instrument, and it projects thereby around itself a cultural world'.[19] These 'natural means' include the habits of the body, which frame one way of life, and the new 'instrument', new bodily skills, which open up a new way of life, cultural achievement. What is considered natural and what is considered cultural, of course, changes over time, through the process by which an acquired skill becomes part of a person's nature. The artistic avant-garde, in reaction against the socially created norms of *not-being-able*, the negative limits imposed on the bodily order, turned to new skills, to new bodily instruments, to create a new world. The simplest, most direct exemplification was dance: the new dance freed the body, especially the woman's body, to do what it had not been able to do before. In turn, the training and achievement of new practice required and promoted a new sensitivity to kinaesthetic perception; conversely, the new sensitivity suggested new work for the body in the creation of art.

This continued to be a pattern in the subsequent development of the modernist arts. For instance, in the middle of the twentieth century, the American dancer and choreographer Merce Cunningham set himself the same task as Shklovsky: 'to turn man to experience the world', to struggle with the mechanism of habit.[20] Just as the Russian so-called artists of the absurd had made familiar the notion of the word twisted on itself or, as one might say, *the word as such*, Cunningham became interested in *movement as such*, the process of completing a movement for the sake of the movement. In practice sessions he busied himself and his dancers with preparing dance stereotypes and then, in their place, creating new 'unnatural' or 'unconventional' movements (as ordinary language says). His dancers took it in turn to research the possibilities of different parts of the body, defining a circle of movements achieved by the parts and striving to widen this circle. They repeated unfamiliar steps until the movements became organic, part of the body. In the course of training the new skill, a reorganization of the bodily schema took place. In the words of a dancer from Cunningham's group, 'everything becomes different, "a non-human existence" . . . a second nature grows'.[21] In such ways, in the course of the twentieth century, the avant-garde re-founded 'the ancient human' and created a new 'second' human nature. As our chapters have set out to show, if drawing in only one part of the historical story, this fed over and over again on the seemingly unbounded resources of the kinaesthetic world. 'The sixth sense', ambiguously but constructively understood as both muscular feeling and embodied intuition and emotion, was exceedingly fertile everywhere that movement had a place in the arts – and where did it not?

In the introduction, we noted the distinction between theoretical knowledge and bodily knowledge given in the polarities of language, '*connaissance*' – '*savoir faire*', 'knowing that' – 'knowing how', '*znanie*' – '*umenie*'. In traditional Western societies, certainly for the educated classes in those societies at the beginning of the twentieth century, the relationship between the two kinds of knowing was not symmetrical: capability, or knowledge labelled 'applied', technical or bodily, had lower status, and those who possessed it were expected to be socially deferential to propositional, theoretical and formal knowledge. Gilbert Ryle, who introduced the language separating knowing that and knowing how into English-language analytic philosophy, wrote:

> To possess *knowledge that* presupposes knowledge about how to use it, when this demands the solution of a theoretical or practical problem. There is a difference between museum knowledge and a craftsman's knowledge. An idiot may be full of information but incapable of deciding a specific question. The uneducated public mistakenly equates education with the transmission of *knowledge that*.[22]

Part of Ryle's critique was that people have to know how to use educated intelligence and scholarly knowledge – even highly informed activity may be stupidly executed; conversely, an illiterate person may act with great intelligence in a practical task. This was, and is, well known. Yet knowledge that, certainly when made the subject of formal theory, has traditionally possessed higher status. One reason is surely that knowledge how has often remained unarticulated and un-verbalized, passed down by apprenticeship rather than by formalized training. In a culture where social status went with highly literate education (to the extent of being education in 'dead' languages), knowing how was by its nature assigned lower status. This did not mean, naturally, that those with lower status and knowledge how did not have their own repertoire of sayings, sometimes amounting to anti-intellectualism, about the ineptitude of the highly educated. Moreover, as Michel de Certeau suggested, there were ways in which capacity in practice created islands of opposition to power that had succeeded in monopolizing language.[23] By focusing on knowledge how in the use of language, the Formalists turned to the gestural, and hence movement qualities of words, and made knowing how into art. Whether they succeeded in subverting power is another matter.

Kinaesthesia in culture

We return to the general themes with which we began. The avant-garde at the beginning of the twentieth century had a marked interest in dynamics and energy, in physical movement, kinetics, and in the inner feeling of movement, kinaesthesia. Also at this time, sport, dance, gymnastics, the circus, cycling, rock-climbing, the motor car and the aeroplane and other activities that centred on movement developed significantly. All this, much influenced by new technologies of representing motion in photography, cinematography and other visual arts, changed perception. This leads to large and to some extent speculative questions. How *new* was this stress on the haptic and the kinaesthetic? And, whether entirely new or not, did this stress begin, and are Western societies now in the midst of, a large-scale change towards a bodily, or *motor*, understanding of perception, intelligence, intuition, imagination, feeling and other capabilities traditionally assigned to what ordinary language names as 'mind'? Is there a shift from a culture dominated by visual perception, and imagery of the human as observer, to a culture of the kinaesthetic and haptic, in which the dominant imagery of a person is of being moved, and moving, in the world? Is knowing how (being able to move), rather than knowing that (being an objective observer), becoming the dominant model of desired human achievement? And is that what people (which people?) want?

It has been a central preoccupation of the social and cultural sciences to understand what makes the modern age different from the centuries that came before. This interest in trying to delineate modernity hardly needs emphasis. There is, however, one claim frequently found in such studies that we want to highlight. This claim is a staple of cultural history, yet, we suggest, it is often asserted with little reflection or clear empirical content. Writers state that visual culture dominates the modern age (here meaning the West since the late medieval period). Sometimes they go further and say that this is at the expense specifically of touch. There is a theoretical, and at times dauntingly abstract, literature about culture which simply takes the generalization for granted. In part, this may derive from the fact that so much social critique, with intellectual roots in Hegel and early Marx, describes the modern age, driven by the power of capital, as separating human practices, labour, from practices and ways of living that would truly address the ideals of human freedom and fulfilment.[24] The Gospels have continued to provide a parallel critique. In the context of such argument, the visual sense, in which the separation between subject and object –

the 'distance' of a person from the world – appears a natural given, has become an embodied metaphor for the separation of people from their true nature and purposes. Building on this, critics then state or imply that visual media – the printed text, the picture, photography, film, television, video – have each in turn achieved a position of social dominance as the technical means for rendering individuals *spectators*, not *participants*, instruments of capital, not self-determining agents. Whatever the importance of such arguments may be (and we are far from denying them), our point now is that, for these or other reasons, the literature on modernity repeats the generalization about the dominance of the visual.

Yet it simply may not be sustainable. Firstly, statements about modern culture at this level of generality all too often have little or no purchase: all the senses play a part in life, and the relative importance attached to one of them, and even the extent to which one sense is distinguished from the others, varies hugely in connection with *local* customs and *particular* practical purposes.[25] This variation, we might surmise, is larger than the capacity of any one sense to dominate. There seems something almost perverse in talking about one sense 'in general', as opposed to recognizing the fabulous richness and variety of sensory life, the multi-coloured and multi-dimensional sensory world, and the mutual influence, or even single system, of the senses. Indeed, in histories of the senses, the history of any one sense inevitably spills over into the history of the others. Common language reflects this, moving unselfconsciously and without any discernible line between reference to a 'sensation' (particular) and reference to 'feeling' (general). The second objection to belief in the dominance of the visual is a simple one: there are, as a matter of fact, wonderfully rich accounts of touch in the modern age, and the metaphors of touch have appeared in all walks of modern life.

Indeed, our writing is a contribution to a wave of enthusiasm for investigating the life of the touch and movement senses, and inquiry keeps turning up more evidence of how important touch was, and is. Constance Classen, in her history of touch in culture, assumed the modern primacy of the visual and referred to 'Western visualism'. She wrote:

The second fall of the sense of touch [the first came with the Fall of Adam and Eve] – which was less of a fall than a gradual displacement from social centrality – began in the late Middle Ages. It was at this time that practices of visual contemplation increased in importance, preparing the way for the more eye-minded culture of modernity.[26]

Yet she compiled a vivid record of the multitude of ways in which touch, as a matter of fact, has had a voice in modern as well as earlier times. Indeed, the very title of her book, *The Deepest Sense*, implied as much, as she used the phrase to indicate the status the sense has had. The 'deepness' of touch is not something that only historians recognize in retrospect, excited as they are by contemporary emphasis on embodiment, but reflects an appreciation repeatedly expressed in earlier centuries.[27] Not least, this appreciation appeared in an extraordinary range of metaphors of high significance in everyday life: being in touch (or in contact), being touched (or moved), the common touch or the king's touch, grasping meaning, taking a grip, and very many more. This does not sound like the language of a culture that has lost 'contact with' the tactile sense. Similarly, Dee Reynolds, in a very thoughtful study of aesthetics and early abstract art, discussing Kandinsky and Mondrian, asserted 'that both are radically opposed to the modernist conception of pictorial space as purely optical'.[28] But, one might think, if *these* artists, so central to everyone's image of modernism, were so 'opposed', there can be no *modernist* conception, in general, as 'purely optical', whatever exclusively visual dimension there may have been in some modernist creations. Reynolds also went on to provide detailed examples of the way in which rhythm, movement and balance, all notions inconceivable without kinaesthetic perception, entered into art. We think our history illuminates major ways in which touch (and movement) were formative in modernist culture. It does not seem necessary to assert that ocular or tactile culture was 'more' important, or dominant; rather, we picture the many ways, not always well recognized, in which *movement* and its perception had a fundamental place. This makes a contribution to cultural studies because even the new historians of touch do not fully appreciate that tactile experience *always* involves an element of movement and the sensing of movement (kinesis and kinaesthesia).

One possible source (among others) for description of the modern age as an ocular one is widespread adoption of Norbert Elias's account of 'the civilizing process'.[29] Concentrating on

European court culture of the seventeenth century, Elias related the refinement of manners to distancing the body and its functions (using a fork, not the fingers). It is easy to see the place that vision might have had in such a culture. As vision is a sense that conveys distance between subject and object, it became valued over the senses like touch and smell, which remind the subject of the body. In the subsequent two centuries, middle-class life further refined conventions of containing and hiding the body. In considerable contrast, in recent decades, in reaction against over-refinement and denaturalization, there has been a return to interest in embodiment and the sense, the touch sense, which gives irreducible knowledge of it. This links with what we have said about re-valuing knowing how and with the appeal of forms of knowledge, and of practice, breaking with traditional, elite culture.

The setting of Ryle's discussion of knowing how is relevant. It was his larger argument to oppose both philosophical and common talk about internal operations of mind, notably reasoning, preceding intelligent action. He argued that reference to intelligence is proper in description of the quality with which something (whether philosophy or dance) is done; it is not proper to refer to a preceding mental capacity, 'intelligence'. Further, he stated:

> There are many activities which directly display qualities of mind, yet are neither themselves intellectual operations nor yet effects of intellectual operations. Intelligent practice is not a step-child of theory. On the contrary theorizing is one practice amongst others and is itself intelligently or stupidly conducted.

He then went on to observe, because mental intelligence is treated as a separate faculty, 'since doing is often an overt muscular affair, it is written off as a merely physical process'.[30] This was stated some time ago. The keen appreciation of bodily intelligence among performers, and the interest of scientists in motor cognition, suggests that Ryle's argument has been well taken. What Ryle said people thought of as 'a merely physical process' is now appreciated, as the first generation of modernist artists appreciated it, as a subtle animated world made possible by feeling of movement. In dance, intelligence is the capacity to do what the dancer does; or it is the spectator's capacity to share some aspect, if in transmuted form, of that capacity. We may call it bodily intelligence, an intelligence involving feeling, kinaesthesia, in both dancer and spectator. That feeling is, in addition, presupposed in the activity of reflecting on and hence, as we are doing, writing about it.

One of the most widely appreciated and generally accessible transitions to modernist art is found in Cézanne's series of studies and paintings of Mont Sainte-Victoire. Here, observers have said, the painter, in order to think about what was before him in the landscape in front of his house, used 'the gesture' of applying his pencil or brush as a guide, using tactile and kinaesthetic feeling in order 'to see'. As Maxine Sheets-Johnstone wrote, 'what Cézanne does with hand and brush, the choreographer does with other bodies'.[31] The truth Cézanne sought required the collaboration of physical feelings. The many studies he produced along the way show how tentative this modernist experiment was. Yet, when Guillemette Bolens introduced her account of the place of gesture in literature, which she brought into relation with contemporary theories of the motor nature of cognition, she found her illustration in a painting from between 1737 and 1738, over a century and a half earlier, the beautiful painting by Chardin of a boy observing the little top he has set in motion.[32] The history of gesture, we are led to understand, has long enacted knowledge of tactile and kinaesthetic perception. We might also look further back, to Velásquez's magnificent painting *Las meninas*, the frontispiece of Foucault's *The Order of Things*. There the portrait of the painter himself emphasizes to the viewer the long handle of the brush he is holding, the material means for transforming the perception of the eye into a painting. The painting is famously about the gaze; but the painter also signals knowledge of the movement of the brush required to put that gaze onto the canvas, the artist's knowing how.

Our interest in these examples is not the one which historians are sometimes accused of, of showing that history repeats itself and that there is nothing new under the sun. On the contrary; when we discuss young women breaking out into free dance, or Mayakovsky composing 'dance poetry', we share the excitement: new aesthetic forms opened up new life. Nevertheless, we need to be clear in what sense something was new and in what particular ways awareness of the kinaesthetic sense found a new voice. It was not new to point to touch or the muscular sense as the source of knowledge of 'the real', or to find in gestural movement, or in rhythmic motion, the symbolic expression of 'higher sensitivity'. But for girls to find these things in dancing in freely flowing tunics, or for poets to find them in verses marching over the page or across the auditorium, was new.

There is a marked contrast between the popular image of a life of movement and the image of scholarship (whether in the natural sciences or the humanities). Scholarship, for most of history, has been the prerogative of elites, and through much of modern Western history scholars have looked on (not to say looked down on) the human body 'through a network of thought grills, categories and practice imposed on the body from without, and contrary to it, with the aim of strengthening the body's power "to become civilized"'. All the same, the human body, 'this object of scattered meaning', is 'a culturally-growing matrix', taking one form rather than another, having one meaning rather than another.[33] As a result, with kinaesthesia becoming the subject of self-conscious attention, both as the subject matter of science and in artistic expression, the body has moved out from the shadows of scholarly regard into the limelight. Not unconnected with this, the whole project of 'civilizing' the body has become highly problematic, and at times simply rejected. It was the artists of the avant-garde who were at the cutting-edge, exploring at one and the same time what awareness of the senses of movement means for cultural life and for a heightened sense of personal experience, for the public and private being of a person.

This still leaves open the question of whether, over the last century, there has been a shift, which can be documented, towards social, artistic, sporting, health-oriented and other practices that recognize and deeply value kinesis and kinaesthesia. It would appear to be so. If so, then this parallels a recent shift in science towards understanding cognition not so much as mental thinking but as a set of practices (sometimes called 'situated' knowledge) embodied in the motor life of the body.[34] This, in turn, signals acknowledgement of the foundational importance of knowledge how rather than knowledge that, knowledge embedded in the capabilities of a person rather than knowledge held 'in the mind'. We earlier cited Merleau-Ponty referring to 'knowledge which is in my hands', and, of course, everyday English says the same in phrases such as 'hands-on knowledge' and 'being handy'. Recognition of the embodied nature of knowledge, the phenomenologists would argue, has its rationale in insight that it is to tactile and movement awareness that a person owes distinctions between 'I' and 'not-I', owes feelings of activity or agency, and owes existential comprehension of being a person 'in contact with' a world and in intimacy with other people.

It is evident that there are very large issues at stake. Whatever one's judgement about them, we hope this book will help recognition, and celebration, of the avant-garde's contribution to forming what we might call kinaesthetic culture. The vitality, energy and dynamism of artists – their bodily intelligence, knowing how – helped them to see and value the rhythmic, gymnastic and aesthetic potential of muscular movement and physical activity as a source of meaning and as a source of techniques for rendering meaning in new forms of life and art. Lidiia Ginzburg called the thoughts that the Formalists of OPOIaZ had about the embodied, 'personal' knowledge of the poet 'the scientific idea of the avant-garde'.[35] The artists of the avant-garde, in all the variety of manifestations they had in the Russian setting, made a turn to movement in the humanities and in the arts. This indeed had its parallels in the sciences, with the turn (then and now) to the motor side of cognition. But the artists constructed their knowledge as technique, knowing how, and they thereby disrupted the social world in which such knowledge was expected to defer to theoretical knowledge.

We face a choice about the way forward, a choice dependent on philosophical argument. In telling the historical story of the involvement of the sixth sense in the lives of the Russian artists of the avant-garde, we create a kind of narrative, an ordered description of the significance of this sense for their art. When we explain why it had this significance, though, we face their arguments or presumptions, and the arguments or presumptions of more recent writers, that kinaesthesia is a special sense because of its primary place in knowledge of self and world. It is necessary to address a philosophical argument about this sense being unmediated in the way the other senses are not. Elements of such an argument have been powerfully articulated at least from the time of John Locke, through Maine de Biran and others in the early nineteenth century, to the present. Husserl restated such a position in phenomenological terms at the time when the artistic avant-garde was expressing it, through practical exemplification rather than formally and systematically, in new practices and media. And in the present it would not be difficult to find practitioners of modern dance, or artists of movement on the streets, for whom movement of the body has status as the primary statement of being alive. In these settings, and for these people, the sense of movement is not the object of a narrative history but is the living expression of vitality. In the social world in which the arts of movement have developed, from the late nineteenth century to the present, there has been an apparently inexorable rise of a public culture of the body – a focus on the body as the defining framework of a person's individual identity and on the body as public persona. There are societies in which people have come to have profound concern with individual diet, exercise, sport, appearance, dress and ornament – that is, with the body as if it were the fundamental, even perhaps the only, means to human flourishing generally. If the ideal of wholeness, that is, the integrated endeavour of body and mind, or of body and spirit, has not gone away, the royal road to achieving it, many people would appear to assume, is through techniques of the body, and especially through movement (or its mirror image, stillness). This is most surely so for the contemporary dancer.

Thus the innovative ways of living of the Russian avant-garde have, with time, become the chosen ways of life of many. Whatever the philosophical validity of argument about the primary, or unmediated, character of the movement sense, there can be no doubt that large swathes of modern life take (if implicitly) this argument as a given. We have drawn attention to what may be a very influential social shift towards the elevation of knowing how above subservience to knowing that, a shift associating democratic political culture with individual bodily powers. Or, if we were to make a critical judgement, we could say a shift towards rendering human capacities, interpreted as embodied, more amenable to commodification or expropriation for profit. However this may be, the philosophical questions remain. Is it right to say life is action and the sense of life therefore the sense of movement? Is it correct to hold that kinaesthesia is unmediated in the way that the other senses are not? Some philosophers, like William James, have certainly held that the *epistemological* question, deciding the grounds on which it can be said people know something, cannot be resolved by attributing knowledge to one sense rather than another.[36] Other philosophers, phenomenologists such as those we cited in our introduction, have held that there is an irreducible difference in the significance and meaning of the movement sense, since it conveys a character of embodied being in a world, rather than of being a mental observer of a world.

On these matters there is an ongoing and divisive debate among philosophers about the naturalization of epistemology.[37] On the grounds of the logic of reason, are logical and scientific knowledge statements to be kept separate, or is knowledge of science essential to the resolution of the problem of knowledge? (This is only the most general form of the debate. Argument about which science is needed in order to address epistemological questions provokes a large dispute, with supporters of the claims of neuroscience at one end of the spectrum of positions and supporters of the sociology of knowledge at the other end.) A parallel range of philosophical issues troubles the literature of dance and performance studies. Here the framework of discussion is not so much that of philosophy of science and science studies, but the reaction to what some people think to be the reckless relativism of postmodern theory. If it were the achievement of postmodern theory to demonstrate the ways in which any claim about the world, or about truth, art or the self, could be shown to be part of a discourse, and discourses themselves be shown to have content by virtue of other discourses, and so on without the possibility of finding a base, then the reaction against this was to turn to the body as the firm base.[38] The claim is, we might say, that the buck stops with the body: the body is real, whatever the discourse about it. Practitioners of the movement arts certainly act as if this is so – and many of them, we think, believe consciously that it is so. Many theorists of performance have gone along with this, even to the extent of being persuaded that brain science is actually the one and true science that provides firm ground for knowledge. The issues remain debated.

The turn to the moving body, to the knowing body, as the immanent ground of knowledge is also, very significantly, an expression of desire for individual agency. This is easy enough to comprehend in public worlds where individual people so often feel powerless to influence events. In the knowing body, and in the acquisition of skills to enhance it, people find, or create, a world in which they do have agency.

An agent who holds sway is a bona fide agent precisely insofar as she/he is aware of her/his own movement, aware not only of initiating it, but aware of its spatio-temporal and energy dynamics, which is to say of its rich and variable qualia [qualitative feels or awareness].[39]

The sense of agency in movement was certainly of great importance to our Russians. Breaking out from a political and cultural world of confinement, seeking a 'higher sensitivity' and, in the radical avant-garde, the embodiment of new ways of life, they found the means, the tools, in movement. Finding movement, the young women in Heptachor found agency. That they and not others achieved this at this time derived from their special, highly educated position in society, as well as from particular force and desire of individual character. But the body was there for everyone as a potential source of agency. 'The pre-reflective awareness of the body in movement as a dynamic form-in-the-making is inherent in any lived experience of sheer body movement. It is not a special kind of awareness which must be cultivated, or which only a select few may achieve.'[40] Dance improvisation has a special place as the language, the gesture, of the free spirit.

Theory in art rests on the back of the practice of art. Twentieth-century aesthetics drew on the practical knowledge of artistic creators. This is perhaps clearest in the theatre, where almost all directors of note articulated their own theory of theatre. In the theatre, the theory of acting was the practice of acting – exemplified in Stanislavsky's 'System'. This aesthetics was, of course, informed by contemporary scientific theories; these people studied in good classical gymnasiums which, often enough, offered a broader and better education than that commonly provided later. Yet, to a significant degree, the theories were based on personal practical, sensuous and emotional experience. This is why kinaesthesia, among the other senses, matters. Shklovsky exemplifies the practitioner of literature who theorizes from his own experience. In his words,

> People say that one doesn't have to be a fish to be an ichthyologist.
>   About myself, I say that I am a fish: a writer that analyses literature as art.[41]

Clearly enough, there is a great deal here that should be taken further. We have tried to create a vivid picture of ways of life in which they *were* taken further – but in *performance* rather than as philosophy or cultural theory. The Russian avant-garde way of life performed the movement sense as the ground of being vital.

It is surely apparent that we would not have written as we have, on the subjects we have, without sympathy for ways of life in which the sense of movement has a primary place. Our descriptive voice as historians is also the evaluative voice of people who have experienced some of the pleasures of movement and, as it may be, an imagination for wholeness or fulfilment in movement. This comes in walking and, in our modest way, in dance, and it comes as spectators of movement from wind in the trees to a running child to an acrobat. Sensitivity to ways of life that emphasize movement, like ways of life generally, must and does go forward while philosophical questions remain there to argue over. (That 'remaining there' is itself a central feature, we would say, of the good life; we are not disparaging philosophy.) If questions about the theory of knowledge remain, we may nevertheless think that practice, knowing how, offers routes, open to all, to achieve something of worth. This is tangible in the lives of our artists.

FURTHER READING

We list a number of sources which might help the reader take topics further. Our references are given in full in the notes. (As a large number of the primary sources, and a fair number of the secondary sources, are in Russian, we do not include a full list of references.)

Modernism and dance

Copeland, Roger and Marshall Cohen, eds. *What Is Dance? Readings in Theory and Criticism*. Oxford: Oxford University Press, 1983.

Duncan, Isadora. *My Life*. The Restored Edition. New York: Liveright, 2013.

Foster, Susan Leigh. 'Dancing Bodies', in *Incorporations*, eds Jonathan Crary and Sanford Kwinter, 480–95. New York: Zone Books, 1992.

Garafola, Lynn. *Diaghilev's Ballets russes*. New York: Oxford University Press, 1990.

Karina, Lilian and Marion Kant. *Hitler's Dancers: German Modern Dance and the Third Reich*. Trans. Jonathan Steinberg. New York: Berghahn Books, 2003.

Kermode, Frank. 'Poet and Dancer before Diaghilev', in *Puzzles and Epiphanies: Essays and Reviews 1858–1961*, 1–28. London: Routledge & Kegan Paul, 1962.

Misler, Nicoletta. *Vnachale bylo telo: ritmoplasticheskie eksperimenty nachala XX veka – Khoreologicheskaia laboratoriia GAKhN* (In the Beginning Was the Body: Rhythmic-Plastic Experiments at the Beginning of the 20th Century – The Choreological Laboratory, GAKhN). Moscow: Izdatel'stvo-XXI vek, 2011.

Reynolds, Dee. *Rhythmic Subjects: Uses of Energy in the Dance of Mary Wigman, Martha Graham and Merce Cunningham*. Alton, Hampshire: Dance Books, 2007.

Schwartz, Hillel. 'Torque: The New Kinaesthetic of the Twentieth Century', in *Incorporations*, eds Jonathan Crary and Sanford Kwinter, 71–126. New York: Zone Books, 1992.

Sirotkina, Irina. *Svobodnoe dvizhenie i plasticheskii tanets v Rossii* (Free Movement and Plastic Dance in Russia). 2nd ed. Moscow: Novoe literaturnoe obozrenie, 2012.

Surits, Elizabeth. *Soviet Choreographers in the 1920s*. Trans. Lynn Visson, ed. Sally Banes. London: Dance Books, 1990.

Veder, Robin. *The Living Line: Modern Art and the Economy of Energy*. Hanover, NH: Dartmouth College Press, 2015.

Performance, theory and the arts

Davis, Tracy C., ed. *The Cambridge Companion to Performance Studies*. Cambridge: Cambridge University Press, 2009.

Fischer-Lichte, Erika. *The Transformative Power of Performance: A New Aesthetics*. Trans. Saskya Iris Jan. London: Routledge, 2008.

Harrison, Charles and Paul Wood, eds. *Art in Theory: An Anthology of Changing Ideas*. Malden, MA and Oxford: Blackwell, 2003.

Noland, Carrie. *Agency and Embodiment: Performing Gestures/Producing Culture*. Cambridge, MA: Harvard University Press, 2009.

Schechner, Richard. *Performance Studies: An Introduction*. London: Routledge, 2013.

Touch, kinaesthesia and the sense of movement

Berthoz, Alain and Jean-Luc Petit. *The Physiology and Phenomenology of Action*. Trans. Christopher Macann. Oxford: Oxford University Press, 2008.

Bolens, Guillemette. *The Style of Gestures: Embodiment and Cognition in Literary Narrative*. Trans. Guillemette Bolens. Baltimore: Johns Hopkins University Press, 2012.

Classen, Constance. *The Deepest Sense: A Cultural History of Touch*. Urbana: University of Illinois Press, 2012.

Ratcliffe, Matthew. 'Touch and the Sense of Reality', in *The Hand, an Organ of the Mind: What the Manual Tells the Mental*, ed. Zdravko Radman, 131–57. Cambridge, MA: MIT Press, 2013.

Sheets-Johnstone, Maxine. *The Primacy of Movement*. 2nd ed. Amsterdam and Philadelphia, PA: John Benjamins, 2011.

Smith, Roger. '"The Sixth Sense": Towards a History of Muscular Sensation'. *Gesnerus: Swiss Journal of the History of Medicine and Sciences* 68, no. 2 (2011): 218–71.

Smith, Roger. 'Kinaesthesia and Touching Reality', in *19: Interdisciplinary Studies in the Long Nineteenth Century*, online journal, no. 19 (2014), at www.19.bbk.ac.uk. (Other articles in this issue are on 'The Victorian Tactile Imagination'.)

NOTES

Introduction: Movement and Exuberant Modernism

1 William Wordsworth, 'Ode ("There Was a Time")' [1807], in *The Major Works*, ed. Stephen Gill (Oxford: Oxford University Press, 2000), 299 (line 64).

2 Maxine Sheets-Johnstone, *The Primacy of Movement*, 2nd edn (Amsterdam and Philadelphia, PA: John Benjamins, 2011), 376.

3 The art of walking is beginning to receive its due. See, for example, Frédéric Gros, *A Philosophy of Walking*, trans. John Hove (2009; London: Verso, 2014); Tim Ingold, 'Culture on the Ground: The World Perceived through the Feet', in *Being Alive: Essays on Movement, Knowledge and Description* (London: Routledge, 2011), 33–50.

4 Maurice Merleau-Ponty, *Phenomenology of Perception*, trans. Colin Smith (1945; London: Routledge, 2002); Sheets-Johnstone, *The Primacy of Movement*; Alain Berthoz and Jean-Luc Petit, *The Physiology and Phenomenology of Action*, trans. Christopher Macann (2006; Oxford: Oxford University Press, 2008); Matthew Ratcliffe, 'What Is Touch?' *Australasian Journal of Philosophy* 90, no. 3 (2012): 413–32; Matthew Ratcliffe, 'Touch and the Sense of Reality', in *The Hand, an Organ of the Mind: What the Manual Tells the Mental*, ed. Zdravko Radman (Cambridge, MA: MIT Press, 2013), 131–57.

5 Sheets-Johnstone, *The Primacy of Movement*, ch. 6.

6 For studies linking the sciences to the modernist arts: Carolyn Burdett (ed.), 'Psychology/Aesthetics in the Nineteenth Century', *19: Interdisciplinary Studies in the Long Nineteenth Century*, online journal, no. 12 (2011), http://www.19.bbk.ac.uk; Jonathan Crary, *Suspensions of Perception: Attention, Spectacle, and Modern Culture* (Cambridge, MA: MIT Press, 1999); Mark S. Micale (ed.), *The Mind of Modernism: Medicine, Psychology, and the Cultural Arts in*

Europe and America, 1880–1940 (Stanford, CA: Stanford University Press, 2004); Dorothy Ross, *Modernist Impulses in the Human Sciences 1870–1930* (Baltimore, MD: Johns Hopkins University Press, 1994). The most direct and original recognition of the importance of movement is Hillel Schwartz, 'Torque: The New Kinaesthetic of the Twentieth Century', in *Incorporations*, ed. Jonathan Crary and Sanford Kwinter (New York: Zone Books, 1992), 71–126.

7   Robert Michael Brain, *The Pulse of Modernism: Physiological Aesthetics in Fin-de-Siècle Europe* (Seattle, WA: University of Washington Press, 2015), xxii.

8   Ibid., xxi.

9   Guillemette Bolens, *The Style of Gestures: Embodiment and Cognition in Literary Narrative*, trans. Guillemette Bolens (2006; Baltimore, MD: Johns Hopkins University Press, 2012); Dee Reynolds, *Rhythmic Subjects: Uses of Energy in the Dances of Mary Wigman, Martha Graham and Merce Cunningham* (Alton, Hampshire: Dance Books, 2007); Robin Veder, *The Living Line: Modern Art and the Economy of Energy* (Hanover, NH: Dartmouth College Press, 2015), 16 and 35.

10 Veder, *Living Line*, 12–13.

11 Robert Michael Brain, 'The Pulse of Modernism: Experimental Physiology and Aesthetic Avant-gardes circa 1900', *Studies in History and Philosophy of Science* 39 (2008): 393–417; Brain, *Pulse of Modernism*; Veder, *Living Line*.

12 Marta Braun, *Picturing Time: The Work of Etienne-Jules Marey (1830–1904)* (Chicago, IL: University of Chicago Press, 1992).

13 Frank Kermode, 'The Dancer', in *Romantic Image* (London: Routledge and Kegan Paul, 1957), 49–91; Frank Kermode, 'Poet and Dancer before Diaghilev', in *Puzzles and Epiphanies: Essays and Reviews 1958–1961* (1958–61; London: Routledge & Kegan Paul, 1962), 1–28.

14 Mark Paterson, for example, in *The Sense of Touch: Haptics, Affects and Technologies* (Oxford: Berg, 2007), said nothing about dance.

15 On Isadora Duncan, Ann Daly, *Done into Dance: Isadora Duncan in America* (Middletown, CT: Wesleyan University Press, 1995); on Laban and 'Labanism', Lilian Karina and Marion Kant, *Hitler's Dancers: German Modern Dance and the Third Reich*, trans. Jonathan Steinberg (1996; New York: Berghahn Books, 2003); on the Ballets russes, Lynn Garafola, *Diaghilev's Ballets russes* (New York: Oxford University Press, 1989).

16 We do not, however, wish to assert the causal, or primary, role of any one sense in anything so nebulous as modernism, in contrast, for instance, to Robert Michael Brain, *Pulse of Modernism*, 201: 'The "modernist" turn around 1910 – the turn toward abstraction – *derived from* the new fascination with kinesthesia as the basis of both artistic creation and spectatorship' (emphasis added). However much there was a pervasive valorization of kinaesthesia in the arts, modernism hardly 'derived' from any one thing. Its scope was much wider (Brain did not discuss dance), and the fascination with kinaesthesia was far from new.

17 For the Russian culture of free dance, Irina Sirotkina, *Svobodnoe dvizhenie i plasticheckii tanets v Rossii* (Free Movement and Plastic Dance in Russia) (Moscow: Novoe literaturnoe obozrenie, 2011); and for the choreographic celebration of the body, with extensive and excellent illustrations, Nicoletta Misler, *Vnachale bylo telo: ritmoplasticheskie eksperimenty nachala XX veka. Khoreologicheskaia laboratoriia GAKhN* (In the Beginning was the Body: Rhythmic-plastic Experiments at the Beginning of the Twentieth Century: The Choreological Laboratory of GAKhN) (Moscow: Iskusstvo-XXI vek, 2011).

18 For the dilemmas of 'turning to nature' in performance, see Alexandra Carter and Rachel Fensham (eds), *Dancing Naturally: Nature, Neo-Classicism and Modernity in Early Twentieth-Century Dance* (Basingstoke, Hampshire: Palgrave Macmillan, 2011).

19 In relation to Russian Formalists, this has been shown by Ilona Svetlikova, *Istoki russkogo formalizma. Traditsiia psikhologizma i formal'naia shkola* (The Origins of Russian Formalism: The Tradition of Psychologism and the Formalist School) (Moscow: Novoe literaturnoe obozrenie, 2005); and by David Romand and Serguei Tchougounnikov, '"Le formalisme russe": Une séduction cognitiviste,' *Cahiers du monde russe* 51, no. 4 (2010): 521–46.

20 The relations of the natural science of energy and work to social transformation at the end of the nineteenth century were influentially discussed in Anson Rabinbach, *The Human Motor: Energy, Fatigue, and the Origins of Modernity* (1990; Berkeley: University of California Press, 1992). Energy was thoughtfully related to dance in Reynolds, *Rhythmic Subjects*.

21 For Russian modernism, see the work and exhibition curatorship of John E. Bowlt and Nicoletta Misler, who also edit *Experiment: A Journal of Russian Culture*. See especially: vol. 2 (1996), 'MOTO-BIO – The Russian Art of Movement: Dance, Gesture, and Gymnastics'; vol. 10 (2004), 'Performing Arts and the Avant-garde';

vol. 17 (2011), 'Sergei Diaghilev and the Ballets Russes'; vol. 20 (2014), 'Kinetic Los Angeles: Russian Emigrés in the City of Self-Transformation'. On movement and the body, see Misler, *Vnachale bylo telo*.

22   Richard Schechner, *Performance Studies: An Introduction* (London: Routledge, 2013), 2.

23   Ibid.

24   Richard Schechner, 'What Are Performance Studies, Anyway?' in *The Ends of Performance*, ed. Peggy Phelan and Jill Lane (New York: New York University Press, 1998), 357–62, on 361.

25   Dwight Conquergood, 'Rethinking Ethnography: Towards a Critical Cultural Politics' [1991] in *The Rise of Performance Studies: Rethinking Richard Schechner's Broad Spectrum*, ed. James M. Harding and Cindy Rosenthal (Aldershot, Hampshire: Palgrave Macmillan, 2011), 351–65, on 358. See also V. Turner, *The Anthropology of Performance* (New York: PAJ Publications, 1986).

26   Nathan Stucky, 'Deep Embodiment: The Epistemology of Natural Performance', in *Teaching Performance Studies*, ed. Nathan Stucky and Cynthia Wimmer (Carbondale, IL: Southern Illinois University Press, 2002), 131–44, on 138–9.

27   Peggy Phelan, 'Introduction: The Ends of Performance,' in *The Ends of Performance*, ed. Peggy Phelan and Jill Lane (New York: New York University Press, 1998), 1–22, on 4.

28   C. M. Soussloff and M. Franko, 'Visual and Performance Studies: A New History of Interdisciplinarity', *Social Text* 20, no. 4 (2002): 29–46, on 33–4.

29   Jane Desmond, 'Embodying Difference: Issues in Dance and Cultural Studies', in *Meaning in Motion: New Cultural Studies of Dance*, ed. Jane Desmond (Durham, NC: Duke University Press, 1997), 29.

30   Conquergood, 'Rethinking Ethnography', 355.

31   Suze Adams, 'The Dwelling Body,' in *Body and Performance*, ed. Sandra Reeve (Axminster, Devon: Triarchy Press, 2013), 67–83, on 71.

32   Philipp B. Zarilli, 'Action, Structure, Task, and Emotion: Theories of Acting, Emotion, and Performer Training from a Performance Studies Perspective', in *Teaching Performance Studies*, ed. Nathan Stucky and Cynthia Wimmer (Carbondale, IL: Southern Illinois University Press, 2002), 145–59.

33   Susan Leigh Foster, 'Movements' Contagion: The Kinesthetic Impact of Performance', in *The Cambridge Companion to Performance*

Studies, ed. Tracy C. Davis (Cambridge: Cambridge University Press, 2009), 46–59, on 49.

34 Naomi Bragin, 'Black Power of Hip Hop Dance: On Kinesthetic Politics', https://www.academia.edu/s/1c07f4bfc7?source=sidebar (accessed 15 April 2016).

35 Jacques Derrida, 'Ou commence et comment finit un corps enseignant?' in *Politiques de la philosophie*, ed. François Châtelet et al. (Paris: Grasset, 1979), 57–89, on 87–8), quoted in Soussloff and Franko, 'Visual and Performance Studies', 29.

36 James Loxley, *Performativity* (London: Routledge, 2007), 153–4.

37 Bragin, 'Black Power of Hip Hop Dance'.

38 Schechner, *Performance Studies*, 2.

39 Conquergood, 'Rethinking Ethnography', 355.

40 Dwight Conquergood, 'Performance Studies: Interventions and Radical Research,' *Drama Review* 46 (2002): 145–56, on 146.

41 Tracy C. Davis, 'Introduction: The Pirouette, Detour, Revolution, Deflection, Deviation, Tack and Yaw of the Performative Turn,' in *The Cambridge Companion to Performance Studies*, ed. Tracy C. Davis (Cambridge: Cambridge University Press, 2009), 1–10, on 2.

42 Bolens, *Style of Gestures*, 1–2.

43 Dee Reynolds and Matthew Reason (eds), *Kinaesthetic Empathy in Creative and Cultural Practices* (Bristol: Intellect Books, 2012).

44 Erika Fischer-Lichte, *The Transformative Power of Performance: A New Aesthetics*, trans. Saskya Iris Jan (2004; London: Routledge, 2008).

45 Sirotkina, *Svobodnoe dvizhenie i plasticheskii tanets*, 85–7.

46 Jacques Rancière, *Aisthesis: Scenes from the Aesthetic Regime of Art*, trans. Zakir Paul (2011; London: Verso, 2013), 193.

47 Some relevant sources include: Viktor Shklovsky, *On Eisenstein*, trans. Benjamin Sher (1991, online at http://www.websher.net/srl/shk-eis-14point.html); Oksana Bulgakova, *Fabrika zhestov* (The Factory of Gestures) (Moscow: Novoe literaturnoe obozrenie, 2005); Ana Olenina-Hedberg, 'Engineering Performance: Lev Kuleshov, Soviet Reflexology, and Labor Efficiency Studies', *Discourse: Journal for Theoretical Studies in Media and Culture* 35, no. 3 (2013): 297–336.

48 For an overview, Birgit Beumers, *A History of Russian Cinema* (Oxford: Berg, 2009).

49 Viktor Shklovsky, *Theory of Prose*, trans. Benjamin Sher (1925; Elmwood Park, IL: Dalkey Archive Press, 1990), 15.

50   Nina Gurianova, *The Aesthetics of Anarchy: Art and Ideology in the Early Russian Avant-garde* (Berkeley: University of California Press, 2012), 3.

51   Sara Pankenier Weld, *Voiceless Vanguard: The Infantilist Aesthetic of the Russian Avant-garde* (Chicago, IL: Northwestern University Press, 2014), 8–9 and 209.

52   Isabel Wünsche, *The Organic School of the Russian Avant-garde: Nature's Creative Principles* (New York: Routledge, 2015), xv and 144.

53   Julia Vaingurt, *Wonderlands of the Avant-garde: Technology and the Arts in Russia of the 1920s* (Chicago, IL: Northwestern University Press, 2013), 6 and 4.

54   Frank Kermode noted the place of modernist dance in healing the world in 'Poet and Dancer'.

55   B. M. Galeev, 'Sinesteziia i muzykal'noe prostranstvo' (Synaesthesia and Musical Space), in *Muzyka–kul'tura–chelovek* (Music – Culture – Man), vol. 2 (Sverdlovsk: Ural'skii gos. universitet, 1991), 36–43 (http://synesthesia.prometheus.kai.ru/yavorsk_r.htm; accessed 12 July 2013).

56   John Martin, extract from *The Modern Dance* [1933], in *What Is Dance? Readings in Theory and Criticism*, ed. Roger Copeland and Marshall Cohen (Oxford: Oxford University Press, 1983), 23–8, on 25.

Chapter 1: The Sixth Sense

1   N. Gumilev, 'Shestoe chuvstvo' (The Sixth Sense) [1920], in *Stikhi. Pis'ma o russkoi poezii* (Poems. Letters about Russian Poetry) (Moscow: Khudozhestvennaia literatura, 1989), 266.

2   Aristotle, *De Anima (On the Soul)*, trans. Hugh Lawson-Tancred (London: Penguin Books, 1986), 160 (413b) and 220 (435a). This is one starting point for an outstanding intellectual history of touch, Daniel Heller-Roazen, *The Inner Touch: Archaeology of a Sensation* (New York: Zone Books, 2007). Aristotle used no concept strictly comparable to either mind or psychology, but referred rather to *psuchē*; for present purposes we may leave the ramifications of this to one side.

3   Aristotle, *De Anima*, 172 (418a).

4   Steven Hsiao, Takasaki Yoshioka and Kenneth O. Johnson, 'Somesthesis, Neural Basis of', in *Encyclopedia of Cognitive Science*, ed. Lynn Nadel (London: Nature Publishing Group, 2003), vol. 4, 92–6.

5   I. Sokolov, *Bedeker po ekspressionizmu* (Baedeker of Expressionism) [1919], in *Russkii ekspressionism. Teoriia. Praktika. Kritika*, ed. V. N. Terekhina (Moscow: IMLI RAN, 2005), 61–4, on 62.

6   Matthew Ratcliffe, 'What Is Touch?' *Australasian Journal of Philosophy* 90, no.3 (2012): 413–32, on 427; also, Aristotle, *De Anima*, 184 (422b).

7   Jacques Derrida, *On Touching – Jean-Luc Nancy*, trans. Christine Irizarry (2000; Stanford, CA: Stanford University Press, 2005), 107, quoting Nancy.

8   Lucretius, *On the Nature of Things*, trans. Martin Ferguson Smith, revised edn (Indianapolis, IN: Hackett, 2001).

9   Aristotle, *De Anima*, 220 (435a–b).

10 Maxine Sheets-Johnstone, *The Primacy of Movement*, 2nd edn (Amsterdam and Philadelphia, PA: John Benjamins, 2011), 51.

11 Alain Berthoz and Jean-Luc Petit, *The Physiology and Phenomenology of Action*, trans. Christopher Macann (2006; Oxford: Oxford University Press, 2008), 121.

12 Edmund Husserl, *Ideas Pertaining to a Pure Phenomenology and to a Phenomenological Philosophy. Second Book. Studies in the Phenomenology of Constitution* (*Collected Works*, vol. 2), trans. Richard Rojcewicz and André Schuwer (Dordrecht: Kluwer, 1989), 24. (Written 1912–28.)

13 Husserl ms, 1931, quoted in Berthoz and Petit, *Physiology and Phenomenology of Action*, 156.

14 Husserl, *Ideas Pertaining to a Pure Phenomenology . . . Second Book*, 61.

15 Edmund Husserl, *Thing and Space. Lectures of 1907* (*Collected Works*, vol. 8), trans. Richard Rojcewicz (Dordrecht: Kluwer, 1997), 136. (The lectures were first published in full in 1973.)

16 Martin Heidegger, *Being and Time*, trans. John Macquarrie and Edward Robinson (1927; Oxford: Basil Blackwell, 1962), 114. By 'ready-to-hand', Heidegger denoted things as they stand in our concern – how they stand as our 'equipment' in the world; see ibid., 95–102.

17 Maurice Merleau-Ponty, *Phenomenology of Perception*, trans. Colin Smith (1945; London: Routledge, 2002), 106.

18 Heidegger, *Being and Time*, 99.

19 Matthew Ratcliffe, 'Touch and the Sense of Reality', in *The Hand, an Organ of the Mind: What the Manual Tells the Mental*, ed. Zdravko Radman (Cambridge, MA: MIT Press, 2013), 131–57, on 151.

20 The phrase was the title of a lecture by Husserl in 1935: 'The Vienna
    Lecture. Appendix I: Philosophy and the Crisis of European
    Humanity', in *The Crisis of European Sciences and Transcendental
    Phenomenology: An Introduction to Phenomenological Philosophy*,
    trans. David Carr (1954; Evanston, IL: Northwestern University
    Press, 1970), 269–99.

21 For an overview of the historical culture of touch, Constance
    Classen, *The Deepest Sense: A Cultural History of Touch* (Urbana,
    IL: University of Illinois Press, 2012). As Classen's book well
    illustrates, it proves impossible to put boundaries to touch as a
    category for historical study: the history of touch constantly
    threatens to become the history of the experiential world generally.

22 Ratcliffe, 'What Is Touch?'; Ratcliffe, 'Touch and the Sense of Reality'.

23 Francisco J. Varela, Evan Tompson and Eleanor Roth, *The Embodied
    Mind: Cognitive Science and Human Experience* (Cambridge, MA:
    MIT Press, 1993), 64; also 113.

24 For vertigo and early work related to the vestibular sense, called, 'the
    search for a sixth sense' (as if there was an intention to find a sixth
    sense, which was not the case), Nicholas J. Wade, 'The Search for a
    Sixth Sense: The Cases for Vestibular, Muscle, and Temperature
    Senses', *Journal of the History of Neurosciences* 12 (2003): 175–202;
    Nicholas J. Wade, 'The Science and Art of the Sixth Sense', in *Art and
    the Senses*, ed. Francesca Bacci and David Melcher (Oxford: Oxford
    University Press, 2011), 19–58. Wade drew on Edwin G Boring,
    Sensation and Perception in the History of Experimental Psychology
    (New York: D. Appleton-Century, 1942).

25 John Bell and Charles Bell, *The Anatomy and Physiology of the
    Human Body*, 5th edn, 3 vols (London: Longman, Hurst, Rees,
    Orme, and Brown, 1823), vol. 3, 9–10. The same account (in both
    cases written by Charles Bell), appeared earlier: John Bell and
    Charles Bell, *The Anatomy and Physiology of the Human Body*, 4th
    edn, 3 vols (London: Longman, Hurst, Rees, Orme, and Brown, and
    T. Cadell, 1816), vol. 3, 1–10, 216–17.

26 Bell and Bell, *Anatomy*, 5th edn, vol. 3, 212–13.

27 There is an intellectual history of psycho-physiology and the
    differentiation of touch, in the last decades of the eighteenth century,
    into tactile and muscular senses. For a preliminary review of the
    sources, Roger Smith, '"The Sixth Sense": Towards a History of
    Muscular Sensation', *Gesnerus: Swiss Journal of the History of
    Medicine and Sciences* 68, no. 2 (2011): 218–71. This contributes to
    a book in progress, Roger Smith, *Force and Resistance: Studies on
    the History of Kinaesthesia* (working title).

28   C. S. Sherrington, 'The Muscular Sense', in *Text-Book of Physiology*,
     ed. E. A. Schäfer (Edinburgh and London: Young J. Pentland, 1900),
     vol. 2, 1002–25, on 1006. See Charles Bell, 'On the Nervous Circle
     which Connects the Voluntary Muscles with the Brain', *Philosophical
     Transactions* [116], part 2 (1826): 163–73.

29   Biran's work, incomplete or unpublished as it often was, is
     complicated to assess; but see François Azouvi, *Maine de Biran. La
     Science de l'homme* (Paris: J. Vrin, 1995); Jerold Seigel, *The Idea of
     the Self: Thought and Experience in Western Europe since the
     Seventeenth Century* (Cambridge: Cambridge University Press, 2005),
     251–68.

30   J. J. Gibson, *The Senses Understood as Perceptual Systems* (Boston,
     MA: Houghton Mifflin, 1966). For an introduction to, and
     assessment of, Gibson's work, see Edward S. Reed, *James J. Gibson
     and the Psychology of Perception* (New Haven, CT: Yale University
     Press, 1988).

31   Charles Bell, *The Hand and Its Mechanism and Vital Endowments as
     Evincing Design* (London: William Pickering, 1833).

32   See Sander L. Gilman, '"Stand up Straight": Notes Toward a History
     of Posture', *Journal of Medical Humanities* 35, no. 1 (2014): 57–83.

33   William James, *The Principles of Psychology*, 2 vols (1890; New
     York: Dover, 1950), vol. 2, 197.

34   H. Charlton Bastian, *The Brain as an Organ of Mind* (London:
     Kegan Paul, 1880), note on 543.

35   *Oxford English Dictionary*, 1st edn (completed 1928).

36   C. S. Sherrington, *The Integrative Action of the Nervous System*, 2nd
     edn, reprint (1906; New Haven, CT: Yale University Press, 1961),
     132; C. S. Sherrington, 'On the Proprio-ceptive System, Especially in
     Its Reflex Aspect', *Brain* 29 (1907): 467–82.

37   I. M. Sechenov, 'Reflexes of the Brain' [first variant 1863], trans. A. A.
     Subkov et al., in *Selected Works*, facsimile reprint (1935; Amsterdam:
     E. J. Bonset, 1968), 263–336, on 286.

38   Ibid., 264.

39   Gilles Deleuze and Félix Guattari, *A Thousand Plateaus: Capitalism
     and Schizophrenia*, trans. Brian Massumi (1980; London:
     Continuum, 2004), 543–7, where the word 'haptic' was attributed to
     Alois Riegl. See also discussion in Mark Paterson, *The Sense of
     Touch: Haptics, Affects and Technologies* (Oxford: Berg, 2007),
     79–102; David H. Warren, 'The Development of Haptic Perception',
     in *Tactual Perception: A Sourcebook*, ed. William Schiff and Foulke
     Emerson (Cambridge: Cambridge University Press, 1982), 82–129.

40   Alois Riegl, *Late Roman Art Industry*, trans. Rolf Winkes (1901; Rome: Giorgio Bretschneider Editore, 1985), 24–8; as the translator's Foreword made clear, though the translator used 'tactile', Riegl used the German word '*haptische*'.

41   For overviews of empathy in relation to modernism, Harry Francis Mallgrave and Eleftherios Ikonomou, *Empathy, Form, and Space: Problems in German Aesthetics, 1873–1893* (Santa Monica, CA: Getty Center for the History of Art and the Humanities, 1994); Robin Veder, *The Living Line: Modern Art and the Economy of Energy* (Hanover, NH: Dartmouth College Press, 2015), ch. 2.

42   See Mallgrave and Ikonomou, *Empathy, Form, and Space*, 99–123.

43   Carolyn Burdett, '"The Subjective Inside Us Can Turn into the Objective Outside": Vernon Lee's Psychological Aesthetics', *19: Interdisciplinary Studies in the Long Nineteenth Century*, online journal, no. 12 (2011), 19 (http://www.19.bbkac.uk/index.php/19/issue/view), quoting Vernon Lee and C. Anstruther-Thomson, *Beauty & Ugliness and Other Studies in Psychological Æsthetics* (London: John Lane, The Bodley Head, 1912), 51 and 53.

44   Bernhard Berenson, *The Florentine Painters of the Renaissance with an Index of Their Works* (New York: G. Putnam's Sons, 1896), 4–5.

Chapter 2: Search for Deeper Knowledge

1   Wassily Kandinsky, 'On the Spiritual in Art and Painting in Particular' [1911], in *Kandinsky: Complete Writings on Art*, ed. Kenneth C. Lindsay and Petger Vergo (New York: Da Capo Press, 1994), 114–219, on 131.

2   F. T. Marinetti, *Critical Writings*, ed. Günter Berghaus (New York: Farrar, Strauss and Giroux, 2006), 374.

3   N. A. Bernshtein, 'Biodinamicheskaia normal' udara' (The Biodynamic Standard of a Stroke), *Issledovaniia TsIT* 1, no. 2 (1924): 54–119, on 101.

4   N. A. Bernstein, *The Co-ordination and Regulation of Movements*, papers trans. from Russian and German (1966; Oxford: Pergamon Press, 1967); see also, A. R. Luria, *The Working Brain: An Introduction to Neuropsychology*, trans. Basil Haigh (Harmondsworth, Middlesex: Penguin Books, 1973), 245–55; Mihai Nadin (ed.), *Anticipation: Learning From the Past. The Russian/ Soviet Contributions to the Science of Anticipation* (New York: Springer, 2014).

5   Yvonne Rainer, 'A Quasi Survey of Some "Minimalist" Tendencies in the Quantitatively Minimal Dance Activity midst the Plethora, or an Analysis of Trio A' [1968], in *What Is Dance? Readings in Theory and Criticism*, ed. Roger Copeland and Marshall Cohen (Oxford: Oxford University Press, 1983), 325–32.

6   Cited in Dee Reynolds, *Rhythmic Subjects: Uses of Energy in the Dance of Mary Wigman, Martha Graham and Merce Cunningham* (Alton, Hampshire: Dance Books, 2007), 65,

7   John Martin, 'The Modern Dance' [1933], in *What Is Dance? Readings in Theory and Criticism*, ed. Roger Copeland and Marshall Cohen (Oxford: Oxford University Press, 1983), 23–8.

8   L. D. Blok, *Vozniknovenie i razvitie tekhniki klassicheskogo tantsa* (Beginning and Development of the Classical Dance Technique) (Leningrad: Iskusstvo, 1987), 255.

9   A. Bely, *Nachalo veka* (The Beginning of the Century) (1933; Moscow: Khudozhestvennaia literatura, 1990), 137.

10   For Theosophy and Anthroposophy, see Maria Carlson, *'No Religion Higher than the Truth': A History of the Theosophical Movement in Russia, 1875–1922* (Princeton, NJ: Princeton University Press, 1993).

11   A. Blok, *Intelligentsiia i revoliutsiia* (The Intelligentsia and Revolution) [1918], in *Sobranie sochinenii* (Selected Works), 8 vols (Moscow and Leningrad: Khudozhestvennaia literatura, 1962), vol. 6, 20.

12   See Irina Sirotkina, 'Conversion to Dionysianism: Tadeusz Zieliński and Heptachor', in *Models of Personal Conversion in Russian Cultural History of the 19th and 20th Centuries. Interdisciplinary Studies on Central and Eastern Europe*, ed. Jens Herlth and Christian Zehndner (Frankfurt: Peter Lang, 2015), 105–22.

13   See Ian Levchenko, *Drugaia nauka: Russkie formalisty v poiskakh biografii* (Another Science: Russian Formalists in Search of a Biography) (Moscow: Vysshaia shkola ekonomiki, 2012), 210; V. Shklovsky, *Eizenshtein* (Eisenstein) (Moscow: Iskusstvo, 1973), 58.

14   E. W. Clowes, *The Revolution of Moral Consciousness: Nietzsche in Russian Literature, 1890–1914* (DeKalb, IL: Northern Illinois University Press, 1988).

15   Friedrich Nietzsche, *Thus Spoke Zarathustra: A Book for Everyone and No One*, trans. R. J. Hollingdale (London: Penguin Books, 1969), 305 ('Of the Higher Man', sect. 19). (Written 1883–5.)

16   Ia. E. Golosovker, 'Imaginativnyi absoliut' (The Imaginative Absolute), in *Logika mifa* (The Logic of Myth) (Moscow: Nauka, 1987), 114–65, on 158.

17 Ibid.

18 Jeanne de Salzmann, *The Reality of Being: The Fourth Way of Gurdjieff*, ed. Stephen A. Grant (Boston: Shambhala, 2011), 68 and 72.

19 See Charlotte Douglas, 'Energetic Abstraction: Ostwald, Bogdanov, and Russian Post-revolutionary Art', in *From Energy to Information: Representation in Science and Technology, Art, and Literature*, ed. Bruce Clarke and Linda Dalrymple Henderson (Stanford, CA: Stanford University Press, 2002), 76–94.

20 Wassily Kandinsky, 'Reminiscences/Three Pictures' [1913], in *Complete Writings on Art*, 355–91, on 371–2; cited in Dee Reynolds, *Symbolist Aesthetics and Early Abstract Art: Sites of Imaginary Space* (Cambridge: Cambridge University Press, 1995), 126–7.

21 Wassily Kandinsky, 'Whither the "New" Art?' [1911], in *Complete Writings on Art*, 96–104, on 101; cited in Reynolds, *Symbolist Aesthetics*, 123.

22 Kandinsky, 'Reminiscences/Three Pictures', 368; cited in Reynolds, *Symbolist Aesthetics*, 125–6.

23 M. Matiushin, 'Novyi prostranstvennyi realizm' (New Spatial Realism) [1916–1920], in *Tvorcheskii put' khudozhnika* (The Creative Way of the Artist), ed. A. V. Povelikhina (Kolomna: Muzei organicheskoi kul'tury, 2011), 220–37.

24 M. A. Chekhov, *To the Actor: On the Technique of Acting* (New York: Harper & Row, 1953), 4.

25 V. V. Mayakovsky, 'Zhivopis' segodniashnego dnia' (Today's Painting) [1914], in *Polnoe sobranie sochinenii* (Complete Works), 12 vols (Moscow: Khudozhestvennaia literatura, 1939), vol. 1, 325–34, on 334.

26 Isadora Duncan, *My Life*, revised edn (1927; New York: Liveright, 2013), 61. For the development of uses of energy in modern dance, Reynolds, *Rhythmic Subjects*.

27 Kandinsky, 'On the Spiritual in Art', 205–6.

28 V. V. Kandinsky, 'Prilozheniia k rabote "O dukhovnom v iskusstve"' (Supplement to the Work, 'On the Spiritual in Art') [1914], in *Izbrannye trudy po teorii iskusstva* (Selected Works on Art Theory), vol. 1, 1901–1914 (Moscow: Gileia, 2008), 171–219, on 211.

29 Wassily Kandinsky, 'Point and Line to Plane' [1926], in *Complete Writings*, 524–699, on 619.

30 Iakov Chernikhov, 'Eksprimatika, 1915–1920', in his, *Moi tvorcheskii put'* (Moscow: S. E. Gordeev, 2011), 44–54, on 44 and 47.

31   Synaesthesia is again at the centre of the interest in linking science
     and the arts: see symposium at Tate Modern, London, February 2014
     (http://www.tate.org.uk/context-comment/video/mirror-touch-
     synaesthesia-social-video-recording).

32   A. Blok, 'Bylo to v temnykh Karpatakh . . .' ('This Was in the Dark
     Carpathians . . .') [1913], in *Polnoe sobranie sochinenii i pisem v 20
     tomakh* (Complete Work and Letters in 20 Volumes), vol. 3
     (Moscow: Nauka, 1997), 195.

33   Studies linking sensory psycho-physiology and visual art include:
     Jonathan Crary, *Suspensions of Perception: Attention, Spectacle, and
     Modern Culture* (Cambridge, MA: MIT Press, 1999); Robert Michael
     Brain, *The Pulse of Modernism: Physiological Aesthetics in Fin-de-
     siècle Europe* (Seattle, WA: Washington University Press, 2015).

34   I. Sokolov, *Bedeker po ekspressionizmu* (Baedeker of Expressionism)
     [1919], in *Russkii ekspressionizm. Teoriia. Praktika. Kritika*, ed. V. N.
     Terekhina (Moscow: IMLI RAN, 2005), 61–4, on 62.

35   B. M. Galeev, 'Sinesteziia v mire metafor' (Synaesthesia in the World
     of Metaphors), in *Obrabotka teksta i kognitivnye tekhnologii* (Text
     Processing and Cognitive Technologies). International Conference,
     Moscow and Varna, 2004, quoted in: http://synesthesia.prometheus.
     kai.ru/sinmet_r.htm (accessed 5 July 2016; we have added the
     emphasis in the passage from Khlebnikov, quoted here).

36   B. M. Galeev, 'Sinesteziia v estetike i v poetike simvolizma' (Synaesthesia
     in the Aesthetics and Poetics of Symbolism, 2004), quoted in: http://
     synesthesia.prometheus.kai.ru/sinest_r.htm (accessed 5 July 2016).

37   Wassily Kandinsky, 'Report to the Pan-Russian Conference, 1920', in
     Complete Writings, 473–4, on 474.

38   T. V. Goriacheva, 'Teatral'naia kontseptsiia UNOVISa na fone
     sovremennoi stsenografii' (UNOVIS's Conception of Theatre against
     the Background of the Contemporary Art of Stage Setting), in *Russkii
     avangard 1910–1920 godov i teatr* (The Russian Avant-garde in the
     Years 1910–1920 and the Theatre), ed. G. F. Kovalenko (Saint-
     Petersburg: Dmitry Bulanin, 2000), 116–28.

39   V. V. Kandinsky, 'Oprosnyi list' (Questionnaire), in *Izbrannye trudy
     po teorii iskusstva* (Selected Works on Art Theory), vol. 1, 1901–1914
     (Moscow: Gileia, 2008), 74–80, on 79–80.

40   Matiushin, 'Novyi prostranstvennyi realizm', 237.

41   A. N. Leont'ev, 'Problema vozniknoveniia oschuscheniia' (The
     Problem of the Emergence of Sensation), in *Problemy razvitiia
     psikhiki* (Problems of Mental Development) (Moscow: Akademiia
     pedagogicheskikh nauk, 1959), 9–158.

42　A. A. Kats (ed.), *Vospominaniia schastlivogo cheloveka. Stefanida Dmitrievna Rudneva i studiia muzykal'nogo dvizheniia 'Geptakhor'* (The Memoirs of a Happy Person: Stefanida Dmitrievna Rudneva and the Studio of Musical Movement 'Heptachor') (Moscow: Glavarkhiv Moskvy, 2007), 297.

43　Ibid., 295–6.

44　M. Matiushin, *Tvorcheskii put' khudozhnika* (The Creative Way of the Artist), ed. A. V. Povelikhina (Kolomna: Muzei organicheskoi kul'tury, 2011), 143.

45　Quoted in Kats (ed.), *Vospominaniia schastlivogo cheloveka*, 297.

46　Ibid., 280–1.

47　Rainer Maria Rilke, *Sonnets to Orpheus*, trans. J. B. Leishman (1923; London: Hogarth Press, 1936), 65.

48　Golosovker, *Imaginativnyi absoliut*, 157.

Chapter 3:　Expression in Dance

1　D. S. Merezhkovsky, 'Griaduschii kham' (The Coming Villain) [1906], in *Intelligentsiia–Vlast'–Narod* (The Intelligentsia–The Authorities–The People), ed. L. I. Novikova and I. N. Sizemskaia (Moscow: Nauka, 1992), 81–118, on 114.

2　Friedrich Nietzsche, *Thus Spoke Zarathustra: A Book for Everyone and No One*, trans. R. J. Hollingdale (London: Penguin Books, 1969), 304 ('The Higher Man', sect. 17). (Written 1883–5.)

3　Quoted in P. Rudnev, *Teatral'nye vzgliady Vasiliia Rozanova* (Vasily Rozanov's Views on Theatre) (Moscow: Agraf, 2003), 67.

4　See I. E. Sirotkina, *Svobodnoe dvizhenie i plasticheskii tanets v Rossii* (Free Movement and Plastic Dance in Russia) (Moscow: Novoe literaturnoe obozrenie, 2011), ch. 2.

5　S. M. Gorodetsky, *Zhizn' neukrotimaia: stat'i, ocherki, vospominaniia* (Indomitable Life: Articles, Sketches, Memoirs) (Moscow: Sovremennik, 1984), 22.

6　Rudolf Arnheim, 'Concerning the Dance' [1946], in *Towards a Psychology of Art: Collected Essays* (London: Faber and Faber, 1966), 261–5, on 261.

7　Quoted in D. O. Torshilov, 'Zritel'noe v yazyke: metody analiza vizual'nogo riada proizvedenii literatury v rabotakh A. Belogo 1916–1934 gg.' (The Visual in Language: Methods of Analyzing Visual Imagery in A. Bely's Literary Works, from 1916 to 1934), in

Trudy Russkoi antropologicheskoi shkoly (Works of the Russian Anthropological School), vol. 3 (Moscow: RGGU, 2005), 303–46, on 322.

8   M. A. Chekhov, 'Zhizn' i vstrechi' (Life and Encounters), in *Literaturnoe nasledie* (Literary Heritage), ed. N. A. Krymova, 2nd edn (Moscow: Iskusstvo, 1995), vol. 1, 122–257, on 169.

9   S. M. Volkonsky, *Moi vospominaniia* (My Memoirs) (Moscow: Iskusstvo, 1992), vol. 1, 66.

10   Quoted in Yu. E. Galanina, *Liubov' Dmitrievna Blok. Sud'ba i stsena* (Liubov' Dmitrievna Blok: Life and Stage) (Moscow: Progress-Pleiada, 2009), 34–5.

11   S. M. Volkonsky, 'Chelovek kak material iskusstva. Musyka–Telo–Plyaska' (Man as Material for Art. Music–Body–*Plyaska*), *Ezhegodnik Imperatorskikh Teatrov* 4 (1911): 125–45, on 135–6.

12   Volkonsky, *Moi vospominaniia*, vol. 1, 169.

13   M. Voloshin, 'Aisedora Dunkan', in *Aisedora. Gastroli v Rossii*, ed. T. S. Kasatkina (Moscow: Akter. Rezhisser. Teatr, 1992), 30–48, on 37.

14   For Rimbaud, Dee Reynolds, *Symbolist Aesthetics and Early Abstract Art: Sites of Imaginary Space* (Cambridge: Cambridge University Press, 1995), 52–4; for Cézanne, Richard Shiff, 'Cézanne's Physicality: The Politics of Touch', in *The Language of Art History*, ed. Salim Kemal and Ivan Gaskell (Cambridge: Cambridge University Press, 1991), 129–80; also Maxine Sheets-Johnstone, *The Primacy of Movement*, 2nd edn (Amsterdam and Philadelphia, PA: John Benjamins, 2011), 428–30.

15   Reynolds, *Symbolist Aesthetics*, 226–7 and 267, n. 62.

16   Friedrich Nietzsche, *The Gay Science*, trans. Walter Kaufmann (2nd edn, 1886; New York: Vintage Books, 1974), Preface to 2nd edn, 38.

17   O. Mandelstam, 'Gosudarstvo i ritm' (The State and Rhythm), in '*I ty, Moskva, sestra moia, legka . . .' Stikhi, proza, vospominaniia, materialy k biografii* ('And You, Moscow, My Sister, Are Light . . .' Poems, Prose, Memoirs, Materials for a Biography) (Moscow: Moskovskii rabochii, 1990), 229–32, on 231.

18   Quoted in F. F. Zelinsky, *Skazochnaia drevnost' Ellady. Mify Drevnei Gretsii* (The Fabulous Antiquity of Hellas. Myths of the Ancient Greeks), ed. G. Ch. Guseinov (Moscow: Moskovskii rabochii, 1993), 3.

19   N. P. Antsiferov, *Iz dum o bylom: Vospominaniia* (From Thoughts on the Past: Memoirs), ed. A. I. Dobkin (Moscow: Feniks, Kul'turnaia initsiativa, 1992), 157.

20 Fyodor Dostoevsky, 'The Pushkin Speech' [1880], in *The Dreams of a Queer Fellow and The Pushkin Speech* (London: Unwin Books, 1960), 43–59, on 55.

21 F. F. Zelinsky. *Drevnegrecheskaia religiia* (Ancient Greek Religion) (1918; Kiev: Sinto, 1993), 51.

22 K. Mochul'skii, 'Pis'ma k V. M. Zhirmuskomu' (Letters to V. M. Zhirmunsky), *Novoe literaturnoe obozrenie* no. 35, 1999, at http://infoart.udm.ru/magazine/nlo/n35/pism.htm (accessed 5 July 2016).

23 A. Ia. Levinson, 'Tretii vecher Duncan' (The Third Evening of Duncan), *Rech'* (23–4 January 1913): 7.

24 Quoted in A. A. Kats (ed.), *Vospominaniia schastlivogo cheloveka. Stefanida Dmitrievna Rudneva i studiia muzykal'nogo dvizheniia 'Geptakhor'* (The Memoirs of a Happy Person: Stefanida Dmitrievna Rudneva and the Studio of Musical Movement 'Heptachor') (Moscow: Glavarkhiv Moskvy, 2007), 717.

25 Ibid.

26 Ibid., 129 and 139.

27 Ibid., 497.

28 Ibid., 126.

29 Antsiferov, *Iz dum o bylom*, 159.

30 O. M. Freidenberg, quoted in N. V. Braginskaia, 'Slavianskoe vozrozhdenie antichnosti' (The Slavic Rebirth of Antiquity), in *Russkaia teoriia, 1920–1930 gody* (Russian Theory in the 1920s and 1930s), ed. S. Zenkin (Moscow: RGGU, 2004), 49–80, on 65.

31 Quoted in Antsiferov, *Iz dum o bylom*, 160.

32 Iu. E. Ozarovskii, *Muzyka zhivogo slova. Osnovy russkogo khudozhestvennogo chteniia* (The Music of the Living Word. Foundations of Russian Artistic Reading) (Saint-Petersburg: T-vo O. N. Popovoi, 1914), 282.

33 Ibid., 123.

34 V. Vsevolodskii-Gerngross, 'Foto-stsenicheskaia korobka i amfiteatr' (Photo-stage Box and the Amphitheatre), in *Teatral'no-dekoratsionnoe iskusstvo v SSSR* (The Art of Stage Design in the USSR) (Leningrad: Komitet vystavki teatral'no-dekoratsionnogo iskusstva, 1927), 141–50, on 142.

35 Quoted in R. K. Vassena, 'K rekonstryktsii istoriii deiatel'nosti Instituta zhivogo slova (1918–1924)' (Towards a Reconstruction of the History of the Activity of the Institute of the Living Word), *Novoe literaturnoe obozrenie* no. 86 (2007): 79–95, on 93.

36 Quoted ibid., 93.

37 I. Odoevtseva, *Na beregakh Nevy* (On the Shores of the Neva) (Moscow; Vladimir: VKT, 2009), 22.

38 RGALI fond 941, *opis'* 4, *delo* 2, sheet 1 (Curriculum vitae S. D. Rudnevoi).

39 GARF fond 2307, *opis'* 4, *delo* 54, sheet 70.

40 Quoted in Kats (ed.), *Vospominaniia schastlivogo cheloveka*, 564.

41 Ibid., 563.

42 Ibid., 263.

43 Ozarovskii, *Muzyka zhivogo slova*, 116.

44 Quoted in S. M. Volkonsky, *Vyrazitel'nyi chelovek. Stsenicheskoe vospitanie zhesta (po Del'sartu)* (The Expressive Person: Stage Training of Gesture According to Delsarte) (Saint-Petersburg: Apollon, 1913), 60–1.

45 A. Bely, 'Teoriia khudozhestvennogo slova. Tvorchestvo rechi (nabrosok lektsii)' (Theory of the Living Word. Creativity of Speech (a Lecture Plan)), in *Zhivoe slovo: Logos, golos, dvizheniie, zhest* (The Living Word: Logos, Voice, Movement, Gesture), ed V. V. Feshchenko et al. (Moscow: Novoe literaturnoe obozrenie, 2015), 138–48.

46 A. Bely, 'Plan lektsii "Zhezl Aarona"' (Plan of the lecture 'Aaron's Crosier'), in *Miry Andreia Belogo* (Andrei Bely's Worlds), ed. Aleksandra Vranesh (Belgrade: Filologicheskii fakul'tet v Belgrade, 2011), 66–82, on 79.

47 Friedrich Nietzsche, *The Birth of Tragedy*, trans. Walter Kaufmann (1872; New York: Vintage Books, 1967), 55 (sect. 6).

48 Bely, '"Plan lektsii"', 79.

49 Inna Skliarevskaia, 'Formirovanie temy: Rannee tvorchestvo Balanchina' (Shaping of the Theme: Balanchine's Early Work), *Teatr* 3 (2004): 82–7.

Chapter 4: Speaking Movement

1 A. Bely, 'Bezrukaia tantsovschitsa' (A Dancer with No Arms), ed. E. V. Glukhova and D. O. Torshilov, *Literary Calendar: The Books of Days* 5, no. 2 (2009): 5–25, on 19.

2 N. Sirotkin, 'Nemetskoiazychnyi avangard' (German-language Avant-garde), in *Semiotika i avangard: antologiia* (Semiotics and the

Avant-garde: An Anthology), ed. Yu. S. Stepanov (Moscow: Akademicheskii proekt; Kul'tura, 2006), 820–5, on 820.

3   Shaun Gallagher, *How the Body Shapes the Mind* (Oxford: Clarendon Press, 2005), 117; cited in Guillemette Bolens, *The Style of Gestures: Embodiment and Cognition in Literary Narrative*, trans. [Guillemette Bolens] (2006; Baltimore, MD: Johns Hopkins University Press, 2012), 22.

4   Quoted in N. Valentinov (N. Vol'skii), *Dva goda s simvolistami* (Two Years with the Symbolists) (Moscow: XXI vek-Soglasie, 2000), 85.

5   A. Bely, 'Zhezl Aarona. O slove v poezii' (Crosier of Aaron. On the Word in Poetry), in *Semiotika i avangard: Antologiia* (Semiotics and the Avant-garde: An Anthology), ed. Yu. S. Stepanov (Moscow: Akademicheskii proekt; Kul'tura, 2006), 376–416, on 415.

6   M. Osorgin, 'Andrei Bely', in *Smert' Andreia Belogo* (The Death of Andrei Bely), ed. M. L. Spivak and E. V. Nasedkina (Moscow: Novoe literaturnoe obozrenie, 2013), 486–94, on 489.

7   F. Stepun, 'Pamiati Andreia Belogo' (A Memory of Andrei Bely), in *Vospominaniia o Serebrianom veke* (Memoirs of the Silver Age), ed. V. Kreid (Moscow: Respublika, 1993), 191–202, on 198.

8   Quoted in Osorgin, 'Andrei Bely', 489.

9   M. A. Chekhov, 'Zhizn' i vstrechi' (Life and Encounters), in *Literaturnoe nasledie* (Literary Heritage), ed. N. A. Krymova (Moscow: Iskusstvo, 1995), vol. 1, 122–257, on 173.

10 Quoted in M. L. Spivak and E. V. Nasedkina (eds), *Smert' Andreia Belogo* (The Death of Andrei Bely) (Moscow: Novoe literaturnoe obozrenie, 2013), 93.

11 A. Bely, *Na rubezhe dvukh stoletii* (At the Turn of Two Centuries) (1931; Moscow: Khudozhestvennaia literatura, 1989), 201.

12 A. Bely, 'Pochemu ia stal simvolistom i pochemu ia ne perestal im byt' vo vsekh fazakh moego ideinogo razvitiia' (Why I Became a Symbolist and Why I Did not Stop Being One at all Stages of My Conceptual Development) [1904], in *Simvolizm kak miroponimanie* (Symbolism as a Worldview), ed. L. A. Sugai (Moscow: Respublika, 1994), 418–93, on 418.

13 Bely, *Na rubezhe dvukh stoletii*, 201.

14 A. Bely, *Nachalo veka* (The Beginning of the Century) (1933; Moscow: Khudozhestvennaia literatura, 1990), 551.

15 Bely, *Na rubezhe dvukh stoletii*, 193.

16 Chekhov, 'Zhizn' i vstrechi', 171.

17 Bely, *Na rubezhe dvukh stoletii*, 221.

18 A. Bely, letter to R. V. Ivanov-Razumnik, 19 April 1914, in *Andrei Bely i Ivanov-Razumnik. Perepiska* (Correspondence) (Saint-Petersburg: Atheneum; Feniks, 1998), 43–5.

19 A. Bely, *Vospominaniia o Shteinere* (Memoirs about Steiner) (Paris: Editions la Presse Libre, 1982), quoted at http://bdn-steiner.ru/modules/Books/files/220.pdf (accessed 6 July 2016).

20 M. V. Voloshina (Sabashnikova), *Zelenaia zmeia* (Green Snake) (Moscow: Enigma, 1993), 226; M. Siegloch, *How the New Art of Eurythmy Began: Lory Maier Smits, the First Eurythmist* (Forest Row, East Sussex: Temple Lodge, 1998). For a summary of Steiner's views on eurythmy, Rudolf Steiner, *A Lecture on Eurythmy. Given at Penmaenmawr on 26th August 1923* (1926; London: Rudolf Steiner Press, 1967). Also, Marjorie Raffe, Cecil Howard and Marguerite Lundgren, *Eurythmy and the Impulse of Dance with Sketches for Eurythmy Figures by Rudolf Steiner* ([London]: Rudolf Steiner Press, 1974).

21 Bely, 'Bezrukaia tantsovschitsa', 19.

22 Umberto Eco, *Art and Beauty in the Middle Ages*, trans. Hugh Bredin (1959; New Haven, CT: Yale University Press, 2002), 39.

23 Steiner, *Lecture on Eurythmy*, 16.

24 See Rudolf Steiner, *Music in the Light of Anthroposophy* [based on lectures, from 1906 to 1924] (London: Anthroposophical Publishing, 1925), 33–4.

25 A. Bely, *Glossolaliia. Poema o zvuke* (Glossolalia. A Poem on Sound) (1922; Moscow: Evidentis, 2002), 10.

26 Bely, 'Bezrukaia tantsovschitsa', 19–20.

27 A. Bely, letter to E. Yu. Fechner, in M. Spivak, *Andrei Belyi – mistik i sovetskii pisatel'* (Andrei Bely – Mystic and Soviet Writer) (Moscow: RGGU, 2006), 260.

28 Osorgin, 'Andrei Bely', 491–2.

29 M. Knebel', 'O Mikhaile Chekhove i ego tvorcheskom nasledii' (On Mikhail Chekhov and His Creative Legacy), in M. A. Chekhov, *Vospominaniia. Pis'ma* (Recollections. Letters), ed. Z. Udal'tsova (Moscow: Lokid-Press, 2001), 9–33, on 18–19.

30 M. A. Chekhov, *To the Actor: On the Technique of Acting.* (New York: Harper & Row, 1953), 63.

31 A. Bely, 'Formy iskusstva' [1902], in *Simvolizm kak miroponimanie* (Symbolism as a Worldview), ed. L. A. Sugai (Moscow: Respublika, 1994), 122–39, on 136.

32 Umberto Eco, *In Search for the Perfect Language*, trans. James Fentress (1993; Oxford: Blackwell, 1995), 18–19.

33 L. V. Ivanova, *Vospominaniia. Kniga ob otse* (Memoirs. A Book about Father), ed. J. Malmstad (Paris: Atheneum, 1990), 35.

34 Bely, *Glossolaliia*, 11–12.

35 E. A. Samodelova et al., 'Kommentarii', in S. A. Esenin, *Polnoe sobranie sochinenii* (Complete Works), 7 vols (Moscow: IMLI RAN, 1997), vol. 5, 325–557, on 476.

36 S. A. Esenin, 'Kliuchi Marii' (The Keys of Maria) [1920], in *Polnoe sobranie sochinenii* (Complete Works), 7 vols (Moscow: IMLI RAN, 1997), vol. 5, 186–213.

37 M. Voloshin, 'Aisedora Dunkan', in *Aisedora. Gastroli v Rossii* (Isadora. Russian Tour), ed. T. S. Kasatkina (Moscow: Akter. Rezhisser. Teatr, 1992), 30–9, on 30.

38 I. Shneider. 'Vstrechi s Eseninym. Vospominaniia' (Encounters with Esenin. Memoirs), in *Aisedora Dunkan*, ed. S. P. Snezhko (Kiev: Mistetstvo, 1989), 217–318, on 256.

39 See, for example, A. B. Mariengof, 'Vospominaniia o Esenine' (Memoirs of Esenin), in *S. A. Esenin v vospominaniiakh sovremennikov* (S. A. Esenin in the Memoirs of His Contemporaries), ed. A. Kozlovskii (Moscow: Khudozhestvennaia literatura, 1986), vol. 1, 310–23, on 322.

40 V. Shalamov, 'Esenin', in *Sobranie sochinenii* (Collected Works), 6 vols (Moscow: Knigovek, 2005), vol. 5, 185–93, on 192.

41 Quoted in *Aisedora Dunkan i Sergei Esenin. Ikh zhizn', tvorchestvo, sud'ba* (Isadora Duncan and Sergei Esenin. Their Lives, Work, Fate), ed. I. Krasnov (Moscow: Terra, 2005), 280–1.

42 A. Sidorov, *Sovremennyi tanets* (Modern Dance) (Moscow: Pervina, 1923), 16.

43 V. Meyerhold, 'Variétés, Cabaret, Uberbrettl' [1908–09], in *Meierhol'dovskii sbornik* (The Meyerhold Collection), ed. O. M. Fel'dman (Moscow: OGI, 2000), vol. 2, 251–3.

44 M. Gerasimov, S. Esenin, S. Klychkov and N. Pavlovich, *Zovushchie zori: Stsenarii v 4 chastiakh* (Calling Dawns: Script in 4 Parts), *Literaturnaia Riazan'* 2 (1957): 289–300, quoted at http://esenin.niv.ru/esenin/text/zovuschie-zori.htm (accessed 13 December 2015).

45 E. Styrskaia, 'Poet i tantsovschitsa' (Poet and Dancer), *Znamia* 12 (1999): 119–28, on 123.

46 A. Mariengof, *Bessmertnaia trilogiia* (Immortal Trilogy) (Moscow: Vagrius, 1998), 47.

47 Quoted in I. Chernetskaia, 'Chestvovanie V. Ia. Briusova' (Celebrating V. Ia. Briusov), in *Aisedora. Gastroli v Rossii* (Isadora. Russian Tour), ed. T. S. Kasatkina (Moscow: Akter. Rezhisser. Teatr, 1992), 341–55, on 347.

48 Quoted in Peter Kurth, *Isadora: A Sensational Life* (2001), in Russian translation: P. Kurt, *Aisedora Dunkan*, trans. S. Losev (Moscow: Eksmo, 2007), 272.

49 A. Rumnev, *Vospominaniia* [Memoirs], ms, The Bakhrushin State Theatre Museum, *fond* 518, *delo* 44, sheet 39.

50 Mariengof, *Bessmertnaia trilogiia*, 47.

51 Ibid.

52 R. Laban, *La Danse moderne éducative*, trans. J. and J. Challet (Villers-Cotterêts: Ressouvenances, 2013), 25.

53 Lol Kinel, quoted in Elena Yushkova, 'Dance and Word in the Art of Isadora Duncan', in *Free Verse and Free Dance: Embodied Sense in Motion* (Moscow: Moscow State University, 2011), 54–7, on 56.

54 Quoted in Philippe Lacoue-Labarthe, *Musica Ficta (Figures of Wagner)*, trans. Felicia McCarren (1991; Stanford, CA: Stanford University Press, 1994), 1.

55 M. L. Gasparov, 'Belyi-stikhoved i Belyi-stikhotvorets' (Bely Poetry Scholar and Bely Poet), in *Andrei Belyi. Problemy tvorchestva* (Andrei Bely. Problems of His Creative Work) (Moscow: Sovetskii pisatel', 1988), 444–60, on 447 and 453.

56 Quoted in ibid., 453.

57 M. Shik, 'Vecher Goleizovskogo' (Goleizovskii Evening), *Teatral'noe obozrenie* 10 (1921): 8–9.

58 I. I. Sollertinskii, quoted in V. M. Krasovskaia (ed.), *Sovetskii baletnyi teatr* (Soviet Ballet Theatre) (Moscow: Iskusstvo, 1976), 84.

59 A. Kviatkovskii, 'Ritmologiia russkogo stikha' (Rhythmology of Russian Poetry), in *Ritmologiia* (Rhythmology) (Saint-Petersburg: Dmitry Bulanin, 2008), 9–338, on 300.

60 Bely, *Glossolaliia*, 113.

61 Voloshina, *Zelenaia zmeia*, 389.

62 A. Bely, 'Arbat' (The Arbat), *Rossiia: Monthly Public and Literary Journal* 2 (1924): 27–66, on 59.

63 S. Esenin and A. Mariengof, cited in *Letopis' zhizni i tvorchestva S. A. Esenina* (The Chronicle of S. A. Esenin's Life and Work), (Moscow: IMLI RAN, 2005), vol. 3, 400–1.

64 O. Lekmanhov and M. Sverdlov, *Sergei Esenin. Biografia* (Sergei Esenin. A Biography) (Moscow: Astrel', Corpus, 2011), 174.

65   Esenin, 'Kliuchi Marii', 213.

66   Isadora Duncan, 'The Dance of the Future' [1903], in *The Art of the Dance*, ed. Sheldon Cheney (New York: Theatre Arts Books, 1969), 54–63, on 54 and 57.

67   F. T. E. Marinetti, 'Manifesto of the Futurist Dance' [1917], in *Marinetti: Selected Writings*, ed. R. W. Flint, trans. R. W. Flint and Arthur A. Coppotelli (London: Secker & Warburg, 1972), 137–41, on 137; quoted in Felicia McCarren, *Dancing Machines: Choreographies in the Age of Mechanical Reproduction* (Stanford, CA: Stanford University Press, 2003), 100.

68   V. Parnakh, 'Opyty novogo tantsa' (Experiences of New Dance) [1922], in *Zhirafovidnyi istukan* (Idol-Giraffe), ed. E. R. Arenzon (Moscow: Piataia strana, Gileia, 2000), 157–8.

69   Quoted in E. Bobrinskaia (ed.), *Futurizm. Radikal'naia revoliutsiya. Italiia-Rossiia* (Futurism. Radical Revolution. Italy-Russia) (Moscow: Gos. Muzei imeni Pushkina, 2008), 32.

70   S. I. Subbotin, 'Kommentarii', in S. A. Esenin, *Polnoe Sobranie sochinenii* (Collected Works), 7 vols (Moscow: IMLI RAN, 1997), vol. 2, 387.

71   Shneider, 'Vstrechi s Eseninym', 260.

72   See E. A. Samodelova, *Antropologicheskaia poetika S. A. Esenina: avtorskii zhiznetekst na perekrestke kul'turnykh traditsii* (S. A. Esenin's Anthropological Poetics: The Author's Life-text on the Crossroad of Cultural Traditions) (Moscow: Iazyki slavianskikh kul'tur, 2006), 585.

73   See A. Kruchenykh, 'O Velimire Khlebnikove' (On Velimir Khlebnikov) [1932–1934; 1964], in *Mir Velimira Khlebnikova: Stat'i. Issledovaniia (1911–1998)* (The World of Velimir Khlebnikov: Papers. Studies (1911–1998)), ed. V. V. Ivanov and Z. S. Papernyi (Moscow: Iazyki slavianskikh kul'tur, 2000), 128–46, on 137.

74   That Mallarmé's poems thus require the reader's constructive imagination is discussed in Dee Reynolds, *Symbolist Aesthetics and Early Abstract Art: Sites of Imaginary Space* (Cambridge: Cambridge University Press, 1995), ch. 3.

75   N. I. Khardzhiev, 'Zametki o Khlebnikove' (Notes about Khlebnikov) [1975], in *Stat'i ob avangarde*, v 2 tomakh (Articles on the Avant-garde, in 2 Vols.) (Moscow: RA, 1997), vol. 2, 273–92, on 278–9.

76   O. M. Freidenberg, *Poetika siuzheta i zhanra: period antichnoi literatury* (Poetics of Plot and Genre: The period of Ancient Greek Literature) (1936; Moscow: Labirint, 1997), 120–2 (emphasis added).

77 A. Kruchenykh, *Apokalipsis v russkoi literature* (The Apocalypse in Russian Literature) (Moscow: Tipografiia TsIT, 1923), 45.

78 V. Kamensky, *Zvuchal' vesneianki. Stikhi* (Moscow: Kitovras, 1918), 186–7. (The title is an example of *zaum'* and untranslatable.)

79 V. V. Feschenko, 'Grafolaliia Zdanevicha-Il'yazda kak khudozhestvennyi eksperiment' (Grapholalia by Zdanevich-Ilyazd as an Artistic Experiment), in *Dada po-russki* (Dada in Russian) (Belgrade: Filologicheskii fakul'tet Belgradskogo Universiteta, 2013), 204–12.

80 V. Kamensky. *Devushki bosikom. Stikhi* (Girls Barefoot. Poems) (Tiflis: [no publisher given], 1916), 1.

81 The words of the artist, David Burliuk, according to Kamensky's widow; see *K 120 letiiu V. V. Kamenskogo* (Towards 120 Years of V. V. Kamensky) (Perm: 2004), quoted at http://refdb.ru/look/ 2752944-pall.html (accessed 14 December 2015).

82 S. Vinogradov, 'Akkordy zhizni' (The Accords of Life), *Ural'skaia zhizn'* [Ekaterinburg] (14 April 1917), 79.

83 N. Anderson, 'Avangard kak telo i predstavlenie: sluchai Goltzschmidt' (The Avant-Garde as Body and Representation: The case of Goltzschmidt), in *Futurist zhizni Vladimir Goltzshmidt. Poslaniia Vladi-mira zhizni s puti k istine* (The Futurist Life of Vladimir Goltzshmidt. The Message by Vladi-mir of Life from the Path towards Truth), ed. N. Anderson (Moscow: Salamandra P.V.V., 2010), 6.

84 Quoted in N. Zakharov-Menskii, 'Kak poety vyshli na ulitsu. Part I (1917–1918 r.)' (How Poets Came Out on the Street. Part I (the Years 1917 to 1918), http://lucas-v-leyden.livejournal.com/108549.html (accessed 15 August 2013).

85 Ibid.

86 V. Khodasevich, 'Vystavka v salone Mikhailovoi' (Exhibition in the Mikhailova Salon), in *Russkii futurizm. Stikhi. Stat'i. Vospominaniia* (Russian Futurism. Poems. Articles. Memoirs), ed. V. N. Terekhina and A. P. Zemenkov (Saint-Petersburg: Poligraf, 2009), 625–55.

87 Kamensky, *Zvuchal' vesneianki*, 9–10.

88 A. Kusikov, K. Bal'mont and A. Sluchanovskii, *Zhemchuzhnyi kovrik* (A Pearl Rug) (Moscow: [no publisher given], 1921), 40–1.

89 S. D. Spasskii, *Maiakovsky i ego sputniki. Vospominaniia* (Mayakovsky and His Circle. Memoirs) (Leningrad: Sovetskii pisatel', 1940), 126–7.

90 Quoted in E. Lazareva (ed.), *Manifesty i programmy ital'ianskogo futurizma, 1915–1933* (Manifestos and Programmes of Italian Futurism) (Moscow: Gileia, 2013), 297.

91   Vladimir Markov, *Russian Futurism: A History* (London:
      MacGibbon and Kee, 1968), 385.

92   Elena Guro, *Nebesnye verbliuzhata* (Heavenly Baby-camels) (Saint-
      Petersburg: Zhuravl', 1914), 54–5.

Chapter 5: By 'the Fourth Way'

1   S. M. Volkonsky, 'Dokladnaia zapiska v Uchenyi komitet po
      fizicheskomu vospitaniiu' (Report to the Physical Culture Committee),
      Listki Kursov ritmicheskoi gimnastiki 6 (1914): 7–11, on 9.

2   S. M. Eisenstein, *Memuary* (Memoirs), ed. N. I. Kleiman (Moscow:
      Trud, Muzei kino, 1997), vol. 1, 164.

3   Jeanne de Salzmann, *The Reality of Being: The Fourth Way of
      Gurdjieff*, ed. Stephen A. Grant (Boston, MA: Shambhala, 2011), 79.

4   P. D. Ouspensky, *Tertium Organum. The Third Canon of Thought. A
      Key to the Enigmas of the World*, revised trans. E. Kadloubovsky and
      the Author (1920; London: Routledge and Kegan Paul, 1981), 277.

5   See R. Whyman, *The Stanislavsky System of Acting: Legacy and
      Influence in Modern Performance* (Cambridge: Cambridge University
      Press, 2008), 78–88; S. D. Cherkasskii, *Stanislavsky i yoga*
      (Stanislavsky and Yoga) (Saint-Petersburg: RATI, 2013).

6   [Anon.], 'O sisteme Dal'croza' (On Dalcroze's System), *Listki Kursov
      ritmicheskoi gimnastiki* 6 (1914): 19–25, on 20.

7   A. Rovner, *Gurdzhiev i Uspenskii* (Gurdjieff and Ouspensky), 2nd
      edn (Moscow: Starlight–Nomos, 2006), 136–7.

8   A. V. Krusanov, *Russkii avangard, 1907–1932. Istoricheskii obzor*
      (The Russian Avant-garde, 1907–1932. Historical Overview), vol. 2
      (Moscow: Novoe literaturnoe obozrenie, 2003), 798.

9   A. Ia. Tairov, *O teatre* (On Theatre) (Moscow: VTO, 1970), 163.

10   A. G. Koonen, *Stranitsy zhizni* (Pages of Life) (Moscow: Iskusstvo,
      1985), 299.

11   N. Chushkin, 'V. V. Dmitriev. Tvorcheskii put', 1948' (V. V. Dmitriev.
      The Creative Way, 1948), in *Mnemozina: Dokumenty i fakty iz istorii
      otechestvennogo teatra XX veka* (Mnemozine: Documents and Facts
      from the History of Russian Theatre), ed. V. V. Ivanov (Moscow:
      Akter. Rezhisser. Teatr, 2004), vol. 3, 601.

12   Yu. A. Golovashenko, *Rezhisserkoe iskusstvo Tairova* (Tairov's Work
      as a Director) (Moscow: Iskusstvo, 1970), 203.

13   S. M. Volkonsky, *Moi vospominaniia* (My Memoirs) (Moscow: Iskusstvo, 1992), vol. 1, 179.

14   Ibid., 186–7.

15   I. E. Sirotkina, N. A. Solntsev, K. G. Iasnova, '"Vse, chto ia khochu vam skazat', ia by luchshe vyrazila v tantse": Pis'ma Aisedory Dunkan K. S. Stanislavskomu' ('All I'd Like to Tell You I would Better Put in a Dance': Isadora Duncan's Letters to K. Stanislavsky), in *Mnemozina: Dokumenty i fakty iz istorii otechestvennogo teatra XX veka* (Mnemozine: Documents and Facts from the History of Russian Twentieth-Century Theatre), ed. V. V. Ivanov (Moscow: Indrik, 2014), vol. 5, 330–62, on 347.

16   P. Claudel quoted (from *Sur le théâtre d'Hellerau*) in C. Schenk, 'Une éducation par le rythme: Émile Jaques-Dalcroze et la cité-jardin d'Hellerau (1911–1914)', in *Créer, ensemble: Points de vue sur les communautés artistiques (fin du XIXe–XXe siècles)* (Montpellier: L'Entretemps, 2013), 197–208, on 206.

17   A. de Salzmann, 'Light, Lighting and Illumination', *Material for Thought* 4 (Spring 1972): 22–4. http://www.farwesteditions.com/mft/mft_04.htm (accessed 15 June 2013).

18   Koonen, *Stranitsy zhizni*, 228.

19   S. V. Vladimirov et al. (eds), *U istokov rezhissury: Ocherki iz istorii russkoi rezhissury XIX – nachala XX veka* (At the Origins of Staging: Essays on the History of Russian Staging from the Nineteenth to the Early Twentieth Century) (Leningrad: Len. gos. institut teatra, muzyki i kinematografii, 1976), 257–8.

20   V. Nicolescu, 'Alexandre de Salzmann, un grand artiste oublié du 20e siècle.' Paper presented at the Halle Saint Pierre, Paris, 24 October 2009. http://www.scribd.com/doc/21983903/Basarab-Nicolescu-Alexandre-de-Salzmann-un-grand-artiste-oublie-du-20e-siecle (accessed 12 August 2013).

21   I. Terent'ev, 'Vecher Zhanny Matinion i Giurdzhieva' (An Evening of Jeanne Matinion [Salzmann] and Gurdjieff), *41°. Ezhenedel'naia gazeta* 1 (14–20 July 1919), 4 (the ellipses after 'Chopin' and after 'relaxation' in the original).

22   M. Ljunggren, *Russkii Mefistofel': Zhizn' i tvorchestvo Emiliia Metnera* (Russian Mephisto: The Life and Work of Emil Medtner) (Saint-Petersburg: Akademicheskii proekt, 2001), 69.

23   Zh. Panova, 'Predislovie' (Foreword), in E. Zhak-Dal'kroz, *Ritm* (Rhythm) (Moscow: Klassika-XXI vek, 2006), 3–19, on 16.

24   Salzmann, *Reality of Being*, 127.

25   Ibid., 63.

26   Ibid., 122.

27   S. Mamontov, 'Demonstratsiia Jaques-Dalcroze' (Demonstration by Jaques-Dalcroze) [1912], quoted in E. Ia. Surits, 'Emile Jaques-Dalcroze v Rossii' (Emile Jaques-Dalcroze in Russia), in *Teatr i russkaia kul'tura na rubezhe XIX-XX vekov* (Theatre and Russian Culture Abroad at the Turn of the Nineteenth and Twentieth Centuries) (Moscow: Teatral'nyi muzei imeni Bakhrushina, 1998), 58.

28   [Charles Stanley Nott], *Teaching of Gurdjieff: The Journal of a Pupil. An Account of Some Years with G. I. Gurdjieff and A. R. Orage in New York and at Fontainbleau-Avon* (London: Routledge & Kegan Paul, 1961), 61.

29   Ibid., 62.

30   Rovner, *Gurdzhiev i Uspenskii*, 160–1.

31   Nott, *Teaching of Gurdjieff*, 85–6.

32   Quoted in M. Voloshin, 'Kul'tura tantsa' (Dance Culture) [1911], in *Zhizn' – beskonechnoe poznan'e* (Life – Endless Knowledge), ed. V. P. Kupchenko (Moscow: Pedagogika-Press, 1995), 289–93, on 292.

33   Quoted in P. I. Rumiantsev, *Stanislavsky i opera* (Stanislavsky and Opera) (Moscow: Iskusstvo, 1969), 407.

34   Salzmann, *Reality of Being*, 73.

35   K. S. Stanislavsky, *An Actor Prepares*, trans. Elisabeth Reynolds Hapgood (New York: Theatre Art Books, 1936), 243 and 275.

36   Ian Driver, *A Century of Dance: A Hundred Years of Musical Movement, from Waltz to Hip Hop* (London: Bounty Books, 2009).

37   G. Simmel, 'The Metropolis and Mental Life' [1903], in *On Individuality and Social Forms: Selected Writings*, ed. D. N. Levine (Chicago, IL: University of Chicago Press, 1971), 324–39.

38   Salzmann, *Reality of Being*, 272 and 123.

39   I. M. Sechenov, 'Reflexes of the Brain' [first variant 1863], trans. A. A. Subkov et al., in *Selected Works*, facsimile reprint (1935; Amsterdam: E. J. Bonset, 1968), 263–336, on 304.

40   E. Levinas, *Basic Philosophical Writings*, ed. A. T. Peperzak, S. Critchley and R. Bernasconi (Bloomington, IN: Indiana University Press, 1996), 80–1.

41   Maurice Merleau-Ponty, *Phenomenology of Perception*, trans. Colin Smith (1945; London: Routledge, 2002), 246.

42   M. M. Bakhtin, 'Avtor i geroi v esteticheskoi deiatel'nosti' (Author and Hero in Aesthetic Activity), in *Estetika slovesnogo tvorchestva*

(Aesthetics of Literary Creation) (Moscow: Iskusstvo, 1986), 9–191, on 127.

43 Erika Fischer-Lichte, *The Transformative Power of Performance: A New Aesthetics*, trans. Saskya Iris Jan (2004; London: Routledge, 2008), 93–101.

44 A critic in 1925, after seeing the actor Gustav Gruendgers, quoted in ibid., 95.

45 E. Barba and N. Savareze, *A Dictionary of Theatre Anthropology: The Secret Art of the Performer*, trans. R. Fowler (London: Routledge, 1991), 74–7.

46 Salzmann, *Reality of Being*, 291.

47 Howard Gardner, *Frames of Mind: The Theory of Multiple Intelligences* (London: Heinemann, 1984), 205–36.

48 V. S. Gurfinkel, interview with Irina Sirotkina, 21 May 2012.

Chapter 6: Thinking with the Body

1 Vladimir Mayakovsky, *How Are Verses Made?* trans. George Hyde (1926; Bristol: Bristol Press, 1990), 68.

2 A. Bely, *Nachalo veka* (The Beginning of the Century) (1933; Moscow: Khudozhestvennaia literatura, 1990), 550.

3 M. Matiushin, *Tvorcheskii put' khudozhnika* (The Creative Way of the Artist), ed. A. V. Povelikhina (Kolomna: Muzei organicheskoi kul'tury, 2011), 86.

4 S. Shamardina, 'Futuristicheskaia yunost' (Futuristic Youth), in V. V. Katanian (ed.), *'Imia etoi teme – liubov'! Sovremennitsy o Mayakovskom* ('The Name of this Theme – Love!' Female Contemporaries on Mayakovsky) (Moscow: Druzhba narodov, 1993), 9–32, on 12; R. M. Kirsanova, *Kostium v russkoi kul'ure XVIII – pervoi poloviny XX veka* (Costume in Russian Culture of the Eighteenth to the First Half of the Twentieth Century) (Moscow: Bol'shaia Rossiiskaia Entsiklopediia, 1995), 269.

5 E. A. Bobrinskaia, 'Futuristicheskii "grim"' (Futurist 'Make-up'), *Vestnik istorii, literatury, iskusstva* (Moscow: RAN, 2005), 88–99, on 93.

6 M. M. Bonch-Tomashevskii, *Kniga o tango. Iskusstvo i seksual'nost'* (A Book on Tango. Art and Sexuality) (Moscow: M. V. Portugalov, 1914), 15 and 31.

7   Quoted in A. V. Krusanov, *Russkii avangard, 1907–1932.*
      Istoricheskii obzor (The Russian Avant-Garde, 1907–32. Historical
      Overview) (Moscow: Novoe literaturnoe obozrenie, 2003), vol. 1,
      book 2, 467.

8   Memoirs of Mayakovsky's women-friends are collected in Katanian
      (ed.), '*Imia etoi teme – liubov'!*, 254, 260 and 278.

9   Quoted in A. Kviatkovsky, 'Osnovnye tipy stikha Mayakovskogo'
      (Main Types of Mayakovsky's Verses), in *Ritmologiia* (Rhythmology)
      (Saint-Petersburg: Dmitry Bulanin, 2008), 495–537, on 514.

10   Iu. N. Tynianov, 'O Mayakovskom. Pamiati poeta' (On Mayakovsky.
      The Memory of the Poet), in *Poetika. Istoriia literatury. Kino* (Poetics.
      History of Literature. Cinema) (Moscow: Nauka, 1977), 196.

11   Mayakovsky, *How Are Verses Made?* 68–9.

12   Kviatkovsky, 'Osnovnye tipy stikha Mayakovskogo', 512–13.

13   Vladimir Mayakovsky, 'It' – 'What It's About'– 'For Her and Me'
      [1923], in *Poems*, trans. Dorian Rottenberg (Moscow: Progress,
      1972), 146; Russian variant quoted in Kviatkovsky, 'Osnovnye tipy
      stikha Mayakovskogo', 520.

14   Vladimir Mayakovsky, 'Vladimir Mayakovsky' [1913], in *Polnoe
      sobranie sochinenii v 13 tomakh* (Complete Works in 13 Volumes),
      vol. 1 (Moscow: Khudozhestvennaia literatura, 1955), 152–72, on
      157–8.

15   Ian Driver, *A Century of Dance: A Hundred Years of Musical
      Movement, from Waltz to Hip Hop* (London: Bounty Books,
      2009), 33.

16   Nina Berberova, *The Italics Are Mine*, trans. Philippe Radley (1969;
      London: Chatto & Windus, 1991), 138–9.

17   M. Gordon, 'Valentin Parnakh, Apostle of Eccentric Dance',
      Experiment: A Journal of Russian Culture 2 (1996): 423–9, on 427.

18   E. Uvarova, *Estradnyi teatr. Miniatiury, obozreniia, muzik-holly,
      1917–1945* (Estrada Theatre. Miniatures, Reviews, Music-Hall,
      1917–1945) (Moscow: Iskusstvo, 1983), 58.

19   O. Brik, 'Agit-holl', *Ermitazh* 4 (1922): 4.

20   V. Parnakh, 'Chernye zhily' (Black Veins) [1919], in *Tri knigi* (Three
      Books), ed. V. Perel'muter (Moscow: Sam & Sam, 2012), 137.

21   See S. Gilman, 'The Fox-trot and the New Economic Policy: A
      Case-study in "Thingification" and Cultural Imports', *Experiment: A
      Journal of Russian Culture* 2 (1996): 443–75, on 465.

22   Quoted in Uvarova, *Estradnyi teatr*, 67.

23 O. Brik, 'Sud'ba tantsa' (Destiny of Dance), *Zrelischa* 23 (1923): 10–11, on 10.

24 *Lilia Brik – El'za Triole. Neizdannaia perepiska (1921–1970)* (Lilya Brik – Elsa Triolet. Unpublished Correspondence), ed. V. V. Katanian (Moscow: Ellis Lak, 2000), 22.

25 Li [A. A. Cherepnin], 'Foregger', *Zrelischa* no. 82 (1924): 11.

26 Li [A. A. Cherepnin], 'Ot fokstrota k "Iablochku"' (From Foxtrot to 'The Little Apple'), *Zrelischa* no. 25 (1924): 5–6, on 6.

27 M. Gorky, 'O muzyke tolstykh' (On the Music of the Fat People) [1928], in his *Sobraniie sochinenii* (Collected Works), 30 vols (Moscow: Khudozhestvennaia literatura, 1953), vol. 24, 351.

28 The Bakhrushin State Theatre Museum, *fond* 517, *opis'* 1, sheet 45.

29 A. Rashkovskii, 'Sud'ba dramaturga i literatora. K 100-letiiu so dnia rozhdeniia I. S. Shura' (The Destiny of a Playwright and Writer. For the Centenary of the Birthday of I. S. Shur), *Topos*. http://www.topos. ru/article/zhizn-kak-est/sudba-dramaturga-i-literatora-k-100-letiyu-so-dnya-rozhdeniya-isaaka-solomonov (accessed 15 January 2014). (Ellipses in original.)

30 I. E. Sirotkina, 'Biomekhanika mezhdu naukoi i iskusstvom' (Biomechanics between Science and Art), *Voprosy istorii estestvoznaniia i tekhniki* no. 1 (2011): 46–70.

31 V. E. Meyerhold, '[Studiia na Borodinskoi]' (The Studio on Borodinskaia Street) [1914], in *Meyerhold: K istorii tvorcheskogo metoda* (Meyerhold: Towards a History of Creative Method), ed. N. V. Pesochinskii (Saint-Petersburg: Kul'tinformpress, 1998), 9–15, on 11.

32 V. E. Meyerhold, 'Lektsii Meierkhol'da o rezhissure' (Meyerhold's Lectures on Directing) [1921], in *Meyerhold: K istorii tvorcheskogo metoda* (Meyerhold: Towards a History of Creative Method), ed. N. V. Pesochinskii (Saint-Petersburg: Kul'tinformpress, 1998), 20–2, on 20.

33 I. E. Sirotkina, *Svobodnoe dvizhenie i plasticheskii tanets v Rossii* (Free Movement and Plastic Dance in Russia) (Moscow: Novoe literaturnoe obozrenie, 2011), ch. 6.

34 V. E. Meyerhold, 'Doklad o sistemakh i priemakh akterskoi igry' (Talk on Systems and Devices of Acting) [1925], in *Meyerhold: K istorii tvorcheskogo metoda* (Meyerhold: Towards a History of Creative Methods), ed. N. V. Pesochinskii (Saint-Petersburg: Kul'tinformpress, 1998), 44–5.

35 Olga Chkalova, quoted in Iu. Zerchaninov, 'Zhiznennyi put' slavnogo russkogo sportsmena doktora Petrova' (The Life Path of the Renowned Russian Sportsman, Dr Petrov), *Iunost'* 11 (1978): 104–8, on 108.

36 *Leonid Sergeevich Vivien. Akter, rezhisser, pedagog* (Leonid Sergeevich Vivien. Actor, Director, Teacher), ed. V. V. Ivanova (Moscow: Iskusstvo, 1988), 170.

37 'Teatr RSFSR I-i. Laboratoriia' (The Theatre RSFSR-I. Laboratory), *Vestnik teatra* nos. 80–1 (1921): 22.

38 V. E. Meyerhold, V. Bebutov, K. Derzhavin, 'Teatral'nye listki-1' (Theatre Notes-1), *Vestnik teatra* nos. 87–8 (1921): 2–3.

39 D. Zolotnitskii, *Meyerhold. Roman c sovetskoi vlast'iu* (Meyerhold: A Love Affair with the Soviets) (Moscow: Agraf, 1999), 79.

40 Ob"iasnitel'naia zapiska k Polozheniiu o Tefizkul'te (Explanatory Note to the Statute of Tefizkul't), Russian State Archive of Literature and Art, *fond* 998 (V. E. Meyerhold), *opis'* 1, *delo* 2921, sheet 4.

41 V. E. Meyerhold, 'V Glavnoe upravlenie Vsevobucha' (In the Main Administration of Vsevobuch), Russian State Archive of Literature and Art, *fond* 998 (V. E. Meyerhold), *opis'* 1, *delo* 2922, list 26.

42 [Minutes of Tefizkul't meetings of 28 July, 10 September and 4 October 1921], Russian State Archive of Literature and Art, *fond* 998 (V. E. Meyerhold), *opis'* 1, *delo* 2921, list 21–3.

43 V. E. Meyerhold, 'Aktior budushchego' (Actor of the Future), *Ermitazh* 6 (1922): 10–11.

44 A. Gastev, 'Narodnaia vypravka' (Posture of the People), *Pravda* (12 July 1922).

45 Quoted in V. Scherbakov, 'Podrazhanie Champolionu' (Imitation of Champolion), in *Ot slov k telu. K 60-letiiu Iuriia Tsiv'iana* (From Words to Body. For the 60th Birthday of Yuri Tsiv'ian), ed. A. Lavrov, A. Ospovat and R. Timenchik (Moscow: Novoe literaturnoe obozrenie, 2010), 393–428, on 427.

46 R. Arnheim, *Art and Visual Perception: A Psychology of the Creative Eye,* new version (Berkeley, CA: University of California Press, 1974), 407.

47 E. Barba and N. Savareze, *A Dictionary of Theatre Anthropology: The Secret Art of the Performer,* trans. R. Fowler (London: Routledge, 1991), 258–9; see also conclusion of our ch. 5.

48 'Biomekhanika' (Biomechanics), in *Teatral'naia entsiklopediia* (Theatre Encyclopaedia), ed. S. S. Mokul'skii (Moscow: Sovetskaia entsiklopediia, 1961), vol. 1, 583.

49 Barba and Savareze, *Dictionary of Theatre Anthropology,* 250.

50 M. Polanyi, *Personal Knowledge: Towards a Post-Critical Philosophy* (London: Routledge & Kegan Paul, 1958).

Chapter 7: Art as Bodily Knowledge

1   Friedrich Nietzsche, *Thus Spoke Zarathustra: A Book for Everyone and No One*, trans. R. J. Hollingdale (London: Penguin Books, 1969), 40 ('Zarathustra's Prologue', sect. 2). (Written 1883–5.)

2   Ibid., 228 ('Of Old and New Law-Tables', sect. 23).

3   L. Ia. Ginzburg, 'Vspominaia Institut istorii iskusstv' (Remembering the Institute for the History of the Arts), in *Rossiiskii institut istorii iskusstv v memuarakh* (The Russian Institute for the History of the Arts in Memories), ed. I. V. Sepman (Saint-Petersburg: Rosiiskii institut istorii iskusstv, 2003), 58.

4   Viktor Shklovsky, 'Kak my pishem' (The Way We Write) [1929], quoted in Vladimir Berezin, *Viktor Shklovsky* (Moscow: Molodaia gvardiia, 2014), 277.

5   S. Zenkin, 'Otkrytie "byta" russkimi formalistami' (The Discovery of 'byt' by Russian Formalists), in *Raboty po teorii* (Works on Theory) (Moscow: Novoe literaturnoe obozrenie, 2012), 305. Zenkin was discussing the work of Gérard Genette.

6   V. E. Meyerhold, 'Doklad o sistemakh i priyomakh aktyorskoi igry' (Talk on Systems and Devices of Acting) [1925], in *K istorii tvorcheskogo metoda* (Towards the History of Creative Methods), ed. N. V. Pesochinsky (Saint-Petersburg: Kul'tinformpress, 1998), 44–5.

7   Quoted in I. Kalinin, 'Istoriia kak iskusstvo chlenorazdel'nosti: istoricheskii opyt i metaliteraturnaia praktika russkikh formalistov' (History as an Art of Articulation: Historical Experience and Metaliterary Practice of the Russian Formalists), *Novoe Literaturnoe Obozrenie* no. 71 (2005): 103–31, on 104.

8   Yury Tsivian, *Na podstupakh k karpalistike: Dvizhenie i zhest v literature, iskusstve i kino* (At the Foot of Carpalistics: Movement and Gesture in Literature, Art and Cinema) (Moscow: Novoe literaturnoe obozrenie, 2010), 264–5.

9   Kalinin, 'Istoriia kak iskusstvo chlenorazdel'nosti', 104.

10 Viktor Shklovsky, *Theory of Prose,* trans. Benjamin Sher (1925; Elmwood Park, IL: Dalkey Archive Press, 1990), 15.

11 Ibid., 16.

12 Quoted in Dee Reynolds, *Rhythmic Subjects: Uses of Energy in the Dance of Mary Wigman, Martha Graham and Merce Cunningham* (Alton, Hampshire: Dance Books, 2007), 65.

13 M. Bakhtin, *Rabelais and His World*, trans. Helene Iswolsky (1965; Cambridge, MA: MIT Press, 1968).

14 Shklovsky, *Theory of Prose*, 15.

15 Maurice Merleau-Ponty, *Phenomenology of Perception*, trans. Colin Smith (1945; London: Routledge, 2002), 166 (emphases added).

16 Ibid., 164–5.

17 F. C. Bartlett, *Remembering: A Study in Experimental and Social Psychology* (1932; Cambridge: Cambridge University Press, 1995), 201.

18 Merleau-Ponty, *Phenomenology of Perception*, 168.

19 Ibid., 169.

20 V. Shklovsky, *Voskreshenie slova* (Resurrection of the Word) (Saint-Petersburg: Tipografiia Z. Sokolinskogo, 1914), 1. Cf. Roger Copeland, 'Merce Cunningham and the Politics of Perception', in *What Is Dance? Readings in Theory and Criticism*, ed. Roger Copeland and Marshall Cohen (Oxford: Oxford University Press, 1983), 307–24, on 314.

21 Quoted in Reynolds, *Rhythmic Subjects*, 202.

22 Gilbert Ryle, 'Knowing How and Knowing That. The Presidential Address', *Proceedings of the Aristotelian Society* 46 (1945–6): 1–16, on 16.

23 M. de Certeau, *The Practice of Everyday Life*, trans. Steven F. Rendall (1980; Berkeley, CA: University of California Press, 1984), xiv–xv.

24 See the influential critique in Guy Debord, *The Society of the Spectacle*, trans. Donald Nicholson-Smith (1967; New York: Zone Books, 1995).

25 David Michael Levine (ed.), *Modernity and the Hegemony of Vision* (Berkeley, CA: University of California Press, 1993), interpreted modernity as the working out of presumptions of visual dominance since the Ancient Greeks.

26 Constance Classen, *The Deepest Sense: A Cultural History of Touch* (Urbana, IL: University of Illinois Press, 2012), 148. Also, Constance Classen, *Worlds of Sense: Exploring the Senses in History and across Cultures* (London: Routledge, 1993), 6–7, on 'Western visualism'.

27 This use of 'deepest' should, however, be distinguished from reference (e.g., in Milton, cited by Classen, *Deepest Sense*, 54) to spiritual knowledge, drawing a contrast with the superficial knowledge of *all* the senses.

28 Dee Reynolds, *Symbolist Aesthetics and Early Abstract Art: Sites of Imaginary Space* (Cambridge: Cambridge University Press, 1995), 123.

29 Norbert Elias, *The Civilizing Process: The History of Manners*, trans. E. Jephcott (1939; Oxford: Basil Blackwell, 1978).

30 Gilbert Ryle, *The Concept of Mind* (1949; Harmondsworth, Middlesex: Penguin Books, 1963), 27 and 32.

31 Maxine Sheets-Johnstone, *The Primacy of Movement*, 2nd edn (Amsterdam and Philadelphia, PA: John Benjamins, 2011), 429.

32 Guillemette Bolens, *The Style of Gestures: Embodiment and Cognition in Literary Narrative*, trans. Guillemette Bolens (2006; Baltimore, MD: Johns Hopkins University Press, 2012), frontispiece.

33 S. Zenkin, 'Sotsial'nyi fakt i vesch'. (K probleme smysla v gumanitarnykh naukakh)' (The Social Fact and the Thing. On the Problem of Meaning in the Human Sciences), in *Raboty o teorii* (Works on Theory) (Moscow: Novoe literaturnoe obozrenie, 2012), 24.

34 Philip Robbins and Marat Aydede (eds), *Cambridge Handbook of Situated Cognition* (Cambridge: Cambridge University Press, 2008); Shaun Gallagher, *How the Body Shapes the Mind* (Oxford: Clarendon Press, 2005).

35 Ginzburg, 'Vspominaia Institut istorii iskusstv', 55.

36 This is an underlying implication of William James's discussion of space perception, in *The Principles of Psychology*, 2 vols (1890; New York: Dover, 1950), vol. 2, 134–203.

37 There is an unusually succinct statement of how the debate has acquired its present form in Nicolas Langlitz, 'On a Not so Chance Encounter of Neurophilosophy and Science Studies in a Sleep Laboratory', *History of the Human Sciences* 28, no. 4 (2015): 3–24; significantly, Langlitz wrote as an anthropologist of science and philosophy, observing but not advocating one side of the argument (while, of course, 'performing', and in this way advocating, anthropological observation).

38 This is not the place to go further into the issues and to engage with the fine discussion in Carrie Noland, *Agency and Embodiment: Performing Gestures/Producing Culture* (Cambridge, MA: Harvard University Press, 2009). Though fully aware of the achievements of discourse studies, Noland finally inclined towards a more realist assessment of the body in movement.

39 Sheets-Johnstone, *The Primacy of Movement*, 51.

40 Maxine Sheets-Johnstone, *The Phenomenology of Dance*, 2nd edn (London: Dance Books, 1979), 137.

41 Viktor Shklovsky, 'Tetiva: O neskhodstve skhodnogo' (Bowstring: On Dissimilarity of the Similar), in *Izbrannoe v 2 tomakh* (Selected Works in 2 Vols) (Moscow: Khudozhestvennaia literatura, 1983), vol. 2, 4–307, on 195.

INDEX